Philadelphia Homestyle

Cover: Weetzie Lamb
Illustrations: Mary Kurtz
Theme Consultant: Kathleen Eastman

Published by
Norwood-Fontbonne Academy
Home and School Association
Philadelphia, Pennsylvania

A portion of the proceeds will go to a special Fund for Philadelphia's homeless.

Just as the intention of **Philadelphia Homestyle** is to add flavor to your cooking repertoire, we hope also to give you a sampling of the flavor of Philadelphia's neighborhoods.

The city which encompasses 130 square miles is a network of neighborhoods, each one having its own distinct and historical roots. Ask a native where he lives and the reponse will not be "Philadelphia" but "Tacony", "Fishtown", "Chestnut Hill" or any of the 109 communities that comprise the city.

We have traced the origins of 13 of these areas. Many have evolved over the years-branching out to form newer or separate areas. Our attempt is to highlight the beginnings and capture the flavor of these streets, homes, factories, businesses and, of course, the most important ingredient-the people.

Library of Congress Catalog Card No.: 84-62632
First Printing 5,000—Second Printing 3,000
Third Printing 5,000—Fourth Printing 5,000
ISBN 0-9614938-0-1

Copyright 1984
Norwood-Fontbonne Home and School Association
Philadelphia, Pennsylvania

Printed by
WIMMER BROTHERS
Memphis   Dallas

COMMITTEE

Chairwoman: Evelyn P. Olivieri
Co-Chairwoman: Susan Miller

ART

Joanne Dhody
Mary Kurtz

Weetzie Lamb
Florence Narducci

EDITORS

Marilyn Anderson
Brighid Blake
Mary Bradley
Alice Brogan
Marylou Bruno
Elaine Cellini
Pat Coscia
Jeanne Dolaway

Mary Jo Egoville
John Egoville
Barbara Forde
Joan Forde
Marie Goldkamp
Ruth Anne Hill
Pat Hughes

Virginia McCuen
Bonnie Piecyk
Barbara Powers
Nancy Pugh
Pru Rawson
Sharyn Vergare
Cheryl Young

MARKETING

Maureen Allu
Peggy Miller   *Co-Directors*
Marshae Murrell

Maria Aduso
Dr. Thomas Balshi
Maura Bock
Alice Anne Bossow
Regina Cassidy
Bonnie Courtney
Joan DeNofa
Lawrence DiFranco
Jean Farlino
Cheryl Fletcher

Evelyn Gorman
Dolores Jordan
Halina Klimowicz
Mary Lou Longo
Valerie McDaniel
Rinda McGoldrick
Florence McLafferty
Marie Milito
J. Scott Miller
Claudia Patterson

Dr. Gerald R. Phelan
Evelyn Redcross
Kathleen Schock
Bonnie Shields
Monica Sinker
Marlene Martin Surrena
Mary Jane Tucker
Joan Walters
Ann Wiser
Rose Marie Zaro

PROMOTION

Joanne Balshi, *Director*

Carol Corson
Judy Marabella
Susan Pagliaro

Susann Undi
Brenda Wilson

Curtis J. Wilson
Maryann Wrubel

PUBLICITY

Susan Miller, *Director*

Sally Beil
Alice Brogan

Pat Castelli
Susan Cinalli

Jacqueline Massari
Marie King Wolfe

THEME

Kathleen Eastman
Muriel Graci

Robbyn O'Neill
Jeanne Roman

TREASURER

Beth Ounsworth

3

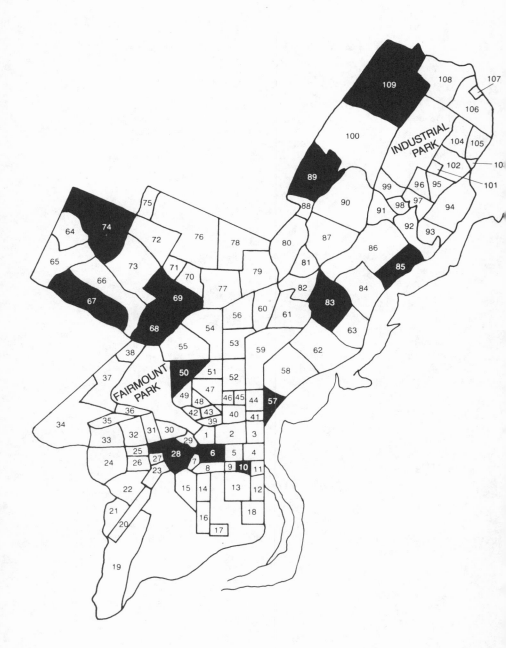

KEY
PHILADELPHIA'S NEIGHBORHOODS

1.	Logan Circle	37.	Wynnefield	73.	West Mt. Airy
2.	Chinatown	38.	Wynnefield Heights	74.	Chestnut Hill
3.	Old City	39.	Spring Garden	75.	Cedarbrook
4.	Society Hill	40.	Poplar	76.	West Oak Lane
5.	Washington Square	41.	Northern Liberties	77.	Logan
6.	Rittenhouse Square	42.	Francisville	78.	East Oak Lane
7.	Schuylkill	43.	Fairmount	79.	Olney
8.	Southwest Center City	44.	Olde Kensington	80.	Lawncrest
9.	Hawthorne	45.	Ludlow	81.	Summerdale
10.	Bella Vista	46.	Yorktown	82.	Northwood
11.	Queen Village	47.	North Central	83.	Frankford
12.	Pennsport	48.	Sharswood	84.	Wissinoming
13.	Wharton	49.	Brewerytown	85.	Tacony
14.	Point Breeze	50.	Strawberry Mansion	86.	Mayfair
15.	Grays Ferry	51.	Stanton	87.	Oxford Circle
16.	Girard Estate	52.	Hartranft	88.	Burholme
17.	Packer Park	53.	Franklinville	89.	Fox Chase
18.	Whitman	54.	Nicetown-Tioga	90.	Rhawnhurst
19.	Eastwick	55.	Allegheny West	91.	Lexington Park
20.	Elmwood	56.	Hunting Park	92.	Holmesburg
21.	Paschall	57.	Fishtown	93.	Upper Holmesburg
22.	Kingsessing	58.	Kensington	94.	Torresdale
23.	Southwest Schuylkill	59.	West Kensington	95.	Academy Gardens
24.	Cobbs Creek	60.	Feltonville	96.	Ashton-Woodenbridge
25.	Garden Court	61.	Juniata	97.	Pennypack Woods
26.	Cedar Park	62.	Richmond	98.	Winchester Park
27.	Spruce Hill	63.	Bridesburg	99.	Pennypack
28.	University City	64.	Andorra	100.	Bustleton
29.	Powelton Village	65.	Upper Roxborough	101.	West Torresdale
30.	Mantua	66.	Roxborough	102.	Morrell Park
31.	Belmont	67.	Manayunk	103.	Crestmont Farms
32.	Mill Creek	68.	East Falls	104.	Millbrook
33.	Haddington	69.	Germantown	105.	Modena Park
34.	Overbrook	70.	Wister	106.	Parkwood Manor
35.	Carroll Park	71.	Morton	107.	Mechanicsville
36.	Parkside	72.	East Mt. Airy	108.	Byberry
				109.	Somerton

"N O R W O O D"
circa 1850
8891 Germantown Avenue
Philadelphia, Pennsylvania

The Gothic Revival villa that is now part of Norwood-Fontbonne Academy, was built about 1850 for Charles Taylor who named his estate "Norwood". It was designed by the noted architect of the time, James C. Sidney, who is credited with a number of other residences in the Chestnut Hill area. Some fine examples of his work can be seen on Summit Street and Chestnut Hill Avenue. The similarity between "Norwood" and the home at 42 Summit Street is apparent in the use of the mansard roof. Sidney was one of the first architects to introduce this change to the Victorian Gothic style.

In approximately 1883, the house became the property of Harriet Benson who made a number of alterations to the original dwelling. She lived at "Norwood" until about 1900 when Reed Morgan became its new owner.

In 1919, the Sisters of St. Joseph purchased the estate from the Morgans to accommodate the increasing enrollment at the Mount St. Joseph Academy for Boys. It was opened in 1920 and called Norwood Academy for Boys. The first student body consisted of fifty-four students.

In 1924, there was a need to expand Mount St. Joseph Academy for Girls, and the Sisters purchased the property adjacent to Norwood Academy from the Harrison family. It became known as Fontbonne Hall, taking the surname of one of the founders of the Order. In January, 1925, the school opened with a student body of forty-four girls.

Fontbonne relocated down the road at Norwood and Sunset Avenues in 1945 in a home purchased from Samuel and Barbara Strawbridge Morris. It continued at this site until 1959 when it closed to make room for the growing number of young women entering the Sisters of St. Joseph as postulants. The building was renamed Assumption Hall. At the same time, a large dormitory building was constructed on the property for the postulants.

In the early 1970's, when this building was no longer needed as a dormitory, it reopened as Fontbonne Academy under the administration of Norwood Academy. The Norwood campus on Germantown Avenue, which now included a gymnasium facility, and the Fontbonne location at Sunset and Norwood Avenues, soon became known as Norwood-Fontbonne Academy, a co-educational day school for children from Montessori Pre-School through eighth grade.

We dedicate this book to the children of Norwood-Fontbonne Academy, their parents and teachers, and to the continuing heritage of excellence in education that has prevailed for more than half a century.

We wish to give special thanks to Mary Ann Powell and her Language Arts Class for soliciting recipes from celebrities.

Shannon Barry
David Billitto
Chuck Bodner
Amy Boris
Christian Bradley
Madeline Clements
Courtney Connell
Al Cunningham
Ali Daly
Nancy DeCamara
Brian Donaghy
Rebecca Garza
Keith Guinta
Milly Himes
Colleen Kelly
Kevin Kelly
John Lambert
Richard Lambert
Richard Lane
Robert Leahy
Dennis Ledwith
Susan Lynch
Mimi Mastrangelo

Ian McDowell
Sean McSweeny
Krista Milito
Mary Monahan
Tracy Moses
Brian Mulroney
Wendy Narducci
Chris Polek
Pamela Richardson
David Shoup
John Stanczak
David Stephens
Kristen Tague
Diane Timm
Kevin Tinneny
Orlando Torres
Paul Towhey
Kathleen Walls
Marty Whalen
Jennifer Wilson
Kate Yanity
Christa Zaro

PATRONS

Mr. and Mrs. Marshall Allu
Mr. and Mrs. R. David Bradley
Mr. and Mrs. Edward Cellini
Mr. and Mrs. John E. F. Corson
Mr. and Mrs. Dinesh Dhody
Dr. and Mrs. David Forde
Mr. and Mrs. George Forde
Dr. and Mrs. Jay Handler
Mr. and Mrs. Stephen Kurtz
Mr. and Mrs. Richard McCuen

Mr. and Mrs. Ronald Miller
Mr. and Mrs. J. Scott Miller
Mr. and Mrs. Jerome Murrell
Mr. and Mrs. Herbert Olivieri
Dr. and Mrs. Gerald Phelan
Mr. and Mrs. H. Denys Rawson
Mr. and Mrs. Charles Schock
Mr. and Mrs. Paul Shoup
Mr. and Mrs. Thomas Wiser
Mr. and Mrs. Walter Zalewski

TABLE OF CONTENTS

BELLA VISTA

Certain areas of Philadelphia are known for their ethnic character, and South Philadelphia has long been considered an Italian stronghold. The Italian immigrants have left their imprint on the city in many forms.

Arriving in Philadelphia, many Italian immigrants sought boarding at Palumbo's, a local boarding house which today is one of the city's landmark restaurants. Their favorite pastime, Bocce, was played in many of the streets of South Philadelphia. Second and third generation Italians still enjoy playing this game.

Also native to this neighborhood are the "Mummers". Started more than 100 years ago on "Two Street" (Second Street to those not from South Philly), this New Year's Day extravaganza is the nation's oldest January 1st observance. Dancing and prancing "up Broad Street", string bands, comic and fancy brigades strut to the applause of many thousands of bundled spectators.

Another tradition in South Philadelphia is the Italian Market, located along Ninth Street. It was set up at the turn of the century, fashioned after European-type markets, where Italian immigrants sold fruits, vegetables and meats. Today's expanded market continues to appeal to Philadelphians and has become a tourist attraction as well.

Ninth Street and South Philadelphia were put on the national map when "Rocky" made his famous run through the market and the city, and up the steps of the Philadelphia Art Museum.

Beverages

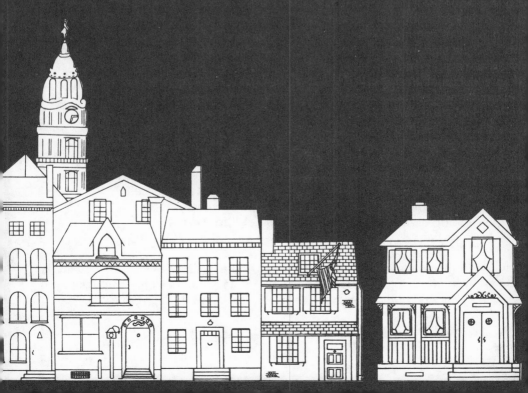

BEVERAGES

TOASTED ALMOND

Easy

Serves: 1
Prep Time: 5 Minutes

1 ounce amaretto
1 ounce kahlúa
2 ounces milk

2 heaping scoops butter almond
   or vanilla ice cream

Combine ingredients in blender. Blend at high speed for 10 seconds or until creamy.

Maria C. Pié - Mt. Airy, Pa.

BOSCO BEAR

Easy

Serves: 2
Prep Time: 5 Minutes

1½ ounces kahlúa
1 ounce crème de cocoa
4 ounces vanilla ice cream

1 ounce half and half
4 ounces ice

Combine ingredients in blender in the order listed. Blend until thick and creamy. Pour into glasses. Top with whipped cream and chocolate syrup.

O'Hara's Dining Saloon - West Philadelphia, Pa.

CAPPUCINO

Moderate

Serves: 2
Prep Time: 5 Minutes

1 teaspoon sugar
1 teaspoon cocoa
¼ cup espresso, or strong
   coffee

¼ cup half and half
2 ounces brandy
Whipped cream

Combine sugar and cocoa in a pan. Add espresso. Stir until cocoa-sugar mixture dissolves. Add half and half. Heat just below simmer. Pour into two cups. Add brandy. Stir until well blended. Top with whipped cream.

Annette M. George - Wyomissing, Pa.

CAPE CODDER

Easy

Serves: 1
Prep Time: 2 Minutes

**2½ ounces cranberry juice
  cocktail**

1 ounce vodka

Pour juice and vodka over cracked ice. Stir until well blended. *Wonderful summer refresher.*

Ave M. Pollak - Sherman, Ct.

COFFEE LIQUEUR

Easy
Make Ahead

Serves: 24
Prep Time: 20 Minutes

4 cups water
4 cups sugar
1 cup brown sugar
**1 (2 ounce) jar instant coffee,
  not decaffeinated**

2 teaspoons vanilla extract
1 quart vodka

Combine water, sugars and coffee in a large pan. Stir until sugars dissolve. Bring to a slow rolling boil over a moderate heat. Reduce heat and continue to boil, uncovered, for 5 minutes. Remove from heat. Stir in vanilla and vodka. Let cool. Pour into decorative bottles. Refrigerate for one week before using. *Make your own and save. Great gift idea!*

Helen Reardon - Newtown, Pa.

BEVERAGES

MELON COLADA

Easy

Serves: 1
Prep Time: 5 Minutes

1 (1½ ounce) jigger light rum
1 ounce cream of coconut
3 ounces pineapple juice
1 (1½ ounce) jigger Midori
  (melon liqueur)

½ cup honeydew melon, cubed
  (optional)

Combine ingredients in a blender. Whip until smooth. Pour over cracked ice.

Evelyn P. Olivieri - Mt. Airy, Pa.

SUMMER'S DELIGHT
(Italian Water Ice)

Easy
Make Ahead

Serves: 8 to 10
Prep Time: 15 Minutes

2 cups water
2 cups sugar
¾ cup fresh lemon juice

1 tablespoon grated lemon peel
4 cups *cold* water

Combine water and sugar in heavy saucepan. Stir until sugar dissolves. Bring to a boil over medium-high heat. Reduce heat and continue to boil for 10 minutes. Set aside. Combine fresh lemon juice, lemon peel and cold water. Add to sugar mixture. Pour into freezer container and freeze stirring every hour until mixture becomes slushy. This takes 4 to 5 hours.

Farlino Family - Miquon, Pa.

FROZEN CRANBERRY SOUR

Easy

Serves: Varies
Prep Time: 5 Minutes

Whiskey or rum
Whiskey sour mix

Cranberry juice

Combine equal parts of whiskey or rum, sour mix and cranberry juice in freezer container. Freeze. Remove from freezer just before serving and stir until slushy.

Claire O'Malley - Jamesburg, N.J.

IRISH CREAM

Easy
Make Ahead

Serves: 10
Prep Time: 10 Minutes

3 eggs, beaten
1 (14 ounce) can sweetened,
  condensed milk
1 tablespoon honey

1 tablespoon chocolate syrup
1 pint heavy cream
1½ cups Irish whiskey or rye
Dash of nutmeg

Place eggs in blender. Add remaining ingredients in order listed and blend until well mixed. Chill overnight. *Extra special and makes a great gift in a nice bottle.*

Barbara Erdmann - Springfield, Il.

JAMAICAN SUNRISE

Easy

Serves: 2
Prep Time: 5 Minutes

4 large ice cubes
4 ounces orange juice
2 ounces dark Jamaican rum

½ ounce grenadine
8 to 10 whole strawberries
1 small ripe banana, peeled

Place all ingredients in a blender. Blend on high for about 20 seconds or until smooth. *Fresh or frozen strawberries can be used. You will think you're relaxing in the islands!*

Bonnie Blackwell - York, Pa.

BEVERAGES

AUNT JO'S EGGNOG

Moderate
Make Ahead

Serves: 30
Prep Time: 30 Minutes

12 eggs
1 cup sugar
1 quart Cognac
1 pint light rum

2 quarts milk
1 pint heavy cream
1 cup powdered sugar
Nutmeg

Separate eggs. Place yolks in a large mixing bowl and 6 whites in each of 2 small mixing bowls. Beat yolks lightly. Gradually, add sugar and beat until well blended. Alternate cognac and rum, adding slowly and stirring carefully after each addition. Add milk and all of cream except for 1 cup. Chill. Beat 6 egg whites until stiff but not dry. Fold into yolk mixture. Beat remaining egg whites adding powdered sugar gradually. Continue to beat until stiff enough to hold peaks. Slowly add remaining cream. Beat just until blended. Fold into yolk mixture. Chill, preferably overnight, before serving. Serve in punch cups with a dash of freshly grated nutmeg. *Smooth, creamy and packs a whallop!!!*

Rinda McGoldrick - Oreland, Pa.

PINK MIST

Easy

Serves: 1
Prep Time: 2 Minutes

Sparkling burgundy
Pink lemonade

Fresh strawberries

Mix equal amounts of sparkling burgundy and lemonade. Pour into glass filled with cracked ice. Garnish with fresh strawberries.

Joanne Balshi - Gwynedd, Pa.

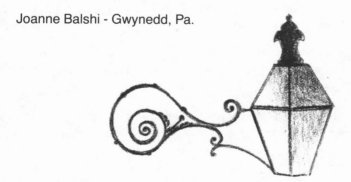

ANNIVERSARY CHAMPAGNE PUNCH

Easy
Make Ahead

Serves: 20 to 25
Prep Time: 10 Minutes

**Rinds from 3 oranges, cut into
  strips
Rinds from 3 lemons, cut into
  strips
3 tablespoons sugar**

**¾ cup cognac or brandy
¾ cup orange-flavored liqueur
3 bottles champagne
2 cups carbonated water**

Place fruit rinds and sugar in punch bowl. Pour in cognac and orange-flavored liqueur. Stir. Chill 2 to 3 hours. Add champagne and carbonated water before serving. Stir gently. Serve over ice.

Maria Aduso - Roxborough, Pa.

MIMOSA

Easy

Serves: 1
Prep Time: 2 Minutes

4 ounces orange juice

2 ounces champagne, chilled

Pour orange juice into wine glass. Add chilled champagne. Stir gently.

Lynne Miller - Penllyn, Pa.

FROSTED CHAMPAGNE PUNCH

Easy

Serves: 25
Prep Time: 5 to 10 Minutes

**1 bottle champagne
1 bottle Rhine wine
1 (32 ounce) bottle club soda
1 (6 ounce) can frozen orange
  juice, undiluted**

**1 (6 ounce) can frozen
  lemonade, undiluted
1 quart pineapple sherbet**

Combine the first 5 ingredients in a large punch bowl. Add scoops of sherbet before serving. *Lemon or lime sherbet may be substituted, if desired.*

Peggy Miller - Chestnut Hill, Pa.

BEVERAGES

PASSEL OF PUNCH

Easy

Serves: 60
Prep Time: 15 to 20 Minutes

3 cups orange juice
1½ cups lemon juice
3 quarts unsweetened pineapple juice
⅓ cup lime juice
1 cup mint leaves
2 cups sugar

4 quarts ginger ale, chilled
2 quarts carbonated water, chilled
2 cups fresh, sliced strawberries
1 cup lemon slices
1 cup lime slices

Combine juices, sugar and mint leaves in large jar or pitcher. Chill several hours or overnight. Strain. Pour over a large cake of ice in a punch bowl. Slowly pour the ginger ale and carbonated water down the side of the bowl. Add strawberries and lemon and lime slices. Stir gently.

Mary Ann Powell - Roxborough, Pa.

PETE'S COLONIAL PUNCH

Easy
Make Ahead

Serves: about 32
Prep Time: 30 Minutes

16 tea bags
2 quarts hot water
2 cups sugar, or to taste

1 dozen lemons
1 fifth light rum
5 pounds ice cubes

Place tea bags in a large mixing bowl or heat-proof jar. Pour in hot water. Allow to steep. Add sugar after removing tea bags. Stir until dissolved. Continue to cool. Peel lemon rinds into spirals. Squeeze juice from lemons. Place rind spirals and juice in a large punch bowl. Add cooled tea and rum. Stir in ice cubes before serving.

Mary D. Kurtz - Mt. Airy, Pa.

SOUTHERN COMFORT PUNCH

Easy

Serves: 25
Prep Time: 10 Minutes

1 (12 ounce) can frozen orange juice
2 lemons, sliced
2 oranges, sliced
1 (6 ounce) jar maraschino cherries
1 (6 ounce) can frozen lemonade, undiluted

1 (12 ounce) can frozen five-juice blend, undiluted
1 fifth southern comfort
4 ounces apricot brandy
1 (11 ounce) can mandarin oranges
1 (64 ounce) bottle lemon-lime carbonated beverage

Mix orange juice according to the directions on the can. Arrange sliced lemons, oranges and cherries in bottom of a mold. Pour orange juice over the fruit and freeze. Before serving, place lemonade and five-juice blend in punch bowl. Mix together. Pour southern comfort and apricot brandy over frozen juices. Stir. Add mandarin oranges and frozen mold. Add bottle of lemon-lime beverage. Stir.

Susann T. Undi - Cheltenham, Pa.

WASSAIL BOWL

Easy

Serves: about 40
Prep Time: 45 Minutes

1 gallon apple cider
1 quart cranberry juice
1½ cups lemon juice
4 cinnamon sticks

2 oranges
4 whole cloves
2 cups vodka
2 cups brandy

Combine cider, juices and cinnamon sticks in a large kettle. Cook over a medium heat until warmed throughout. Slice oranges and insert cloves. Float in the mixture. Cover and heat over a low heat for 30 minutes. Add vodka and brandy. Mix well. When heated, place in heat-resistant punch bowl and serve.

Joanne Balshi - Gwynedd, Pa.

CHESTNUT HILL

Tucked quietly in the northwest corner of Philadelphia is one of its loveliest neighborhoods, Chestnut Hill. The character of this community with its tree-lined streets and stately homes was carved from the 19th century development of the Pennsylvania Railroad, and the contributions of Henry Howard Houston, a wealthy businessman and philanthropist. Designed by him as an uppercrust suburb of Philadelphia, it continues today within the city's borders as one of its most prestigious areas.

Cobblestoned Germantown Avenue is the main thoroughfare. Winding through Chestnut Hill, Germantown Avenue exhibits many colonial-styled buildings that house a charming assortment of shops, boutiques, galleries and restaurants.

During the last quarter century, Chestnut Hill has adopted many strong and viable community organizations. Residents tackle problems themselves rather than relying on city or government agencies. The community has its own newspaper, a resident's organization, a businessmen's organization and countless groups devoted to improving the quality of life in Chestnut Hill.

In the summer, there are concerts in the park, and in the winter, the trees along the Avenue are lit with sparkling white lights announcing the holiday season. The Chestnut Hill Flower Show is held in the spring and the Main Street Fair is held in the autumn. This is truly a neighborhood for all seasons!

Appetizers

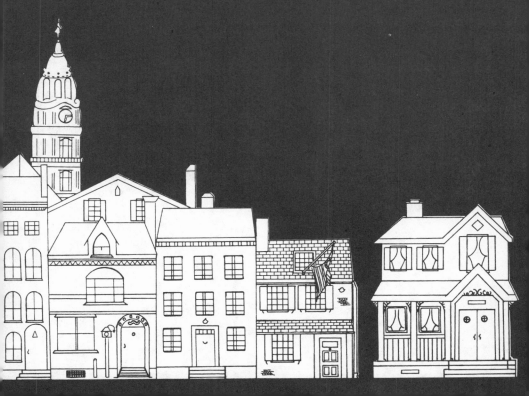

APPETIZERS

SPANAKOPITA
(Spinach Cheese Triangles)

Moderate
Make Ahead
Freeze

Serves: 15 to 20
Prep Time: 1½ Hours
Oven Temp: 350°
Baking Time: 10 to 15 Minutes

1 medium-sized onion, finely chopped
¼ cup olive oil
2 (10 ounce) packages frozen, chopped spinach, thawed, drained and finely chopped
½ pound feta cheese

¼ cup finely chopped scallions
6 ounces ricotta cheese
3 eggs, beaten
¼ cup breadcrumbs
1 pound phyllo pastry sheets
½ cup butter, melted

Sauté onion in olive oil for 5 minutes. Add spinach which has been squeezed as dry as possible. Simmer with onion over a low heat, stirring occasionally, until most of the moisture has evaporated. Crumble the feta cheese into small pieces. Add cheese, scallions and ricotta cheese. Mix until well blended. Add eggs. Mix well. Toss breadcrumbs into spinach-onion mixture. Add the spinach-onion mixture to the cheese mixture. Stir until all ingredients are well blended. Remove one sheet of phyllo pastry. Place it on a flat surface and brush with melted butter. Fold in long sides toward the middle making a strip about 2 inches wide. Place 1 tablespoon of spinach-cheese mixture in the bottom right-hand corner of the strip. Fold over into a triangle shape. Continue folding, making sure with each fold that the bottom edge is parallel with the alternate side edge in the same way that a flag is folded. Lightly butter the finished triangle. Continue in this manner until all the spinach mixture or phyllo sheets are used. Bake the spanakopita at 350° for 10 to 15 minutes or until puffed and golden. Allow to cool about 5 minutes before serving. *To make smaller triangles, cut sheets of phyllo into thirds, measuring across the widest part; fold sides toward center and fill with 1 teaspoon of mixture. Follow flag-folding procedure. N.B. Freeze on buttered cookie sheets for 30 minutes and store in plastic bags in freezer. Keep phyllo sheets between two sheets of waxed paper and covered with a damp cloth to prevent drying. Work quickly.*

A Friend of Norwood-Fontbonne

SPINACH BALLS WITH MUSTARD SAUCE

Easy to Moderate
Make Ahead
Refrigerate or Freeze

Serves: 20 to 25
Prep Time: 30 Minutes
Oven Temp: 350°
Baking Time: 10 to 15 Minutes

Spinach Balls:

2 (10 ounce) packages frozen, chopped spinach, thawed and squeezed dry
2 cups herbed stuffing mix, crushed
1 cup firmly packed, freshly grated Parmesan cheese

½ cup butter, melted
4 small green onions, finely chopped
3 eggs, slightly beaten
Dash freshly grated nutmeg

Mustard Sauce:

½ cup Dijon mustard
2 tablespoons mustard powder
4 tablespoons sugar
3 tablespoons vinegar
1 cup oil

3 tablespoons chopped dill
3 tablespoons chopped parsley
1 hard-cooked egg, chopped
1 tablespoon capers, optional

Spinach Balls: Combine all ingredients except mustard sauce in a large mixing bowl. Mix until well blended. Shape into 1 inch balls. Cover. Refrigerate or freeze until ready to use. Place balls on ungreased baking sheet. Bake at 350° for 10 minutes or until golden brown. Serve with mustard sauce.

Mustard Sauce: Combine mustards, sugar and vinegar. Mix until well blended. Add oil slowly, beating constantly. Fold in herbs and egg. Refrigerate several hours to allow flavors to blend.

Bea Wilson - Mt. Airy, Pa.

APPETIZERS

HOT ARTICHOKE DIP

Easy

Serves: 20
Prep Time: 10 Minutes
Oven Temp: 325°
Baking Time: 15 Minutes

**2 (14 ounce) cans artichoke
  hearts in water**

**1 cup mayonnaise
1 cup grated Parmesan cheese**

Chop artichoke hearts. Combine with mayonnaise and Parmesan. Mix until well blended. Pour into a lightly buttered 1½ quart casserole dish. Bake at 325° for 15 minutes. Serve warm with garlic rounds and crackers. *This recipe is easy to do and is always a favorite with guests.*

Deborah Knapp - WCAU-TV, Channel 10
Toby McDowell - Chestnut Hill, Pa.

ASPARAGUS ROLLS

Moderate
Make Ahead
Freeze

Serves: 25
Prep Time: 15 Minutes
Oven Temp: 350°
Baking Time: 10 to 15 Minutes

**1 (8 ounce) package cream
  cheese, softened
1 (4 ounce) package blue
  cheese, softened
1 loaf thin sliced melba bread**

**Boiled ham, sliced thin
  (optional)
1 (14 ounce) can asparagus
  spears
½ cup butter**

Combine the cream cheese and blue cheese. Mix until well blended. Spread on bread forming a heavy rim at the edges. If using ham, place ham on top of cheese. Place asparagus on top. Roll and press. Slice in 4 one-inch pieces. Dip in melted butter. Place on an ungreased 15x10x1 inch baking sheet. Bake at 350° for 10 to 15 minutes.

Kathy Gallagher - Manayunk, Pa.

HERB-COTTAGE CHEESE DIP

Easy
Make Ahead

Serves: 8 to 10
Prep Time: 10 Minutes

1 cup cottage cheese
½ cup sour cream
1 cup mayonnaise
2 tablespoons chopped chives
1 tablespoon chopped parsley
2 cloves garlic, minced

2 tablespoons grated onion
½ teaspoon Worcestershire
¼ teaspoon hot pepper sauce
Salt to taste
Pepper to taste

Combine cottage cheese and sour cream in a small mixing bowl. Beat until smooth and creamy. Add remaining ingredients. Mix until well blended. Cover bowl. Refrigerate several hours or overnight. Serve with raw vegetables.

Marilyn Anderson - Roxborough, Pa.

CURRY DIP FOR RAW VEGETABLES

Easy
Make Ahead
Refrigerate

Serves: 8 to 10
Prep Time: 10 Minutes

2 cups mayonnaise
3 teaspoons curry powder
3 tablespoons chili sauce
1 tablespoon Worcestershire
**   sauce**

½ teaspoon salt
Pepper
½ teaspoon garlic salt
1 teaspoon instant onion

In a medium-sized mixing bowl, combine ingredients in order listed. Mix until well blended. Cover and refrigerate until chilled. Serve with assorted raw vegetables like carrots, string beans, cauliflower, green pepper pieces or other raw vegetables.

Mrs. Dick Thornburgh - Wife of the Governor of Pennsylvania

APPETIZERS

CAPONATA ALLA SICILIANA

Moderate
Make Ahead

Serves: 16 to 20 (1 quart)
Prep Time: 30 Minutes

⅔ cup olive oil
½ teaspoon garlic powder
1 large eggplant, washed and
  cubed, skin left on
2 teaspoons salt, divided
1 cup chopped onions
½ cup diced green pepper
½ cup diced celery
½ cup halved ripe olives
1 (15½ ounce) can Italian
  tomatoes

1 tablespoon capers
2 teaspoons oregano, crushed
1 teaspoon sweet basil, crushed
¼ teaspoon black pepper
5 tablespoons garlic flavored
  red wine vinegar
¼ cup toasted pine nuts
Crusty Italian or French bread,
  buttered
Parmesan cheese

Heat olive oil with garlic powder in a large, heavy skillet. Sauté eggplant in oil until golden. Remove from pan. Sprinkle with 1 teaspoon salt. Add onions, green peppers and celery to remaining oil in pan. Sauté until lightly golden. Stir in olives, tomatoes, capers, oregano, basil, pepper, vinegar and remaining salt. Add sautéed eggplant; simmer, uncovered, for 20 minutes. Remove from heat. Stir in pine nuts. Cool. Pour into a covered container and refrigerate overnight. To serve, butter small pieces of crusty Italian or French bread, sprinkle with Parmesan cheese and top with chilled Caponata. This Sicilian cold vegetable Hors d'Oeuvres is delicious. 1 (16 ounce) can solid packed tomatoes may be substituted for the Italian tomatoes.

Alice Brogan - Ambler, Pa.

"PLAINS SPECIAL" CHEESE RING

1 pound sharp cheese, grated
1 cup finely chopped nuts
1 cup mayonnaise
1 small onion, finely grated

Black pepper, to taste
Dash cayenne
Strawberry preserves, optional

Combine ingredients in mixing bowl in the order listed. Beat until well blended. Mold into a ring or desired shape. Chill. To serve, fill ring center with strawberry preserves. *Can be served as a complement to a main meal or as an hors d'oeuvre with crackers.*

Jimmy Carter - Former President - U.S.A.

CHESSBOARD CAVIAR

Moderate
Make Ahead

Serves: 10 to 12
Prep Time: 20 Minutes

1 (8 ounce) package cream
  cheese, softened
⅓ cup sour cream
⅓ cup mayonnaise
2 tablespoons onion, finely
  grated

1 tablespoon lemon juice
Freshly ground pepper to taste
3 hard-cooked eggs, finely
  chopped, divided
3 to 4 ounces fresh black or red
  salmon caviar

Combine first 6 ingredients. Whip until blended. Add 1 chopped egg and spread into a 6 or 7 inch square dish. Refrigerate. Before serving, mark off 9 equal sections. Top each section alternately with either caviar or remaining chopped egg. Serve with thinly sliced black bread. *Be creative and make your own colorful design.*

Evelyn P. Olivieri - Mt. Airy, Pa.

CHEESE PUFF HORS D'OEUVRES

Moderate
Make Ahead

Serves: 12 to 15
Prep Time: 25 Minutes
Oven Temp: 400°
Baking Time: 10 to 12 Minutes

1 loaf firm, unsliced white bread
1 (3 ounce) package cream
  cheese
¼ pound sharp Cheddar cheese,
  cut into chunks

½ cup butter
2 egg yolks, slightly beaten
2 egg whites, stiffly beaten

Trim crusts from bread and cut into 1 inch cubes. Melt cheeses and butter in top of a double boiler. Add half the cheese mixture to the slightly beaten egg yolks. Mix well. Return to remainder of mixture and continue to cook for 1 minute. Remove from heat. Fold in stiffly beaten egg whites. Dip bread cubes into cheese mixture until well coated. Place on an ungreased, 15x10x1 inch jelly roll pan. Refrigerate overnight. Bake at 400° for 10 to 12 minutes before serving.

Debbie Formica-Anella - Holland, Pa.

APPETIZERS

MADEIRA CHEESE SPREAD

Easy
Make Ahead

Serves: 10 to 12
Prep Time: 20 Minutes

1 (8 ounce) package cream
  cheese, softened
1 to 1½ pounds cold pack
  Cheddar cheese

1 teaspoon horseradish
1 teaspoon Worcestershire
  sauce
2 ounces Madeira

Place cold pack Cheddar in a mixing bowl. Gradually add cream cheese, beating well after each addition. Add horseradish, Worcestershire sauce and Madeira. Beat until smooth and creamy. Place in a crock or glass jar with a tight-fitting lid. Serve with crackers.

Bernie Handler - Huntingdon Valley, Pa.

CHICKEN LOG

Moderate
Make Ahead

Serves: 6 to 8
Prep Time: 15 Minutes

2 (8 ounce) packages cream
  cheese, softened
1 tablespoon steak sauce
½ teaspoon curry powder
1½ cups minced, cooked
  chicken

⅓ cup minced celery
¼ cup chopped parsley, divided
¼ cup toasted almonds

Combine cream cheese, steak sauce and curry powder. Beat until smooth and creamy. Add chicken, celery and 2 tablespoons parsley. Mix until well blended. Refrigerate remaining parsley. Shape cheese mixture into a 9 inch log. Wrap in plastic wrap. Chill 4 hours or overnight. Toss remaining parsley and almonds. Roll cheese log in parsley/almond mixture until coated. Serve with crackers. *May add 2 tablespoons chopped green pepper to this for added flavor.*

Sister Beatrice De Santis - Principal, Norwood-Fontbonne Academy

CHICKEN WINGS CANTONESE

Easy

Serves: 4
Prep Time: 20 Minutes

12 chicken wings
1 clove garlic, minced
2 tablespoons vegetable oil
4 tablespoons soy sauce
3 tablespoons dry sherry
1 teaspoon white vinegar

2 tablespoons honey
2 scallions, including green
 tops, minced
¼ teaspoon cayenne pepper
1 teaspoon freshly grated ginger
 root

Sauté chicken wings and garlic in oil over medium heat until chicken is browned on all sides. Discard grease. Add remaining ingredients in order listed. Stir. Reduce heat. Simmer, covered, for 30 minutes or until sauce thickens and clings to the wing pieces. Turn chicken occasionally while cooking. *I recommend wingettes when prepared as a main course. Smaller wings will suffice when prepared as an appetizer. DO NOT substitute cooking sherry or powdered ginger in this recipe.*

Diane R. Dobbins - North Wales, Pa.

CHILI CON QUESO DIP

Easy
Make Ahead

Serves: 6 to 8
Prep Time: 20 Minutes

1 (16 ounce) can stewed
 tomatoes
1 (4 ounce) can chopped green
 chilies
1 medium-sized onion, chopped

1 tablespoon vegetable oil
2 cups evaporated milk or cream
1 (16 ounce) package
 pasteurized processed cheese
Dash garlic salt

Place tomatoes, chilies, onions and oil in skillet. Cook over a medium-high heat until mixture bubbles, stirring constantly. Reduce heat. Simmer, stirring often, until most of the liquid has evaporated. Add milk. Stir until well blended. Add cheese. Continue to simmer, stirring constantly, until cheese has melted. Add garlic salt. Serve hot in fondue pot or chafing dish. Good with corn chips. *Perfect after a family hayride.*

Loretta Burton - Plymouth Meeting, Pa.

APPETIZERS

CLAM DIGGERS

Easy
Make Ahead

Serves: 24 to 30
Prep Time: 20 Minutes
Oven Temp: 350°
Baking Time: 15 Minutes

½ cup chopped green pepper
½ cup butter, melted
1 teaspoon chopped parsley
1 tablespoon Worcestershire
   sauce
½ teaspoon dried mustard
1 teaspoon oregano

Dash onion salt
1 cup fresh clams or 2 (6½
   ounce) cans minced clams,
   undrained
12 slices bread, crumbed
Paprika
Clam shells

Sauté green pepper in butter until tender. Add next 6 ingredients. Simmer over a medium heat for 5 to 8 minutes. Work bread crumbs into the mixture with a fork. Remove from heat and pack into clam shells or a greased 1½ quart casserole. Sprinkle with paprika. Bake at 350° for 15 minutes.

Leigh Narducci - Blue Bell, Pa.

CRAB DIP

Easy

Serves: 16 to 20
Prep Time: 15 Minutes
Oven Temp: 325°
Baking Time: 30 Minutes

2½ (8 ounce) packages cream
   cheese
4 teaspoons minced onion
2 tablespoons horseradish
½ teaspoon salt

½ teaspoon pepper
2 tablespoons milk
1 pound fresh crabmeat,
   cartilage removed

Melt cream cheese over medium-to-low heat, stirring constantly. Add remaining ingredients in order listed, except for the crab. Mix until well blended. Fold in crabmeat. Pour into a buttered 1½ quart casserole. Bake at 325° for 30 minutes. Serve in chafing dish to keep warm. *Great party dip for those special occasions!*

Lois Wilson - Chestnut Hill, Pa.

DIPPIN BREAD

Easy
Make Ahead

Serves: 10 to 12
Prep Time: 30 Minutes

1⅓ cups mayonnaise
1½ cups sour cream
2 teaspoons salt
2 tablespoons parsley
2 tablespoons dill weed

2 tablespoons minced onion
4 ounces black olives, pitted and
  chopped
1 or 2 (16 ounce) loaves rye
  bread, unsliced

Combine all ingredients except bread. Mix until well blended. Chill overnight. Hollow out the center of rye bread loaf and fill with dip. Cube the removed bread. Arrange around dip-filled loaf to be used as crackers for the dip.

Eileen DiFranco - Mt. Airy, Pa.
Katie Eastman - Lansdale, Pa.

SHRIMP MOLD

Moderate
Make Ahead

Serves: 10 to 12
Prep Time: 30 Minutes

½ (10¾ ounce) can tomato soup
1 envelope unflavored gelatin
¾ cup mayonnaise
1 (3 ounce) package cream
  cheese, softened

½ cup chopped celery
¼ cup chopped onion
2 cups coarsely chopped shrimp

Place soup in saucepan. Heat over a medium heat until hot but not boiling. Add gelatin, stirring constantly, until gelatin dissolves. Remove from heat. Combine mayonnaise, cream cheese, celery and onion in a mixing bowl. Add tomato mixture and shrimp. Mix until well blended. Pour into a lightly greased, 1 quart mold. Refrigerate several hours or overnight. Serve with rye bread rounds or other party-type crackers. *Great party recipe since it can be made a day or 2 before. Guests will ask for the recipe.*

Pat Coscia - Lafayette Hill, Pa.

APPETIZERS

BOURBON FRANKS

Easy

Serves: 8
Prep Time: 10 Minutes
Baking Time: 2 Hours

¾ **cup bourbon**
½ **cup brown sugar**
½ **cup chili sauce**

1 (16 ounce) package cocktail or
   bite-sized franks

Combine all ingredients in a saucepan in order listed. Simmer over a low heat for 2 hours, stirring occasionally. Serve hot in a fondue pot or chafing dish.

Marie Hamilton - East Falls, Pa.

JOSEPHINAS

Easy

Serves: 16 to 20
Prep Time: 20 Minutes
Oven Temp: Broil
Baking Time: 5 to 6 Minutes

1 party loaf French bread, sliced
   in ¼ inch rounds or 1 (8
   ounce) bag corn tortilla
   rounds, quartered
½ **(4 ounce) can chopped green**
   chilies
½ **cup butter**

1 clove garlic, finely chopped
1 cup mayonnaise
4 ounces Monterey Jack cheese
   or Cheddar cheese or
   combination of both
Radish, sliced
Parsley

Toast the bread rounds at 350° for 10 minutes or until browned. Combine chilies, butter and garlic in small bowl. Mix until well blended. Spread on toasted bread or tortilla rounds. Combine mayonnaise and cheese. Spread over the butter mixture. Place on a baking sheet. Place under broiler for 5 to 6 minutes or until browned. Garnish with radish slices and parsley. *So easy kids will love to make this one!*

Weetzie Lamb - North Hills, Pa.

TERIYAKI MEATBALLS

Easy

Serves: 6 to 8
Prep Time: 20 Minutes

1 tablespoon soy sauce
1 tablespoon water
2 teaspoons sugar
¼ teaspoon dehydrated onion

Dash garlic powder
Dash ginger
½ pound ground beef
½ cup bread crumbs

Combine first 6 ingredients in a small mixing bowl. Allow to stand for 10 minutes. Combine ground beef and bread crumbs. Work together until well blended. Add soy sauce mixture. Roll into ¾ inch balls. Deep fry at 350° for 10 minutes. Drain well. Serve with warmed catsup and mustard. *Always a crowd pleaser!*

Diane R. Dobbins - North Wales, Pa.

HAMBURGER TWIRLS

Easy
Make Ahead
Can Be Frozen

Serves: 8 to 10
Prep Time: 25 Minutes
Oven Temp: 425°
Baking Time: 20 Minutes

¼ cup chopped onions
1 teaspoon chopped green
    pepper
⅓ cup chopped celery
2 tablespoons butter, melted
1 pound ground beef

¾ tablespoon salt
Dash pepper
2 teaspoons flour
1 teaspoon bouillon
½ cup water
1 recipe biscuit mix dough

Sauté onion, green pepper and celery in butter over a medium heat until tender. Add meat, salt and pepper. Stir until blended. Cook until meat is medium rare. Sprinkle flour over mixture. Add bouillon and water. Reduce heat. Simmer mixture until thickened. Remove from heat. Allow to cool to room temperature. Spread on biscuit mix dough which has been rolled to form 12x18 inch rectangle. Roll up as a jelly roll. Cut into 1 inch slices. Place on a cookie sheet. Bake at 425° for 20 minutes. Serve with your favorite sauce. *For biscuit mix dough, follow directions on box. Slices can be frozen and heated later for serving.*

Harold S. Mohler - Former Chairman of the Board - Hershey Foods Corp.

APPETIZERS

PARMESAN STUFFED MUSHROOMS

Easy

Serves: 6 to 8
Prep Time: 15 Minutes
Oven Temp: 350°
Baking Time: 20 to 25 Minutes

**20 large mushrooms, washed
  and drained
1 clove garlic, minced
¼ cup olive oil**

**½ cup soft bread crumbs
½ cup Parmesan cheese
1 tablespoon dried parsley
  flakes**

Remove mushroom stems. Set aside caps and chop stems. Sauté stems and garlic in oil over a medium heat until tender. Remove from heat. Stir in remaining ingredients. Spoon into caps. Place in 13x9x2 inch baking dish. Bake at 350° for 20 to 25 minutes.

Pam Shriver - Riderwood, Md.

PEPPERONI STUFFED MUSHROOMS

Moderate
Make Ahead

Serves: 6
Prep Time: 15 Minutes
Oven Temp: 325°
Baking Time: 25 to 30 Minutes

**12 large mushrooms
2 tablespoons butter
1 medium-sized onion, chopped
¼ cup chopped green peppers
½ cup (2 ounce) diced
  pepperoni
1 garlic clove, minced
½ cup round butter crackers,
  crushed**

**3 tablespoons Parmesan cheese
1 tablespoon chopped parsley
½ teaspoon salt
¼ teaspoon oregano
Dash pepper
¾ cup chicken broth**

Remove mushroom stems. Set caps aside and chop stems. Melt butter over a medium heat. Add stems, onion, green peppers, pepperoni and garlic. Sauté until tender. Add cracker crumbs, cheese, parsley and seasonings. Mix well. Stir in chicken broth. Stuff caps. Place on a generously greased baking sheet. Bake at 325° for 25 to 30 minutes.

Phyllis Mastrangelo - Plymouth Meeting, Pa.

SEAFOOD STUFFED MUSHROOMS

Moderate

Serves: 12 to 16
Prep Time: 30 Minutes
Oven Temp: 400°
Baking Time: 6 to 8 Minutes

Mushrooms:
**2 pounds medium fresh
mushrooms, washed and
drained**

**½ cup butter, melted
Parmesan cheese**

Seafood Filling:
**¼ pound scallops
¾ to 1 pound cooked bay
shrimp
2 ounces crabmeat, cartilage
removed
2 (3 ounce) packages cream
cheese, softened**

**2 eggs, slightly beaten
½ teaspoon garlic powder
1 teaspoon dry mustard
¼ teaspoon white pepper
½ teaspoon salt**

Seafood Filling: Blanch scallops in boiling water for 30 seconds. Cool. Finely chop scallops, shrimp and crab. Squeeze out any excess moisture through a clean towel or cheesecloth. Place seafood in a mixing bowl. Add cream cheese, chopped mushroom stems, eggs and seasonings. Mix until well blended.

Mushrooms: Remove stems and chop. Arrange caps on baking sheet. Place 1 tablespoon of filling mounded in each cap. Drizzle melted butter over each cap. Sprinkle lightly with cheese. Bake at 400° for 6 to 8 minutes or until mushrooms are hot and cheese is lightly browned.

Sis Milito - Norristown, Pa.

APPETIZERS

PIER 4 MUSHROOMS

Easy

Serves: 6 to 8
Prep Time: 20 Minutes

½ cup wine vinegar
⅔ cup salad oil
1 teaspoon oregano
1 clove garlic, minced
½ teaspoon salt

½ teaspoon sugar
½ teaspoon pepper
1 tablespoon fresh lemon juice
1 pound fresh mushrooms

Combine all ingredients in order listed, except for the mushrooms. Mix until well blended. Clean and cut ends from mushrooms. Pour marinade over mushrooms. Cover. Refrigerate overnight. Before serving, drain mushrooms. *Great appetizer! Always a pleaser!*

Nancy Minehan - Wyndmoor, Pa.

STUFFED MUSHROOM CAPS

Easy

Serves: Varies (See note)
Prep Time: 20 Minutes
Oven Temp: 350°
Baking Time: 15 Minutes

**Mushrooms, washed and
   stemmed**
Bread crumbs

Minced onions
Shredded blue cheese
¼ cup butter

Chop mushroom stems. Combine with next 3 ingredients. Sauté over medium heat in butter until mushrooms and onions are tender. Stuff mushroom caps. Place in a lightly greased casserole dish. Bake at 350° for 15 minutes. *What's great about this recipe is that you can add as much or as little as you desire with any of the four ingredients. 1 pound mushrooms will serve approximately 6 to 8 people as appetizers.*

Carolyn M. Williams - V⁀st Oak Lane, Pa.

SWEDISH DIP

Easy
Make Ahead
Food Processor

Serves: 10 to 12
Prep Time: 15 to 20 Minutes

1 (10 ounce) package frozen,
  chopped spinach, thawed and
  squeezed dry
1 (8 ounce) can water chestnuts,
  coarsely chopped
1 (1⅝ ounce) package Swiss
  vegetable soup mix

1 cup mayonnaise
1 cup sour cream
2 tablespoons chopped onions
1 tablespoon grated Parmesan
  cheese

Combine ingredients in order listed in a medium-sized mixing bowl. Beat until well blended or process for a few seconds in a food processor. *"Smaklig maltid"*

Lisa Lindbom Fetterman - Wyndmoor, Pa.

BREAD-PIZZA APPETIZER

Easy
Make Ahead

Serves: 10 to 15
Prep Time: 10 Minutes
Oven Temp: 350°
Baking Time: 10 Minutes

6 ounces Swiss cheese,
  shredded
6 ounces Cheddar cheese,
  shredded
1 pound bacon, cooked and
  crumbled
3 (4 ounce) cans chopped
  mushrooms

⅔ cup mayonnaise
1 tablespoon oregano
2 tablespoons parsley
½ teaspoon rosemary
½ teaspoon salt
½ teaspoon pepper
2 loaves French bread, halved
  lengthwise

Combine all ingredients except bread in order listed in a large mixing bowl. Mix until well blended. Cover. Refrigerate overnight. Spread the cheese mixture on the bread halves. Bake at 350° for 10 minutes. Remove from the oven and allow to stand 5 minutes before slicing and serving.

Margaret Piszek - Lafayette Hill, Pa.

APPETIZERS

SPINACH AND PORK PÂTÉ WITH FINE HERBS

Moderate
Make Ahead

Serves: 20 to 25
Prep Time: 1 hour
Oven Temp: 325°
        300°
Baking Time: 30 Minutes - 325°
        40 Minutes - 300°

1 large onion, diced
¼ cup butter, divided
½ pound frozen spinach,
   defrosted
4 eggs, slightly beaten
¼ cup heavy cream
½ teaspoon salt
½ teaspoon pepper
2 cloves garlic, minced
2 tablespoons basil
2 tablespoons parsley
2 tablespoons tarragon

1 tablespoon rosemary
¼ teaspoon cayenne pepper
Dash nutmeg
2 tablespoons unflavored
   gelatin
¼ cup cold water
¼ pound chicken liver
1 pound pork, cut into 1 inch
   cubes, uncooked
½ pound ham, finely diced
1 pound button mushrooms
2 pounds bacon

Sauté onion in 2 tablespoons butter over a medium heat until tender and transparent. Add the spinach. Cook for 5 minutes, stirring constantly, being careful not to burn the mixture. Combine eggs and cream. Add salt, pepper, garlic and spices. Mix until well blended.

Soften gelatin in cold water. Sauté the chicken liver in remaining butter until lightly browned. Place the pork in a food processor. Process for 2 minutes. Add the onion mixture, egg mixture and gelatin. Process for an additional 2 minutes. Scrape down the sides of the processor container. Process until mixture is smooth. Fold in the ham, mushrooms and chicken liver.

Line a 9x5x3 inch pan by laying bacon strips flat on the bottom of the pan. Lay bacon strips over the sides. Pour pâté mixture into the bacon-lined pan. Fold the bacon strips over the top. Bake at 325° for 30 minutes. Reduce temperature to 300° and continue to bake an additional 40 minutes. Refrigerate for 24 hours before slicing.

Heino Koberg - Chef, Le Champignon - Philadelphia, Pa.

BAKED VEGETABLE PÂTÉ

Moderate to Difficult
Make Ahead

Serves: 12
Prep Time: 1½ Hours
Oven Temp: 375°
Baking Time: 1 Hour

Pâté Dough:
1 cup milk
1 cup water
1 (1¾ ounce) package yeast
2 tablespoons sugar
2 eggs, slightly beaten
½ teaspoon salt

2 tablespoons oil
¾ cup wholewheat flour
¾ cup bran flour
1½ cups all-purpose flour
1 egg white

Filling:
3 pounds cream cheese
½ cup celery
½ cup hazelnuts
8 stalks asparagus

¼ pound broccoli
¼ pound cauliflower
½ cup raisins
Cream, as needed

Pâté Dough: Scald milk. Add water. Cool to room temperature. Add yeast, stirring until yeast is completely dissolved. Add sugar. Mix until well blended. Cover. Allow to set 15 to 20 minutes or until mixture begins to bubble. Add eggs and salt. Mix well. Add wholewheat and bran flour. Mix until smooth and elastic. Add enough of the all-purpose flour to make a dough which is dry to the touch and easy to handle. Cover and allow to rise in a warm place for 45 minutes to 1 hour or until almost double in bulk. Roll out and line a 12 inch pâté tin. Fill with cream cheese filling. Fold dough over filling. Wash with egg white. Bake at 375° for 1 hour. Cool. Refrigerate overnight. Remove from the pan, slice and serve.

Filling: Soften cream cheese. Beat until smooth and creamy. Fold in remaining ingredients. Pour into the dough lined pâté pan.

Jon Atkin - Executive Chef, Black Bass Hotel - Lumberville, Pa.

APPETIZERS

CHUTNEY PÂTÉ

Easy
Make Ahead

Serves: 8
Prep Time: 10 Minutes

2 (3 ounce) packages cream
  cheese, softened
1 cup shredded sharp Cheddar
  cheese
1 tablespoon + 1 teaspoon
  sherry
½ teaspoon curry powder

¼ teaspoon salt
1 (8 ounce) jar mango chutney,
  finely chopped
4 green onions and tops, finely
  sliced
Sesame or wheat wafers

Combine first 5 ingredients in mixing bowl in order listed. Beat until well blended and smooth. Spread on a serving platter about ½ inch thick. Chill until firm. Before serving, spread with chutney. Sprinkle with green onions. Serve with sesame or wheat wafers.

Pru Rawson - Wyndmoor, Pa.

SALMON MOUSSE #I

Easy

Serves: 6 to 8
Prep Time: 20 Minutes

1 envelope unflavored gelatin
¼ cup cold water
¾ cup mayonnaise
1 cup salmon, separated into
  flakes
½ cup chopped celery

½ green pepper, finely chopped
2 tablespoons chopped olives
½ teaspoon salt
1 tablespoon vinegar
¼ teaspoon paprika
Pinch cayenne pepper, if desired

Soften gelatin in cold water. Place bowl over boiling water. Stir until gelatin is dissolved. Cool. Add mayonnaise, flaked salmon, celery, pepper, olives, salt, vinegar, paprika and cayenne. Turn into a 1½ quart mold that has been rinsed in cold water. Refrigerate until firm. Remove to a bed of lettuce leaves and garnish as desired. *Tuna or crabmeat may be used in place of salmon. I put the salmon and mayonnaise in the food processor and add melted gelatin. Add vegetables by hand if using the processor.*

John Cardinal Krol - Archbishop of Philadelphia

SALMON MOUSSE #II

Easy

Serves: 15 to 20
Prep Time: 30 Minutes

1 (16 ounce) can salmon,
   drained and flaked, reserve
   liquid
2 hard-cooked eggs, chopped
½ cup diced celery
1½ tablespoons gelatin
1 cup mayonnaise

1 cup sour cream
1 teaspoon salt
2 tablespoons lemon juice
½ cup parsley, chopped
1 tablespoon grated onion
2 teaspoons horseradish
½ teaspoon paprika

Combine salmon, eggs and celery. Soak gelatin in reserved salmon liquid for 5 minutes until it softens. Dissolve over a low heat, stirring constantly. Cool slightly. Stir into mayonnaise. Add sour cream, onion, salt, lemon juice, horseradish, paprika and parsley. Combine with fish mixture. Place in a 1½ quart mold which has been lightly oiled. Cover. Refrigerate several hours or overnight until firm.

Beth Ounsworth - Mt. Airy, Pa.

SHRIMP CHEESIES

Easy
Make Ahead
Can Be Frozen

Serves: 16 to 18
Prep Time: 10 Minutes
Oven Temp: Broil
Baking Time: 3 to 5 Minutes

1 (4 ounce) jar Old English
   pasteurized processed cheese
   spread
½ cup butter, softened

1 tablespoon mayonnaise
½ teaspoon garlic powder
1 (4 ounce) can shrimp, diced
6 English muffins

Combine first 5 ingredients in mixing bowl or blender container. Mix until well blended and fairly smooth. Cut each muffin half into 4 pieces. Spread each ¼ muffin with 1 teaspoon of cheese mixture. Broil for 3 to 5 minutes or until golden brown. *These can be frozen by placing on a baking sheet and allowing to freeze. They can then be placed in a freezer bag and stored until needed. Broil while still frozen.*

Patrice Panebianco - North Hills, Pa.

APPETIZERS

CREAMY TACO DIP

Easy
Make Ahead

Serves: 8 to 10
Prep Time: 15 Minutes

2 (8 ounce) packages cream
   cheese, softened
1 envelope taco seasoning mix
⅓ head lettuce, chopped
2 tomatoes, chopped

2 cups shredded Cheddar
   cheese
½ to 1 cup olives, chopped
1 (4 ounce) jar mild taco sauce
Round corn chips

Combine cream cheese and taco seasoning mix in a medium-sized mixing bowl. Mix until well blended. Spread on the bottom of a 1 quart casserole dish. Top this mixture with a layer of each of the following ingredients in the order listed: lettuce, tomatoes, cheese and olives. Pour taco sauce over the olive layer. Serve with round corn chips.

Sue Miller - Philadelphia, Pa.

AVOCADO TACO SPREAD

Easy
Make Ahead

Serves: 10 to 12
Prep Time: 20 Minutes

2 (8 ounce) cans bean dip
3 ripe avocados, peeled and
   puréed
2 teaspoons lemon juice
1 cup sour cream
½ cup mayonnaise
1 envelope taco seasoning mix
4 tomatoes, chopped

1 bunch scallions, chopped
1 (16 ounce) can black olives,
   chopped
2 cups shredded Cheddar
   cheese
2 (8 ounce) bags round corn
   chips

Spread bean dip in a plate or in the bottom of a 13x9x2 inch pan. Top with puréed avocados combined with lemon juice. Mix sour cream, mayonnaise and taco seasoning mix. Spread over the avocados and lemon juice. Add a layer of tomatoes, followed by scallions and finally black olives. Top with a layer of Cheddar cheese. Serve with round corn chips.

Joan G. Wachlin - Fairmount, Pa.

PEPPER CHEESE

Easy
Make Ahead

Serves: 6 to 8
Prep Time: 10 Minutes

**1 (8 ounce) package cream
    cheese, softened**
½ cup butter, softened

½ clove garlic, minced
**1¼ teaspoons freshly cracked
    pepper**

Combine all ingredients in mixing bowl. Beat until well blended. Pack into a crock or container with tight-fitting lid. Refrigerate. Serve with crackers.

Susan Miller - Philadelphia, Pa.

RUMAKI

Moderate
Make Ahead

Serves: 12
Prep Time: 10 Minutes
Oven Temp: Broil
Baking Time: 5 Minutes

Teriyaki Sauce:
¼ cup vegetable oil
¼ cup soy sauce
2 tablespoons catsup

1 tablespoon vinegar
¼ teaspoon pepper
2 cloves garlic, crushed

Rumaki:
**6 chicken livers, washed and
    halved**
**4 water chestnuts, cut into 3
    pieces**

Teriyaki sauce
6 slices bacon, halved

Teriyaki Sauce: Combine ingredients in order listed in a jar with a tight fitting lid. Shake until well blended.

Rumaki: Combine chicken livers and water chestnuts in a mixing bowl. Pour on Teriyaki sauce. Cover and refrigerate for 4 hours or overnight. Drain. Wrap a piece of liver and a piece of water chestnut in each bacon piece. Secure with a wooden pick. Broil 3 to 4 inches from the broiler unit for 5 minutes or until bacon is crisp. Turn occasionally.

Nancy Murphy - Chestnut Hill, Pa.

EAST FALLS

East Falls is appropriately named for the community clinging to the banks of the Schuylkill River. The river was its very life, providing the community with a wealth of fish and water through the once turbulent falls.

Today the residents are not dependent on the waterway for their livelihood, but the strong sense of community that existed in the 19th century is still in evidence.

In close proximity to center city, it was once an enjoyable day trip up the Schuylkill River to East Falls, where picnickers could dine in the many taverns on "catfish and waffles"—the local delicacy. The catfish has long been identified with East Falls so much so that a bronze catfish weathervane was installed atop the local library on Midvale Avenue.

East Falls is a quiet residential area. There are few shopping streets, banks or theatres to disturb the peaceful setting. It has often been referred to as "Kellytown" because of its once well-known residents, the John B. Kellys, the family of the late Grace Kelly.

Soups
& Salads

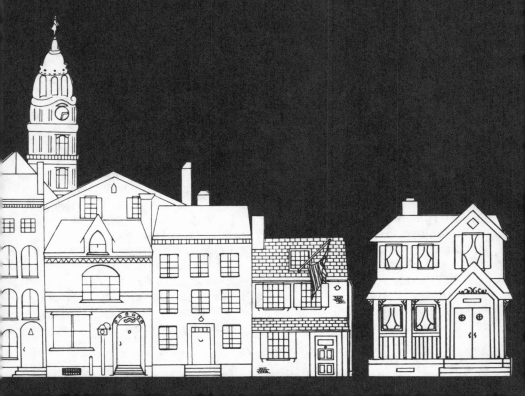

GRAMMY'S VEGETABLE SOUP

Moderate
Make Ahead
Freeze

Serves: 8 to 10
Prep Time: 30 Minutes
Cooking Time: 2½ Hours

1 soup bone
¼ cup barley
1 pot herb
6 turnips, cleaned and diced
6 carrots, peeled and diced
1 onion, diced
1 stalk celery, diced
1 small head cabbage, diced
1 quart tomatoes

1 (8 ounce) can tomato sauce
¼ to ½ teaspoon garlic salt
¼ to ½ teaspoon dill
¼ to ½ teaspoon sweet basil
¼ to ½ teaspoon thyme
¼ to ½ teaspoon marjoram
1 (20 ounce) bag frozen mixed
   vegetables

Cover soup bone with water. Bring to a boil over high heat. Reduce heat and simmer for 40 minutes. Bring back to a boil. Skim fat off surface. Add the barley, pot herb, vegetables, tomatoes, tomato sauce and seasonings. Reduce heat. Simmer soup mixture for 2 hours. Add the frozen vegetables and simmer an additional 15 minutes. Remove soup bone and pot herb before serving. *The whole family loves this one!*

Katie Eastman - Lansdale, Pa.

TARRAGON SPINACH SOUP

Moderate

Serves: 6
Prep Time: 20 Minutes
Cooking Time: 30 to 40 Minutes

3 large onions, sliced
6 tablespoons butter, melted
2 large potatoes, peeled and
   sliced
1 (10½ ounce) can chicken broth
   or bouillon
2½ cups milk
Salt to taste

3 sprigs fresh tarragon, or 1½
   teaspoons dried
1 (10 ounce) package frozen,
   chopped spinach
2 teaspoons soy sauce
¼ to ¾ teaspoon curry powder,
   to taste
1 cup heavy cream, optional

Sauté onion in butter until tender and transparent. Add potatoes, milk, broth, salt and tarragon. Reduce heat. Simmer, covered, for 20 minutes or until potatoes are tender. Add spinach. Continue to simmer 10 minutes or until spinach is defrosted and just cooked. Pour soup mixture into food processor or blender. Blend on high 30 seconds or until mixture is thoroughly blended but still has some texture. Return soup to the pan. Add soy sauce and curry powder. Chill if to be served cold. Add the cream before serving. *Good for St. Patrick's Day. May be served hot or cold. To add extra color, garnish with minced radishes.*

Alice Brogan - Ambler, Pa.

TOMATO AND FONTINA SOUP

Easy

Serves: 6
Prep Time: 20 Minutes
Cooking Time: 1 Hour

6 pounds ripe tomatoes, peeled and seeded
1 tablespoon olive oil
1½ pounds Italian fontina cheese, diced

4 egg yolks, slightly beaten
6 leaves fresh basil, crushed

Combine tomatoes and olive oil in a heavy saucepan. Bring mixture to a boil over a medium high heat. Reduce the heat, cover and simmer for 1 hour. Place the tomato mixture in a food processor or blender. Blend on high 45 seconds or until the mixture is smooth. Return to the saucepan. Add cheese. Cook over a low heat, stirring constantly, until the cheese has melted. Remove from the heat. Add egg yolks to the hot tomato mixture. Mix until well blended. Garnish with basil. *Be sure to remove the mixture from the heat before adding the egg yolks to prevent curdling.* (This soup is good hot or cold.)

Prudence Rawson - Wyndmoor, Pa.

LEEK AND POTATO SOUP

Easy
Make Ahead
Freeze

Serves: 4 to 6
Prep Time: 15 Minutes
Cooking Time: 30 to 40 Minutes

2 tablespoons butter or
  margarine, melted
3 medium leeks, cut into ½ inch
  pieces
1 tablespoon flour
2 cups chicken stock

2 cups water
1 pound potatoes, peeled and
  diced into ½ inch cubes
1 teaspoon salt
½ teaspoon white pepper

Place butter in a 3 to 4 quart saucepan. Add leeks. Sauté over a low heat, stirring often, until they soften. Add flour. Continue cooking, stirring constantly, until mixture thickens. Slowly add the stock and water. Increase heat and cook until simmering. Add the potatoes and seasonings. Cover. Simmer an additional 30 to 40 minutes or until leeks and potatoes are tender. Serve hot, garnished with fresh parsley or chives or grated Swiss cheese. *2 (13¾ ounce) cans chicken broth may be substituted for the chicken stock.*

Mary Bradley - Mt. Airy, Pa.

ULANA'S MUSHROOM SOUP

Moderate

Serves: 4 to 6
Prep Time: 30 Minutes

Mushroom Soup:
1 medium-sized onion, diced
4 tablespoons butter, melted
  and divided
3 cups cultivated mushrooms,
  sliced
1 cup chopped carrots

1 cup chopped celery
4 wild mushrooms, soaked
  overnight, optional
1 tablespoon flour
5 cups chicken stock or water
¼ cup sour cream

Dumplings:
1 egg
1 tablespoon water

1 tablespoon flour
⅛ teaspoon salt

48

In a skillet over a medium heat, sauté onion in 2 tablespoons butter until tender and golden in color. Add 3 cups mushrooms. Sauté until these turn dark. Remove mixture from skillet. Set aside. Sauté carrots, celery and wild mushrooms in remaining butter until celery is translucent but still firm. Sprinkle 1 tablespoon flour over the carrot-celery mixture. Mix until well blended. Place stock in a heavy Dutch oven or stew pot. Bring to a boil over a medium high heat. Add mushrooms and vegetables. Return soup to boiling. Reduce heat and simmer while preparing dumplings. Drop dumplings into the simmering soup. Cook an additional 2 to 3 minutes. Stir in the sour cream.

Dumplings: Combine egg, water, flour and salt in mixing bowl. Stir until ingredients are smooth and mixture is elastic, but still thin. Drop slowly from the end of a spoon. *Batter will form thin dumplings when cooked in the soup.*

Olga Cybriwsky - Oak Lane, Pa.
Ulana's Restaurant - Center City Philadelphia, Pa.

PEPPERPOT SOUP

Easy
Make Ahead

Serves: 6
Prep Time: 1 Hour

1½ to 2 pounds fresh
   honeycomb tripe
1 medium-sized onion, chopped
3 tablespoons butter, melted
Salt to taste
⅛ teaspoon pepper
6 cups boiling water

1 cup grated carrot
½ cup diced celery
6 medium potatoes, diced
1 tablespoon chopped parsley
1 tablespoon pickling spice,
   wrapped in cheese cloth

Thoroughly wash tripe. Remove fat and cover with fresh cold water in heavy saucepan. Cover. Bring to a boil over medium high heat. Reduce heat and simmer for 5 minutes. Drain, rinse and pat dry. Cut tripe into desired serving-sized pieces or put through a meat grinder. Sauté onion in butter until golden brown. Add tripe, salt and pepper. Sauté for an additional 5 minutes. Add boiling water, carrots, celery, potatoes, parsley and pickling spice. Bring to a full boil over a medium high heat. Reduce heat and simmer, covered, for 1 hour.

Vilma Marcolina - Chestnut Hill, Pa.

CRAB ASPARAGUS SOUP

Easy
Make Ahead

Serves: 6
Prep Time: 10 Minutes
Cooking Time: 15 Minutes

1 (6 to 8 ounce) package
   Alaskan King crab, thawed
   and drained
¼ cup chopped green onions
½ teaspoon curry powder

1 tablespoon butter, melted
2 (10¾ ounce) cans condensed
   cream of asparagus soup
2 cups half and half
¼ cup sherry

Slice crab, reserving leg pieces for garnish. Sauté green onions and curry powder in butter over a medium heat. Stir in soup, half and half and crab meat. Heat, stirring occasionally. Blend in sherry. Serve garnished with reserved crab legs, cut into bite-sized chunks. *If cooking for a larger number of people, triple the recipe.*

Mary D'Angelo - Roxborough, Pa.

ROSEMONT FARM CHOWDER

Easy

Serves: 4
Prep Time: 15 Minutes

Pea/Corn Chowder:
1 bag of frozen baby peas
1 bag of frozen baby corn -
   preferably white kernels
1½ cups of chicken broth (more
   or less depending on
   consistency)

1 tablespoon butter
Tabasco
Pinch of onion salt
Light cream (optional)

Defrost peas and corn. Add the vegetables to the chicken broth in a saucepan and bring almost to a boil. Remove from heat, and pour into a blender. Blend well and strain. Return the mixture to the stove and heat for approximately 5 minutes, making sure that the color does not change. Season with a dash of Tabasco and a pinch of onion salt. Add light cream if desired. Be careful not to overcook the soup. *This soup can be enjoyed either hot or cold.*

John and Teresa Heinz - U.S. Senate - Pa.

CARROT AND ORANGE SOUP

Easy

Serves: 6
Prep Time: 20 Minutes
Cooking Time: 40 Minutes

2 tablespoons butter
½ teaspoon fresh ginger, grated
1 pound carrots, peeled and
    cubed
½ cup sliced leeks, white part
    only

3 cups chicken broth, divided
1½ cups orange juice
Salt to taste
Pepper to taste
Orange slices
Mint leaves

Melt butter over medium heat. Add ginger, carrots and leeks. Sauté until leeks are tender. Add 2 cups chicken broth. Heat until mixture boils. Lower heat, cover and simmer for 30 minutes or until carrots are soft. Remove from heat. Pour mixture into blender. Blend on high until mixture is smooth. Return to the saucepan. Add remaining 1 cup chicken broth and orange juice. Salt and pepper to taste. Heat through without boiling. Garnish with orange slices and mint leaves before serving.

Joanne Dhody - Chestnut Hill, Pa.

PASTA CECI

Easy

Serves: 6 to 8
Prep Time: 3 to 3½ Hours

2 garlic cloves, minced
2 stalks celery, chopped
2 large green peppers, chopped
¼ cup olive oil
3 (29 ounce) cans tomato sauce
1 or 2 (19 ounce) cans ceci
    beans (chick peas)

1 (16 ounce) package ditalini,
    cooked *al dente* and drained
Freshly grated Parmesan
    cheese

Sauté garlic, celery and green pepper in olive oil in a large, covered pot on low for 20 to 25 minutes. Add tomato sauce. Cook on low for 2½ to 3½ hours. Add ceci beans to pot. Cook until heated through. To serve: Place pasta in serving bowl, ladle on sauce with beans and top with grated cheese.

Elizabeth Mongelli - Ventnor, N. J.

STRACCIATELLA ALLA ROMANA
(Italian Consommé with Eggs)

Easy

Serves: 3
Prep Time: 20 Minutes

2 large eggs, beaten
3 tablespoons fine, soft
breadcrumbs
3 tablespoons grated Parmesan
cheese

1 teaspoon grated lemon rind
3 cups hot bouillon
Salt
Ground black pepper

Combine eggs, breadcrumbs, cheese and lemon rind in a saucepan. Mix well. Gradually beat in the hot bouillon. Bring mixture to a boil, stirring constantly. Reduce heat. Simmer 15 minutes or until soup thickens slightly. (Do not boil.) Add salt and pepper to taste. Serve hot.

Giuseppina Malatesta - Mt. Airy, Pa.

BISQUE IN CHEESE BREAD BOWLS

Moderate
Make Ahead: Cheese Bowls

Serves: 4
Prep Time: 1 Hour
Oven Temp: 400°
Baking Time: 20 to 25 Minutes

Luncheon Bisque:
1 (10¾ ounce) can cream of
shrimp soup
⅔ can milk or half and half
1 (6½ ounce) can tuna
1 (10 ounce) box frozen
asparagus, cooked and
drained

3 tablespoons sherry
Croutons

Cheese Bread Bowls:
4 to 4½ cups all-purpose flour
1 package active dry yeast
1½ cups milk
1 tablespoon sugar
1 teaspoon salt

2 cups shredded American
cheese
1 egg yolk
1 tablespoon water

Bisque: Combine all ingredients except for the croutons. Pour into a greased, oven-proof tureen or casserole dish. Bake at 400° for 20 to 25 minutes. Add croutons to bisque before serving in edible cheese bowls.

Cheese Bread Bowls: In a large mixer bowl, combine 2 cups of flour and the yeast. Heat milk, sugar and salt over low heat until warm (115 to 120°). Add the warm liquid to the flour mixture along with the cheese. Beat at a low speed of the electric mixer for 30 seconds, scraping the bowl constantly. Beat an additional 3 minutes on high speed. Stir in as much of the remaining flour as you can mix in with a spoon. Turn the dough onto a lightly floured surface. Knead in enough remaining flour to make a moderately stiff dough that is smooth and elastic. (This will take about 6 to 8 minutes.) Place dough in a greased bowl. Turn once to grease the surface. Cover. Let rise in a warm place for 1½ hours or until double in bulk. Punch down. Divide into 8 portions. Shape each into a smooth ball. Cover. Let rise for 10 minutes. For each bowl, roll 1 ball of dough into a 6 inch circle. Fit the dough circles over the bottoms of 8 well-greased, 5 inch foil tart tins or 10 ounce custard cups. Arrange on baking sheets. Bake at 375° for 10 minutes. (If the dough begins to puff up, press down gently with a pot holder.) Remove bowls from the oven. Remove bread from the pans with a narrow metal spatula. Invert right side up on baking sheet. Brush the inside of bowls and rims with a mixture of egg yolk and water. Bake for 5 additional minutes. Turn bowls and bake 4 minutes longer to brown edges. Cool on rack. *Bowls can be baked ahead of time and reheated just before serving. To reheat bake at 350° for 5 to 8 minutes.*

Maura Bock - Hatboro, Pa.

NEW ENGLAND CLAM CHOWDER

Moderate
Make Ahead
Freeze

Serves: 12
Prep Time: 30 Minutes
Cooking Time: About 35 Minutes

3 dozen chowder clams
1 cup water
½ pound sliced bacon, diced
3 medium onions, sliced
4 tablespoons flour, divided
8 potatoes, peeled and diced
¼ teaspoon pepper

4 cups milk
2 cups heavy whipping cream,
   divided
3 tablespoons butter
1 large egg yolk
Paprika, optional

Scrub clams until free of sand. In an 8 quart Dutch oven, heat water to boiling. Add clams. Reduce heat to low, cover and steam for 10 minutes or until the clams open. Remove from heat. Reserve all liquid. Cool clams until they are easily handled. Chop clams. Set aside. In the same pan, cook diced bacon until lightly browned. Add the onions. Sauté until tender. Stir 3 tablespoons flour into onion mixture until blended. Add enough water to reserve clam liquid to make 6 cups. Gradually, stir liquid into flour mixture and cook over a medium heat, stirring constantly, until the mixture has thickened. Stir in potatoes. Add pepper. Cover and cook 10 minutes or until the potatoes are just tender. Stir in the clams, milk, 1 cup cream and butter. Cook until heated through, stirring often. Combine the egg yolk, remaining cream and flour. Gradually, add egg mixture to hot soup, stirring constantly. Sprinkle with paprika before serving. *Great for a rainy day at the shore. Time consuming, but worth the effort.*

Connie Nowak - Lafayette Hill, Pa.

CAPE COD FISH CHOWDER

Easy

Serves: 8
Prep Time: 20 Minutes
Cooking Time: 1 Hour

2 pounds haddock
2 cups water
2 tablespoons shortening or 2
   ounces salt pork, diced
2 onions, sliced
1 cup chopped celery
4 large potatoes, diced

1 bay leaf, crumbled
4 cups milk
2 tablespoons butter
1 teaspoon salt
Freshly ground black pepper, to
   taste

54

Simmer haddock in water for 15 minutes. Drain, reserving broth. Remove bones from the fish. Sauté diced pork until crisp or melt shortening. Sauté onions in shortening or pork until golden brown. Add fish, potatoes, celery, bay leaf, salt and pepper. Add reserved broth, plus enough boiling water, to make 3 cups liquid. Reduce heat and simmer for 30 minutes. Add milk and butter. Simmer for an additional 5 minutes or until heated through. Add pepper to taste.

Edward M. Kennedy - U. S. Senate - Massachusetts

JOE'S MINESTRONE SOUP

Easy
Make Ahead
Freezes Well

Serves: 10 to 12
Prep Time: 2½ Hours

Minestrone Soup:

2 cups cranberry beans
5 quarts plus 2 cups water, divided
1 cup diced potatoes
1 cup diced celery
1 cup diced rutabaga
1 cup diced zucchini
1 cup diced string beans
1 cup chopped onions
2 cups shredded curly cabbage
¼ cup finely diced carrots

½ cup diced leeks
2 teaspoons salt
¼ teaspoon pepper
½ cup tomato sauce
¼ cup plus 2 tablespoons butter
3 tablespoons olive oil
1½ cups uncooked macaroni
¼ cup pesto sauce (see page 80)
Grated Parmesan cheese

Minestrone Soup: Boil the cranberry beans in 2 cups water. Reduce heat and simmer for 1 hour or until beans are tender. Strain. Set aside reserved liquid. Puree beans in blender. Combine vegetables, salt, pepper, pureed beans, reserved bean liquid and 5 quarts of water in a large stock pot. Bring to a boil over high heat. Reduce heat and simmer mixture, uncovered, for 2 hours. Add tomato sauce, butter and olive oil. Stir occasionally while adding the pesto sauce and uncooked macaroni. Cook for 15 minutes or until macaroni is tender. Sprinkle with Parmesan cheese before serving.

Joe Carcione - The Greengrocer - TV, Radio, Newspaper Columns

AVOCADO WITH TAHINI-YOGURT DRESSING

Easy

Serves: 6
Prep Time: 10 Minutes

1 (8 ounce) carton plain yogurt
⅓ cup tahini
⅜ teaspoon ground cumin
⅛ teaspoon ground coriander
¼ teaspoon minced garlic
1 tablespoon lemon juice
¼ teaspoon salt

¼ teaspoon pepper
⅛ teaspoon cayenne pepper
3 ripe avocados, peeled, cut in
   half lengthwise and pits
   removed
⅜ cup slivered almonds, toasted

Combine yogurt and tahini in a small mixing bowl. Whisk until well combined. Add the remaining ingredients, except for the avocados and almonds. Just before serving, thinly slice each avocado in half lengthwise and fan out the slices on individual salad plates. Spoon dressing over each serving. Sprinkle with the toasted almonds. *This is an old FROG recipe that is still a crowd pleaser. Beautiful creamy avocados come to life under this tangy, nutty dressing which would also be delicious for chicken-bacon-avocado salad, as a dip for crudités or with a mixed vegetable salad in pita bread.*

FROG - Center City - Philadelphia, Pa.

TANGY VINAIGRETTE

Easy
Make Ahead

Servings: 6 to 8
Prep Time: 10 Minutes

⅓ cup white tarragon vinegar
Salt to taste
Lemon pepper to taste

1 clove garlic, minced
1 to 2 teaspoons mustard
⅔ cup vegetable oil

Combine first 5 ingredients in a jar with a tight-fitting lid. Cover and shake vigorously. Add oil. Shake again. Allow to sit for ½ hour before serving. Refrigerate unused portion. *Hot or sweet mustard can be used in this dressing to suit your individual tastes.*

Jo Ann Seeger - Oreland, Pa.

SESAME-SEED DRESSING

Easy
Make Ahead

Serves: 6 to 8
Prep Time: 10 Minutes

¼ cup sesame seed
1 cup oil
⅔ cup wine vinegar

3 tablespoons soy sauce
2 tablespoons sugar

Sauté sesame seed in oil over a low heat until golden brown. Scrape seeds into a jar with a tight-fitting lid. Cool. Add vinegar, soy sauce and sugar. Cover. Shake until sugar completely dissolves. Refrigerate. *This will keep up to 1 week in the refrigerator. 1 tablespoon honey may be substituted for the sugar in this recipe.*

Alice Brogan - Ambler, Pa.

KANPAI GINGER SALAD DRESSING

Easy
Make Ahead

Serves: 4 to 6
Prep Time: 10 Minutes

½ cup soy oil
¼ cup soy sauce
⅓ cup diced onion
¼ cup diced celery
3 tablespoons plus 1 teaspoon
 rice vinegar
2 tablespoons peeled, diced
 fresh ginger

2 teaspoons sugar
1½ teaspoons grated lemon rind
½ teaspoon catsup
¼ teaspoon black pepper
¼ teaspoon Aji-no-moto
 (Japanese monosodium
 glutamate), optional

Place ingredients into blender container or food processor in order listed. Blend on high for 60 seconds or until vegetables are puréed. Pour into a jar or container with a tight-fitting lid. Shake before serving.

KANPAI - Philadelphia, Pa.

PEA SALAD

Easy
Make Ahead

Serves: 8
Prep Time: 10 Minutes

**1 (10 ounce) package frozen
green peas, thawed**
¼ cup chopped onion
½ cup chopped green pepper
½ cup chopped celery
**2 (6 ounce) cans sliced water
chestnuts**

1 teaspoon sugar
**8 ounces large curd cottage
cheese**
½ cup mayonnaise

Combine ingredients in order listed. Mix until well blended. Cover and refrigerate until well chilled.

Julie Camburn - East Falls, Pa.

APPLE-ROQUEFORT SALAD

Easy
Make Ahead (Dressing)

Serves: 6
Prep Time: 15 Minutes

Mustard Vinaigrette Dressing:
1 tablespoon Dijon mustard
2 to 3 tablespoons white vinegar
½ cup light olive oil

**⅛ teaspoon freshly ground
pepper**

Apple-Roquefort Salad:
**2 to 3 medium-sized, firm red
Delicious apples, unpeeled,
quartered lengthwise and
cored**
**½ cup crumbled Roquefort
cheese**
**3 tablespoons coarsely chopped
walnuts**

**1 small head Belgian endive,
trimmed**
**1 bunch watercress, rinsed,
dried, stems removed**
Freshly ground pepper

Mustard Vinaigrette Dressing: Whisk mustard, vinegar and pepper in small bowl until well blended. Slowly add oil, drop by drop, whisking constantly. *Dressing can be stored, covered, in refrigerator for up to 2 days.*

Apple-Roquefort Salad: Slice each apple quarter into 8 thin slices. Toss with Roquefort cheese, walnuts and 3 tablespoons of dressing. Cover bowl and refrigerate 3 hours, tossing ingredients occasionally. Before serving, cut endive into quarters, separate and add to the apple mixture along with the watercress. Shake dressing. Pour over salad. Toss. Serve immediately with freshly ground pepper.

Dorothea Duncan - Toms River, N. J.

WILD MUSHROOM SALAD

Easy

Serves: 6
Prep Time: 20 Minutes

½ pound chantrelle mushrooms
½ pound shitake mushrooms
½ pound oyster mushrooms
½ cup walnut oil
1 head radicchio, washed and torn
3 bunches mâche, washed and torn
2 bunches arugala, washed, leaves only
2 heads limestone, washed
1 bunch watercress, washed, leaves only

1 head curly endive, washed, hearts only
¼ cup pine nuts
2 tablespoons shallots, minced
1 tablespoon garlic, minced
¼ cup sherry wine vinegar
2 tablespoons basil, minced
2 tablespoons tarragon, minced
2 tablespoons thyme, minced
2 tablespoons chives, minced
Salt to taste
Pepper to taste

Mix greens in large salad bowl. Sauté mushrooms in hot, smoking oil for 5 to 8 minutes or until tender. Add to the greens. Toss gently to mix. In same skillet used to sauté mushrooms, sauté pine nuts, shallots and garlic for 1 minute or until pine nuts brown. Add vinegar to deglaze the pan. Add herbs, salt and pepper. Pour over mushrooms and greens. Toss to mix.

MICHAEL'S - Los Angeles, Ca.

SPINACH SALAD

Easy

Serves: 4 to 6
Prep Time: 15 to 20 Minutes

Salad:
1 pound fresh spinach
1 small onion, sliced in thin
rings
1 (8 ounce) can bean sprouts,
optional

1 (6 ounce) can water chestnuts,
optional
2 hard-cooked eggs, cut up
8 slices bacon, fried crisp and
crumbled

Dressing:
½ cup salad oil
¼ cup vinegar
1 tablespoon sugar or to taste

Dash salt
Dash pepper

Salad: Combine spinach, onions, bean sprouts and water chestnuts in a large salad bowl. Toss to mix. Pour dressing over spinach mixture. Toss. Top with eggs and bacon.

Dressing: Combine ingredients in order listed in a jar with a tight-fitting lid. Cover. Shake until well blended. Chill until just before serving salad.

Elaine Richardson - Lafayette Hill, Pa.

BROCCOLI SALAD

Easy
Make Ahead

Serves: 6
Prep Time: 15 Minutes

1 pound bunch of broccoli
10 to 12 cherry tomatoes, halved
1 small onion, diced
¼ teaspoon salt, or to taste

Dash white pepper
½ cup salad dressing
¼ cup chopped water chestnuts

Rinse broccoli. Cut off tough part of stem. Cut the rest into flowerets, small pieces and stem in ¼ inch slices. Steam or cook in a small amount of boiling, salted water for 10 minutes or until barely tender. (Do not overcook.) Drain and chill. Combine the remaining ingredients. Add to chilled broccoli. Toss until well blended. Chill several hours before serving.

Herb Clarke - WCAU-TV - Channel 10

DILL CUCUMBER SALAD

Easy
Make Ahead

Serves: 4
Prep Time: 15 Minutes

2 tablespoons oil
1 tablespoon lemon juice
2 teaspoons red wine vinegar
½ teaspoon salt
⅛ teaspoon pepper

2 medium-sized cucumbers,
   peeled, halved, seeded and
   thinly sliced
1 tablespoon snipped fresh dill
   weed

In a medium-sized bowl, combine the oil, lemon juice, vinegar, salt and pepper. Mix until well blended. Add the cucumbers and dill weed. Toss to mix. Refrigerate.

Justine Schaedler - Havre de Grace, Md.

CASHEW SALAD

Easy
Make Ahead (Dressing)

Serves: 8
Prep Time: 15 Minutes

Salad:
1 head lettuce
2 (2 ounce) packages salted
   cashews

Dressing:
2 tablespoons sugar, or to taste
1 teaspoon dry mustard
½ teaspoon minced onion

1 teaspoon celery seed
¼ cup vinegar
1 cup oil

Dressing: Combine all ingredients in a jar with a tight-fitting lid. Shake until well blended. Refrigerate until ½ hour before serving.

Salad: Break lettuce into small, bite-sized pieces. Pour dressing over salad. Sprinkle with cashews.

Sue Miller - Philadelphia, Pa.

SEVEN LAYER SALAD

Easy
Make Ahead

Serves: 8 to 10
Prep Time: 30 Minutes

1 head lettuce	**½ cup grated carrot**
1 cup sliced celery	**2 cups mayonnaise**
1 cup chopped onion	**3 teaspoons sugar**
1 (10 ounce) package frozen peas	**1 (4 ounce) package grated sharp Cheddar cheese**

Layer first 5 ingredients in a 13x9x2 inch glass pan. Combine the mayonnaise and sugar. Mix until well blended. Spread over carrot layer. Top with Cheddar cheese. Cover and refrigerate. *For a decorative touch, layer in a clear, tall serving dish. The peas do not need to be defrosted as they will thaw on their own.*

Pat Benvenuto - Mt. Airy, Pa.

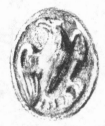

RAW VEGETABLE SALAD

Easy
Make Ahead

Servings: 6 to 8
Prep Time: 25 Minutes

1 medium-sized head cauliflower, chopped into bite-sized pieces	**1 small red onion, thinly sliced and halved**
1 bunch broccoli, chopped into bite-sized pieces	**1 cup mushrooms, halved**
4 carrots, chopped into bite-sized pieces	**½ cup celery, chopped**
	½ cup black olives, halved
	1 (8 ounce) bottle Italian dressing

Mix first 7 ingredients in a large salad bowl. Add Italian dressing. Cover and allow vegetables to marinate overnight. Mix before serving. *This makes a great snack for kids.*

Joanne Dhody - Chestnut Hill, Pa.

NEW POTATO SALAD

Easy
Make Ahead

Serves: 4 to 6
Prep Time: 45 Minutes

**1 pound small red potatoes,
  boiled in jackets and
  quartered**
1 large onion, chopped
**½ cup Spanish olives, coarsely
  chopped**

⅓ cup chopped parsley
Mayonnaise
Dijon mustard to taste
Salt to taste
Pepper to taste

Combine the first 4 ingredients in mixing bowl. Add enough mayonnaise to which a few teaspoons of mustard have been added to coat the potato mixture. Salt and pepper to taste. Cover and chill until serving. *Colorful and different.*

Joan Forde - Chestnut Hill, Pa.

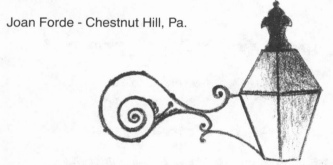

GERMAN-AMERICAN POTATO SALAD

Easy

Serves: 6 to 8
Prep Time: 1 Hour

15 medium-sized potatoes
1 small onion, finely chopped
1 teaspoon salt
**6 strips bacon, cut into small
  pieces**

¼ cup vinegar
¼ cup water
Mayonnaise

Cook potatoes with skin on. When tender, skin, cool and dice. Place onion in a large mixing bowl. Add salt and diced potatoes. Fry bacon pieces in a small skillet until crisp. Add vinegar and water to the hot bacon and grease. Pour immediately over the cold potatoes. Mix lightly. Cool mixture. Add mayonnaise to taste. Cover and refrigerate until serving.

Sister Helen Wiegmann - Former Principal, Norwood-Fontbonne Academy

SOUPS & SALADS

RASPBERRY SWIRL SALAD

Easy
Make Ahead

Serves: 12
Prep Time: 30 Minutes

1 (6 ounce) package raspberry-
   flavored gelatin
2 cups boiling water

2 (10 ounce) packages
   raspberries
⅔ cup sour cream

Dissolve flavored gelatin in boiling water. Add raspberries. Mix well. Chill until thickened, but not set. Pour ½ thickened gelatin into a lightly oiled, 6 cup mold. Spoon sour cream over gelatin. Cover with remaining gelatin. Swirl with a knife to marble. Chill 4 hours or longer. *This colorful salad can also be used as a dessert.*

Maureen Allu - Fort Washington, Pa.

PINEAPPLE VEGETABLE CROWN

Easy
Make Ahead

Serves: 10 to 12
Prep Time: 25 Minutes

1 (3 ounce) package strawberry-
   flavored gelatin
2½ cups boiling water, divided
1 (20 ounce) can pineapple
   chunks, drained
½ cup pineapple juice, reserved
   from chunks
1 (3 ounce) package lemon-
   flavored gelatin

2 cups grated cabbage
1 cup grated carrot
1 tablespoon lemon juice
1 (3 ounce) package cream
   cheese, softened
Pineapple slices or chunks
Salad greens

Place strawberry-flavored gelatin in a medium-sized mixing bowl. Add 1 cup of boiling water. Stir until gelatin dissolves. Add pineapple chunks and juice. Stir until well blended. Turn into a 1½ quart, lightly oiled, mold. Chill until firm. Dissolve lemon-flavored gelatin in remaining 1½ cups boiling water. Chill until slightly thickened. Stir in cabbage, carrot, lemon juice and cheese which has been thinned with a teaspoon of pineapple juice. Turn onto the strawberry layer in the mold. Chill until firm. Serve with pineapple slices or chunks on beds of salad greens. *For rapid setting: set mold in a pan of ice and water.*

Mildred L. Hager - Jenkintown, Pa.

MARINATED FRUIT CUP

Easy
Make Ahead

Serves: 8 to 10
Prep Time: 30 Minutes

3 cups cantaloupe or honeydew
melon balls
1 (13¼ ounce) can pineapple
chunks, drained

1 cup strawberries, hulled
1 (6 ounce) can grapefruit juice
¼ cup orange marmalade
2 tablespoons orange liqueur

Combine melon, pineapple and strawberries in a large mixing bowl. Toss gently to mix. Combine remaining ingredients in a small mixing cup or bowl. Pour over fruits. Stir gently until fruits are coated. Cover. Chill in refrigerator for 1 to 2 hours before serving, stirring occasionally.

Barbara Powers - Roxborough, Pa.

FESTIVE CHICKEN AND FRUIT SALAD

Moderate
Make Ahead

Serves: 6
Prep Time: 1 Hour

Salad:
1 (5 pound) roasting chicken or
chicken breasts
¾ cup diced celery
1 cup seedless white grapes,
halved

1 cup mandarin orange
sections, drained
¼ cup toasted, slivered almonds
Lettuce

Dressing:
½ cup mayonnaise
½ cup sour cream
2 tablespoons finely chopped
parsley

2 tablespoons lemon juice
½ tablespoon salt
½ tablespoon pepper

Salad: Steam chicken for 1 hour or until tender, being careful not to let it boil. Cool. Remove skin. Bone and cut into large bite-sized pieces. Place in a medium-sized mixing bowl and add celery, grapes, and orange sections. Chill. Pour dressing over chicken and fruit. Toss to coat chicken and fruit with dressing. Cover. Chill for several hours to allow flavors to blend. Serve on lettuce cups. Sprinkle with almonds. Can be garnished with extra grapes and orange sections. Dressing: Combine ingredients and blend.

Betsy Ledwith - Oreland, Pa.

FISHTOWN

The community of Fishtown has been making its own history for over 16 generations. So important is it to the city's development that the statue of William Penn gazes down upon Fishtown from atop the City Hall tower.

Originally called Shackamaxon (the Meeting Place of Chiefs), it featured an abundance of trees. Prominent among them was the "Great Elm", under which Penn signed his treaty negotiating the purchase of Pennsylvania from the Indians in 1682. Long gone, the tree has now been replaced by a monument and a beautiful park along the banks of the Delaware.

Fishtown was a popular fishing center in the 18th and 19th centuries. This seafaring economy was reflected in the local architecture, and Fishtown literally grew up from the river's bank. The Green Tree Inn (now the Marlboro Inn) has been designated a historic landmark as the oldest continuous inn in the country. It is a reminder of those days when ships were announced from the octagonal watchtower (called a belvedere). As its fishing industry increased, so did its mills, blacksmiths and lumberyards. Fishtown, a factory town, grew with the city.

Today called home by a great many diverse people, Fishtown identity has come to supersede ethnic identity. Most residents feel it is more important to be a Fishtowner than anything. They are more interested in what's happening down the block than in their city of Brotherly Love.

Eggs, Cheese, Pasta & Rice

EGGS, CHEESE, PASTA & RICE

BAKED BREAKFAST

Easy
Make Ahead

Serves: 8
Prep Time: 35 Minutes
Oven Temp: 350°
Baking Time: 45 Minutes

Butter or margarine
12 slices bread, crusts removed
1½ pounds bulk pork sausage,
  cooked, crumbled, and
  drained

6 eggs, beaten
2 cups milk
2 cups shredded Cheddar
  cheese

Butter one side of bread slices. Line a 13x9x2 inch baking dish with bread, buttered side up. Sprinkle with cooked sausage. Combine eggs and milk; pour over bread. Top with cheese. Cover and refrigerate overnight. Bake at 350° for 45 minutes. Uncover last 15 minutes. *This is great to make ahead. May be used for lunch with a salad.*

Marge Solarski - Roxborough, Pa.

BACON AND CHEESE OVEN OMELET

Easy

Serves: 5
Prep Time: 20 to 30 Minutes
Oven Temp: 350°
Baking Time: About 40 Minutes

12 slices bacon, cooked and
  drained
6 slices cheese

8 eggs, beaten
1 cup milk

Curl 1 slice bacon, chop 4 slices and leave remaining slices whole; set aside. Cut cheese slices in half and line bottom of a lightly buttered 9 inch pie pan. Combine eggs and milk; beat with a fork until well blended. Add chopped bacon. Pour over cheese and bake at 350° for 30 minutes. Arrange whole bacon slices on top around curled bacon. Bake 10 minutes longer; let stand 5 minutes before cutting.

Sister Beatrice DeSantis - Principal, Norwood-Fontbonne Academy - Chestnut Hill, Pa.

FRITTATA

Easy
Make Ahead

Serves: 4 to 6
Prep Time: 20 Minutes
Oven Temp: 375°
Baking Time: About 45 Minutes

1 large onion, sliced
1 tablespoon butter or
  margarine
1 large loaf French or Italian
  bread
2 cups (8 ounces) Swiss cheese,
  shredded
6 ounces ham, sliced thin

1 cup (4 ounces) grated
  Parmesan cheese
6 eggs, beaten
3 cups milk
½ teaspoon salt
Freshly ground pepper to taste
Dash of freshly grated nutmeg

Sauté onion in butter until tender. Cut bread into ½ inch slices; arrange in bottom of a greased 2 quart casserole dish. Sprinkle bread with half the onions. Add layer of half the Swiss cheese, all of the ham and a layer of half the Parmesan. Repeat layers of bread slices and onions. Mix the last 5 ingredients and pour over all. Top with remaining cheeses. Refrigerate until ready to bake. Bake at 375° for approximately 45 minutes or until golden brown. *Great way to use leftover bread or rolls or for a change of pace meal.*

Evelyn P. Olivieri - Mt. Airy, Pa.

RED BEET EGGS

Easy
Make Ahead

Serves: 4 to 6
Prep Time: 15 Minutes

1 (16 ounce) can beets
1 cup vinegar
¼ cup sugar
½ teaspoon salt
4 cloves

Cinnamon to taste
6 or 8 hard-cooked eggs
½ cup thinly sliced sweet red
  onions (optional)

Drain beets reserving juice and adding water if necessary to make 1 cup. Add vinegar, sugar, salt, cloves and cinnamon; bring to a boil. Pour hot solution over beets; cool. Add peeled eggs and onions. Cover and refrigerate 1 to 3 days. Invert jar or carefully stir eggs occasionally.

Sharon Avato - Roxborough, Pa.

BRUNCH OMELET

Moderate

Serves: 4
Prep Time: 10 Minutes
Oven Temp: 200°
Baking Time: To Warm

Filling:
1 bunch watercress
1 pound shelled, deveined
  shrimp
1 tablespoon butter or
  margarine

Salt
Pepper

Omelet:
8 eggs, divided
4 teaspoons water, divided
2 tablespoons butter or
  margarine

Salt and pepper
¾ cup sour cream

Filling: Wash and thoroughly dry watercress. Chop leaves coarsely, avoiding stems; set aside. Sauté shrimp in butter until they turn pink. Do not overcook or they become tough. Season with salt and pepper to taste; keep warm.

Omelet: Beat 4 eggs with 2 teaspoons water and season as desired. Heat butter until foaming but not brown in a large non-stick frying pan. Add egg mixture. As edges begin to set, draw them towards center and tilt pan so the rest of the egg cooks. When top is creamy but not runny, loosen with spatula and slide out onto a large plate, creamy side up. Add sour cream spreading to edges. Cover with foil and keep warm in 200° oven. Repeat cooking process with remaining eggs except cook until eggs are slightly firmer. Place a plate over pan and invert. Add watercress and shrimp to omelet in oven. Slide top of omelet onto filling. Cut into 4 to 6 wedges. *Great for brunch with tomatoes stuffed with zucchini or creamed spinach.*

Cheryl Young - Chestnut Hill, Pa.

APPLE CHEDDAR QUICHE

Easy

Serves: 4 to 6
Prep Time: 10 Minutes
Oven Temp: 375°
Baking Time: 40 to 50 Minutes

**1 large Granny Smith apple,
  shredded
½ cup white port or sauterne
  wine
1½ cups shredded Cheddar
  cheese**

**1 (10 inch) deep dish pastry
  shell
3 eggs
1½ cups heavy or light cream
¼ teaspoon nutmeg**

Marinate apples in wine for at least 1 hour; drain. Sprinkle shredded apple and cheese in bottom of pastry shell. Combine eggs, cream and nutmeg; beat until well blended. Pour into shell. Bake at 375° for 40 to 50 minutes. Let stand 15 minutes before cutting. Garnish with apple slices and Cheddar cheese if desired.

Ann Gray - East Falls, Pa.

CHEDDAR BISCUIT QUICHE

Easy

Serves: 6
Prep Time: 20 Minutes
Oven Temp: 350°
Baking Time: 50 to 55 Minutes

**1 (4.5 ounce) can buttermilk
  biscuits
2 cups shredded Cheddar
  cheese
2 tablespoons flour
3 eggs, slightly beaten**

**1¼ cups milk
½ cup chopped ham
2 tablespoons chopped pimento
½ teaspoon salt
Dash of pepper**

Line bottom and sides of an ungreased 9 inch pie pan with biscuits; press together to seal. Combine cheese and flour. Add eggs, milk, ham, pimento and seasonings; mix until well blended. Pour into biscuit shell. Bake at 350° for 50 to 55 minutes.

Ruth Anne Hill - Roxborough, Pa.

MUSHROOM QUICHE

Easy
Make Ahead
Freeze

Serves: 4 to 6
Prep Time: 15 Minutes
Oven Temp: 350°
Baking Time: 35 Minutes

**4 tablespoons butter or
    margarine, divided**
2 tablespoons minced shallots
**1 pound fresh mushrooms,
    thinly sliced**
1½ teaspoons salt, divided
1 teaspoon lemon juice

4 eggs
1 cup heavy cream
⅛ teaspoon pepper
⅛ teaspoon nutmeg
½ cup shredded Swiss cheese
1 (10 inch) baked pastry shell

Melt 3 tablespoons butter in a large skillet. Add the shallots and sauté for 1 minute until tender, stirring constantly. Stir in the mushrooms, 1 teaspoon salt and lemon juice. Cover and simmer over low heat for 10 minutes. Uncover, increase heat to medium, and cook for 5 to 10 minutes until liquid is completely evaporated and the mushrooms begin to sauté. Stir to prevent scorching. Beat the eggs and cream together; add remaining ½ teaspoon salt, pepper and nutmeg. Stir in the mushrooms. Pour this mixture into the baked pastry shell. Sprinkle with grated cheese and dot with remaining 1 tablespoon butter. Bake at 350° for 35 minutes or until the quiche is puffy and browned. A knife inserted in it comes out clean when done.

Frank L. Rizzo, Mayor of Philadelphia 1972 to 1980

BLEU CHEESE AND GREEN APPLE CRÊPES

Moderate

Serves: 4
Prep Time: 15 Minutes

Crêpe Batter:
1 tablespoon flour
**1 tablespoon melted butter or
    margarine**

1 tablespoon milk
1 egg

Crêpe Filling:
¼ cup butter or margarine
4 or 5 peeled and sliced apples

Crumbled bleu cheese
1 ounce apple jack (optional)

Crêpe Batter: Combine flour and butter; beat in milk and egg. Beat until well blended and smooth. Make crêpes and stack on warm tray.

Crêpe Filling: Melt butter over medium high heat. Add sliced apples and sauté until tender. Add cheese and liqueur if desired. Reduce heat and continue to cook, stirring constantly, until melted. Place apples in warm crêpes; roll up crêpes. Place on serving plates and drizzle excess sauce in pan over crêpes; serve while warm. *Excellent for breakfast or luncheon.*

Garry W. Waldie, CEC - Mt. Airy, Pa.

ALPINE OVEN OMELET

Moderate

Serves: 6 to 8
Prep Time: 10 Minutes
Oven Temp: 325°
Baking Time: 10 to 15 Minutes

6 eggs, separated
2 tablespoons milk
½ teaspoon salt
2 tablespoons chopped chives

1 (8 ounce) package Swiss cheese slices, cut into thin strips
1 (2½ ounce) jar mushrooms, drained

Combine egg yolks, milk and salt; beat until thick and lemon colored. Add chives and ⅔ of cheese. Beat egg whites until they hold peaks. Fold yolk mixture into beaten egg whites. Pour into hot, well-greased 10 inch oven-proof skillet. Cook over low heat 10 minutes or until underside is golden brown. Bake at 325° 10 to 15 minutes or until top is firm. Remove from oven; make deep crease across top. Place mushrooms and remaining cheese on half of omelet. Slip spatula underneath, tip skillet to loosen and fold in half. *Great for brunch.*

Ruth Anne Hill - Roxborough, Pa.

"ST. POLYCARP" ROULADE

Moderate
Make Ahead

Serves: 8 to 10
Prep Time: 20 Minutes
Oven Temp: 325°
Baking Time: 25 Minutes

¼ cup butter or margarine
⅓ cup flour
2 cups milk
4 eggs, separated
Breadcrumbs
1 (10 ounce) package frozen,
  chopped spinach, cooked
4 ounces cream cheese

Salt
Pepper
Garlic powder
Nutmeg
1 (8 ounce) carton yogurt or
  sour cream
Bacon, chives, parsley or
  salmon caviar for garnish

Melt butter in saucepan; add flour and cook 2 minutes, stirring constantly. Add milk. Cook until mixture thickens and continue to cook 2 minutes, stirring constantly. Remove from heat. Slowly pour hot cream sauce into yolks. Mix until blended. Return to heat and cook 1 minute. Remove from heat; season. Beat egg whites until stiff. Gently fold into cream sauce. Pour into waxed paper-lined, crumb covered 11x8x2 inch pan. Bake 25 minutes at 325° until brown. Turn out on waxed paper covered with breadcrumbs. Combine spinach and cream cheese; season to taste with seasonings. Spread spinach mixture over roulade. Roll lengthwise jelly-roll style. Slice log. Serve with yogurt. Garnish with bacon, chives, parsley, or salmon caviar. May be served hot or cold.

Garry W. Waldie, CEC - Mt. Airy, Pa.

GIANT APPLE POPOVER

Easy
Make Ahead

Serves: 8 to 10
Prep Time: 15 Minutes
Oven Temp: 425°
Baking Time: 20 to 25 Minutes

6 eggs
1½ cups flour
¼ teaspoon salt
1 tablespoon sugar
1½ cups milk
¾ cup butter or margarine,
  divided

3 large apples, peeled, cored
  and thinly sliced
Lemon juice
¾ cup sugar
2 tablespoons cinnamon

Beat eggs; add flour, salt and sugar. Stir until smooth; gradually stir in milk. (Batter may be made ahead.) Divide butter between two (9 inch) skillets with oven proof handles. Sprinkle apple slices with lemon juice and divide between the 2 pans. Sprinkle sugar and cinnamon over apples and sauté until glazed and golden. Add half the egg batter to each pan. Bake at 425° for 20 to 25 minutes until puffed and golden brown. Serve at once.

Arlen Specter - U. S. Senate, Pa.

HERBED SANDWICHES

Easy
Make Ahead

Yield: 2 Cups
Prep Time: 5 Minutes

1 bunch fresh mixed herbs, such
  as tarragon, parsley, chives,
  oregano, marjoram, basil,
  watercress-whatever is
  available from the garden
1 (8 ounce) container cottage
  cheese or cream cheese

1 hard-cooked egg, quartered
1 (2 ounce) package walnut
  pieces
Salt and pepper to taste

Finely chop herbs in food processor. Add cheese, egg, nuts and seasonings. Blend until smooth. Serve on black bread with tomato or cucumber slices. *This makes a nice late spring or early summer lunch or light cocktail snack when the herb garden is bountiful.*

Marie King Wolfe - Chestnut Hill, Pa.

EGGS, CHEESE, PASTA & RICE

SHIRRED EGGS WITH SCRAPPLE

Easy

Serves: 4
Prep Time: 10 Minutes
Cooking Time: 10 to 15 Minutes

2 tablespoons butter
8 eggs
Salt and pepper, to taste

Cheese slices
½ pound Scrapple

Melt butter in skillet over low heat. Crack eggs in pan. Cover and cook slowly until eggs turn "white". Remove from heat. Season with salt and pepper. Place cheese slices over eggs and slice into wedges.

Scrapple: Slice in ⅜ inch slices. Brown in non-stick pan until crisp on the outside and soft on the inside.

John B. Kelly, Jr., President, U.S. Olympic Committee

TERIYAKI STEAK SANDWICH

Easy
Make Ahead

Serves: 4
Prep Time: 5 Minutes
Oven Temp: Broil
Baking Time: 8 Minutes

⅔ cup oil
⅓ cup honey
⅓ cup soy sauce
2 cloves garlic, chopped
2 tablespoons green onions,
chopped

Dash of ground ginger
1 pound flank steak/London
Broil
Sandwich rolls

Mix first 6 ingredients. Pour over steak in a non-metal baking dish. Marinate for a minimum of 6 hours or overnight. Grill or broil 4 minutes per side or until medium rare. Slice on diagonal and serve on rolls. *Sauce may also be used on chicken.*

Gay E. Simpson - Mt. Airy, Pa.

WILD MUSHROOM SAUCE

Easy

Serves: 4 to 6
Prep Time: 1 Hour
Cooking Time: 45 Minutes

1 ounce dried Porcini
  mushrooms
2 tablespoons finely chopped
  shallots
5 tablespoons unsalted butter or
  margarine

¼ pound ham, minced
2 cups canned, whole tomatoes
  with juice
Salt and freshly ground pepper
1 pound fresh spaghetti
Grated Parmesan cheese

Soak mushrooms in 1 cup water for 40 minutes. Reserve liquid. Rinse and chop them finely. Sauté shallots in butter until pale gold. Add the ham, tomatoes with juice and the strained mushroom liquid. Cook, uncovered, for 45 minutes. Add salt and pepper and keep at a simmer. Cook spaghetti for 1 minute; drain and place in warmed serving dish. Toss with sauce; top with grated Parmesan cheese.

Primarily Pasta, Inc. - Philadelphia, Pa.

MUSSEL SAUCE

Easy

Serves: 4
Prep Time: 20 Minutes
Cooking Time: 11 Minutes

4 tablespoons unsalted butter or
  margarine
1 leek, cleaned and finely
  chopped
3 tablespoons onions, finely
  chopped
1 teaspoon loose stem saffron

2 tablespoons red wine vinegar
3 pounds mussels, well
  scrubbed
½ cup heavy cream
¼ cup minced parsley
1 pound spinach linguine

Melt butter in large pan. Add leek, garlic and onions and sauté for 3 minutes. Add saffron, vinegar and mussels. Cover and cook for 3 minutes. Add cream and parsley. Simmer for 5 minutes or until mussels open. (Discard unopened ones.) Keep warm. Serve over linguine.

Primarily Pasta, Inc. - Philadelphia, Pa.

EGGS, CHEESE, PASTA & RICE

NEOPOLITAN TOMATO SAUCE

Easy

Serves: 4 to 6
Prep Time: 15 Minutes
Cooking Time: 15 to 45 Minutes

12 fresh tomatoes
3 tablespoons olive or vegetable
oil
4 cloves garlic, sliced

1 medium white or yellow onion,
sliced
1 bay leaf
Salt and pepper to taste

Blend tomatoes in electric blender until juice forms. Pour juice into sauce-pan and bring to a boil over medium high heat. Heat oil in frying pan and sauté garlic until golden brown. Pour hot tomato juice into garlic mixture. Add sliced onion, bay leaf and salt and pepper to taste. For spaghetti sauce, simmer 1 hour. For vegetable dishes, simmer 15 minutes, then add your favorite vegetable and continue to cook until tender. *This delicious, all-purpose sauce is the foundation of all good Italian cooking-for spaghetti, vegetable dishes or casseroles.*

Joe Carcione, GreenGrocer - TV/Radio/Newspaper Column

WHITE CLAM SAUCE FOR PASTA

Easy

Serves: 4 to 6
Prep Time: 15 Minutes
Cooking Time: 10 Minutes

¼ cup butter or margarine
1 large clove garlic, finely
chopped
2 tablespoons flour
2 (6½ ounce) cans minced
clams, drained and liquid
reserved

¼ cup chopped parsley
Salt and pepper to taste
1½ teaspoons dried thyme

In a saucepan heat the butter over medium heat. Add garlic and sauté 1 minute. With a wire whisk stir in the flour. Add the clam juice stirring con-stantly. Cook until smooth. Add the parsley, salt, pepper and thyme. Re-duce heat and simmer 10 minutes. Add the minced clams and heat through. Serve over linguine or spaghetti.

Beth Ounsworth - Mt. Airy, Pa.

FETTUCCINE PRIMAVERA

Moderate
Make Ahead

Serves: 6 to 8
Prep Time: 30 Minutes
Cooking Time: 15 to 20 Minutes

½ cup butter or margarine
1 medium shallot, minced
1 large clove garlic, minced
6 ounces cauliflower, cut into
  small pieces
6 ounces broccoli *or* 1 pound
  asparagus
1 cup carrots, thinly sliced
½ pound mushrooms, sliced

2 small zucchini, unpeeled and
  thinly sliced
1 pound fettuccine noodles
1 cup heavy cream
½ cup chicken stock or bouillon
2 tablespoons basil
1 cup grated Parmesan or
  Romano cheese

Melt the butter in a large skillet or wok; sauté the shallot and garlic. Sauté the vegetables 1 at a time just until crunchy. (Start with those that take the longest to cook.) Boil the fettuccine noodles. Combine cream, stock and basil until well blended. Heat slightly; pour over vegetables. Drain the fettuccine and toss with the vegetables. Top with cheese.

Mary Lou Longo - Chestnut Hill, Pa.

PASTA CALDA

Easy

Serves: 6
Prep Time: 15 Minutes
Cooking Time: 20 Minutes

1 medium onion
4 cloves garlic
1 (35 ounce) can Italian
  tomatoes
1 pound rigatoni pasta

½ cup olive oil
1 cup (4 ounces) shredded
  mozzarella cheese
Fresh basil (optional)

Mince onion and garlic; set aside. Drain the tomatoes and cut into chunks. Cook rigatoni until *al dente*. While rigatoni is cooking, prepare the sauce. Pour olive oil into pan; add garlic and onion and simmer for 2 minutes. Add cut tomatoes and continue cooking for 4 minutes. Drain rigatoni and add to tomato mixture. Stir in mozzarella cheese until melted. Garnish with fresh basil if desired.

Susann T. Undi - Cheltenham, Pa.

PAGLIA E FIENO
(Straw and Hay)

Easy

Serves: 4
Prep Time: 20 Minutes
Cooking Time: 15 to 20 Minutes

3 ounces green noodles
3 ounces white noodles
1 cup heavy cream
2 tablespoons unsalted butter
¼ cup cooked ham, cut in
  julienne strips

¼ cup cooked peas
¼ cup grated Parmesan cheese
2 well-beaten egg yolks

Cook noodles in boiling salted water about 5 minutes; drain. In large saucepan combine cream, butter, ham and peas; heat to melt butter. Stir in noodles. Cook about 5 minutes or until noodles are tender. Stir in cheese and egg yolks. Cook and stir until slightly thickened.

Ann Wiser - Fort Washington, Pa.

PESTO

Easy
Make Ahead
Freeze

Yield: 2½ Cups
Prep Time: 15 Minutes

1 cup fresh basil leaves, washed
  and dried
6 sprigs parsley
½ cup pine nuts or slivered
  almonds
2 cloves garlic, peeled and
  mashed

⅓ cup grated Parmesan cheese
⅓ cup grated Pecorino or
  Romano cheese
4 tablespoons olive oil
4 tablespoons butter or
  margarine, softened
¼ teapoon salt

Combine all ingredients in container of blender or food processor. Blend until a smooth paste is formed. Put the paste in a jar with a lid and store in the refrigerator. It will keep about a week or a couple of months in the freezer. *Besides being good on pasta, Pesto may be spread on slices of French or Italian bread and toasted.*

Chef Tell Erhardt, "Quick Cuisine" (Copyright © 1985)

TORTELLINI IN CREAM SAUCE

Moderate

Serves: 4 to 6
Prep Time: 30 to 40 Minutes

1 (16 ounce) frozen tortellini
½ pound fresh mushrooms
¼ cup butter or margarine,
   divided
¼ pound proscuitto, thinly
   sliced

1 (10 ounce) package frozen or
   fresh tiny peas
1 cup heavy cream
2 tablespoons fresh grated
   Parmesan cheese

Cook tortellini according to package directions. Chop mushrooms and sauté in 2 tablespoons butter. Add proscuitto and set aside. Steam peas; set aside. When all ingredients are prepared, mix cream and remaining butter. Add cheese; mix until well blended. Add mushrooms and peas; heat gently and pour over tortellini.

Bonnie A. Shields - Roxborough, Pa.

LASAGNA ROLLS

Easy
Make Ahead

Serves: 6
Prep Time: 1 Hour
Oven Temp: 350°
Baking Time: 30 Minutes

1 (8 ounce) package lasagna
   noodles
1 (2 pound) container ricotta
   cheese
1 (10 ounce) package frozen
   chopped spinach, thawed and
   drained

1 egg
Grated Parmesan cheese
Lemon juice
Salt
Pepper
Spaghetti sauce

Cook lasagna noodles according to package directions. Take one noodle, lay flat and spread with some of the mixture of ricotta, spinach, egg, grated cheese, lemon juice and salt and pepper to taste. Roll up jelly-roll style and place in greased 13x9x2 inch baking dish. Cover with spaghetti sauce and more grated Parmesan. Cover loosely with foil and bake at 350° for 30 minutes. *Serve with salad and Italian garlic bread.*

Marylou Bruno - Plymouth Meeting, Pa.

EGGS, CHEESE, PASTA & RICE

PRESIDENT REAGAN'S FAVORITE MACARONI AND CHEESE

Serves: 4
Prep Time: 20 Minutes
Oven Temp: 350°
Baking Time: 45 Minutes

1 (8 ounce) package macaroni
1 teaspoon butter or margarine
1 egg, beaten
1 teaspoon dry mustard

1 teaspoon salt
1 tablespoon hot water
1 cup milk
3 cups shredded sharp cheese

Boil macaroni in water until tender and drain thoroughly. Stir in butter and egg. Mix mustard and salt with 1 tablespoon hot water and add to milk. Add cheese, leaving enough to sprinkle on top. Pour into buttered casserole, blend in milk, sprinkle with cheese. Bake at 350° for about 45 minutes or until custard is set and top is crusty.

Ronald Reagan, President of the United States

TAGLIOLINI VERDI AL PROSCIUTTO COTTO
(Green Noodles with Cooked Ham)

Moderate

Serves: 4
Prep Time: 1 Hour 15 Minutes

8¾ cups all-purpose flour
6 ounces boiled spinach,
　squeezed and chopped
8 eggs
Salt

1½ teaspoons oil
¼ cup butter
¼ cup cooked ham, julienned
Béchamel sauce
Grated Parmesan cheese

Knead together flour, spinach, eggs, salt and oil. Roll into rectangle about ¼ inch thick. Cut the pasta into fine strips. Cook the noodles in boiling water for 3 minutes; drain. In a pan, combine butter, ham and noodles. Transfer everything to a glass, oven-proof dish. Spread with béchamel sauce and grated Parmesan cheese. Place under broiler until browned.

Hotel Cipriani - Venice, Italy

BÉCHAMEL SAUCE

Easy   Prep Time: 15 Minutes

4 tablespoons butter   **¼ cup white wine**
3 tablespoons flour   **¼ teaspoon salt**
1 cup chicken broth   **1 cup heavy cream**

Melt butter in a saucepan over medium heat. Add flour and whisk for one minute, stirring constantly. In a separate pan, heat the chicken broth, wine and salt. Add the flour/butter mixture to the heated broth and stir until well blended. Add the heavy cream. Simmer for 20 minutes. "The longer cooking time eliminates that floury taste."

Marabella's - Center City Philadelphia, Pa. and Stone Harbor, N.J.

MANICOTTI CASSEROLE

Moderate   Serves: 6 to 8
Make Ahead   Prep Time: 1 Hour
                                        Oven Temp: 350°
                                        Baking Time: ½ Hour

Batter:
2 extra large eggs   **¼ teaspoon salt**
½ cup milk   **¾ cup flour**

Filling:
1 pound ricotta cheese   **1 (16 ounce) jar spaghetti sauce**
2 extra large eggs   ** or your own recipe**
2 teaspoons chopped parsley   **Grated Parmesan cheese**
Salt and pepper

Batter: Combine ingredients in order listed. Beat until smooth. In a hot, well-oiled 6 inch skillet, pour ¼ cup batter. Fry on 1 side only until the batter holds the shape of the pan. Place separately on cloth until all pancakes are cooked.

Filling: Combine all ingredients and mix well. Place about 1 tablespoon of filling on each manicotti and roll up. Arrange in a shallow 13x9x2 inch baking pan which has been lined with your favorite spaghetti sauce. Cover with additional sauce and sprinkle with grated cheese over top. Bake, covered, at 350° for 30 minutes.

Pat Coscia - Lafayette Hill, Pa.

NOODLE-SOUR CREAM CASSEROLE

Easy

Serves: 4 to 6
Prep Time: 20 Minutes
Oven Temp: 350°
Baking Time: 45 Minutes

1 (16 ounce) package broad egg noodles
¼ cup butter or margarine
2 cups sour cream

1 cup cottage cheese
2 tablespoons cinnamon
¼ cup firmly packed brown sugar

Cook noodles as directed on package. Add butter, sour cream, cottage cheese, cinnamon and brown sugar; mix well. Sprinkle with additional sugar and cinnamon. Place in a greased 2 quart casserole. Bake at 350° for 45 minutes.

Mary Monahan - Doylestown, Pa.

SAUSAGE LASAGNA

Moderate
Make Ahead

Serves: 6
Prep Time: 1 Hour
Oven Temp: 350°
Baking Time: 40 Minutes

1 pound Italian sausage
1 medium onion, chopped
1 small clove garlic, minced
1 (16 ounce) can tomatoes, crushed
1 (6 ounce) can tomato paste
1 teaspoon salt
1 teaspoon oregano leaves

1 (8 ounce) package lasagna noodles
2 cups (8 ounces) sliced mozzarella cheese
1½ cups Ricotta cheese or small curd cottage cheese
½ cup grated Parmesan cheese
Freshly ground pepper

Brown sausage in pan for 10 minutes per side. Drain excess oil; add onion, garlic and sauté for 1 to 2 minutes. Add tomatoes, tomato paste and seasonings. Cook, uncovered, for an additional 20 minutes. Cook noodles according to package directions; drain well. Combine cheeses and pepper. Remove sausage from pan and slice very thin. Pour a little sauce in bottom of 13x9x2 inch baking dish. Alternate layers of noodles, cheese mixture, sliced sausage and sauce, ending with noodles covered with sauce. Sprinkle with additional Parmesan cheese. Refrigerate until ready to bake. Bake at 350 degrees for 40 minutes.

Mary Fox - Norristown, Pa.

PASTA SALAD

Easy
Make Ahead

Serves: 8
Prep Time: 20 Minutes

1 (.63 ounce) package mild
Italian salad dressing mix
1 (16 ounce) bottle Italian salad
dressing
1 (16 ounce) package rotini
macaroni, cooked and drained

Chopped fresh vegetables
(tomatoes, broccoli, peppers,
onion, olives) of your choice

Combine salad dressing mix with bottled salad dressing. Mix until well blended. Pour over rotini; add vegetables. Toss to coat; refrigerate. *Try different combinations of vegetables or leftover meat or seafood. Makes for wonderful summer dining.*

Barbara Ray - Kimberton, Pa.

NOODLES MARMADUKE

Moderate
Make Ahead

Serves: 4
Prep Time: 30 Minutes
Oven Temp: 350°
Baking Time: 45 Minutes

¼ cup sliced onions
1 clove garlic, minced
½ pound fresh mushrooms,
sliced
1 pound ground chuck
½ cup butter or margarine

3 tablespoons lemon juice
3 tablespoons burgundy wine
1 cup consommé
Salt and pepper
¼ pound medium noodles
1 cup sour cream

Sauté separately onions, garlic, mushrooms and beef in butter. Combine in saucepan; add lemon juice, wine, consommé, salt and pepper. Simmer over low heat 5 minutes stirring occasionally. Add uncooked noodles, cook over medium heat for 9 minutes. Cool slightly. Add sour cream and mix. Refrigerate 4 hours or overnight. Bake, covered, at 350° for 35 to 45 minutes.

Eleanor W. Briggs - Chestnut Hill, Pa.

EGGS, CHEESE, PASTA & RICE

CLAM SHELL SALAD

Easy

Serves: 10
Prep Time: 10 Minutes

1 (16 ounce) package large
  macaroni shells
2 (.63 ounce) packages zesty
  Italian salad dressing mix
1 (6½ ounce) can minced clams
1 (12 ounce) can pitted black
  olives, sliced

Parmesan cheese, grated
Dash of garlic powder
Dash of salt
Seasoned croutons

Cook macaroni in boiling salted water until tender; drain. Mix salad dressing mix according to package directions; pour over shells and mix. Add
minced clams and olives. Sprinkle Parmesan cheese, garlic and salt to
taste. Top with seasoned croutons. *If you make ahead of time, don't add
dressing until just before serving.*

Mary Ann Powell - Roxborough, Pa.

NOODLE KUGEL

Moderate

Serves: Buffet
Prep Time: 40 Minutes
Oven Temp: 350°
Baking Time: 1 Hour 10 Minutes

1 (16 ounce) package very thin
  noodles
10 eggs, separated
1 cup butter or margarine,
  softened
1 (8 ounce) package cream
  cheese, softened

1 (16 ounce) carton small curd
  cottage cheese
1 pint sour cream
2 tablespoons vanilla extract
1¼ cups sugar
½ cup golden raisins

Topping:
4 teaspoons butter or
  margarine, melted

¼ cup graham cracker crumbs
½ teaspoon cinnamon

EGGS, CHEESE, PASTA & RICE

Cook noodles in boiling water over low heat for 1 hour; drain. Whip egg yolks and beat in remaining ingredients, except egg whites and raisins. Fold in stiffly beaten whites and noodles. Add raisins. Mix until well blended. Pour into greased large deep casserole dish. Mix topping ingredients until crumbly. Sprinkle topping over noodle mixture. Bake at 350° for 1 hour, 10 minutes or until inserted toothpick comes out dry. Cut into squares.

Evie Barson - Bryn Mawr, Pa.

MITSUI'S JAPANESE FRIED RICE

Moderate

Serves: 6 to 8
Prep Time: 10 Minutes
Cooking Time: 15 Minutes

4 slices bacon
½ cup thinly sliced carrots
½ cup diced onions
1 (4 ounce) can mushrooms, or
  ½ cup fresh
½ cup sliced water chestnuts
  (optional)

3 cups cold cooked rice
¼ cup soy sauce
½ cup Chinese pea pods,
  crisped (optional)
½ cup bean sprouts (optional)

Cook bacon until crisp; remove from pan. Retain enough bacon fat to cover bottom of pan. Sauté carrots until limp; add onions and sauté until they start to brown. Add mushrooms, sauté slightly, then water chestnuts. Add rice and soy sauce. Cook for 5 minutes stirring constantly. Before serving add pea pods, bean sprouts and crumbled bacon. *For larger amounts of rice use a 5 quart Dutch oven. To use as a main dish, just add any leftover meat and/ or vegetables. I also use a lot of pepper; no salt as soy sauce is very salty.*

Joan Mulroney - Roxborough, Pa.

RISOTTO ALLA MILANESE

Moderate

Serves: 8 to 10
Prep Time: 15 Minutes
Cooking Time: 40 Minutes

1 small onion, chopped fine
½ cup clarified butter or
   margarine, divided
1 ounce bone marrow
½ cup dry white wine
3 cups Italian Arborio rice

7 cups boiling veal stock
Pinch of saffron (soaked in
   stock)
3 ounces grated Locatelli
   cheese

Sauté onion in half the butter. Gently add bone marrow and cook until onion is transparent and golden. Add wine and cook until reduced. Stir in the rice; sauté gently until rice begins to brown. Pour in 1 cup boiling stock. Continue cooking until liquid has been absorbed. Add all remaining boiling stock, continue to cook about 20 minutes until all the liquid has been absorbed. Add the saffron, stirring into the rice to add flavor and color. Turn off heat and gently stir in the remaining butter and cheese; serve with additional cheese.

Vincent J. Alberici, Executive Chef, Bellevue Stratford - Philadelphia, Pa.

RICE BOWL

Easy

Serves: 6
Prep Time: 15 Minutes
Cooking Time: 1 Hour 15 Minutes

1 cup sliced carrots
3 tablespoons vegetable oil
1 cup sliced green onions
2 cups sliced, cored, unpeeled
   apples

3 cups cooked brown rice
1 teaspoon salt
½ cup seedless raisins
1 tablespoon sesame seeds

Brown Rice:
1 cup brown rice
2¼ cups water

1 teaspoon salt
1 tablespoon butter or oil

Sauté carrots in oil over medium heat for 10 minutes. Add onions and apples. Cook 10 minutes longer. Stir in rice, salt and raisins. Cook, stirring constantly, until rice is heated through. Add sesame seeds and toss lightly.

Brown Rice: Combine ingredients in saucepan with tight-fitting lid. Bring to boil over high heat, stirring once or twice; cover. Reduce heat to simmer for 45 to 55 minutes or until rice is tender and liquid is absorbed. *Brown rice is used because it is tastier and more nutritious. A salad added to this would make a completely balanced meal.*

Maura Bock - Hatboro, Pa.

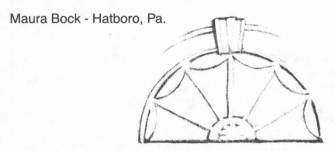

GREEN AND YELLOW RICE CASSEROLE

Easy
Make Ahead

Serves: 6
Prep Time: 15 Minutes
Oven Temp: 350°
Baking Time: 45 Minutes

3 cups cooked rice
¼ cup melted butter or
  margarine
4 eggs, beaten
1 pound sharp Cheddar cheese,
  shredded
1 cup milk
1 (10 ounce) package frozen
  chopped spinach, cooked and
  drained

1 tablespoon onion, chopped
1 tablespoon Worcestershire
  sauce
½ teaspoon marjoram
½ teaspoon thyme
½ teaspoon rosemary
½ teaspoon salt

Combine rice and butter; set aside. In a large bowl combine eggs and cheese. Pour in milk; mix. Add spinach, onion, Worcestershire and seasonings. Gently add rice and pour into 2 quart casserole. Set aside 45 minutes. Place casserole uncovered in a pan of warm water and bake at 350° for 45 minutes.

Julius and Turquoise Erving, Philadelphia 76'ers

RICOTTA BALLS

Moderate

Yield: 25 Balls
Prep Time: About 45 Minutes

Balls:
3 pounds ricotta cheese
½ cup grated Locatelli cheese
¼ cup fresh parsley, chopped
Pinch of salt

Freshly ground pepper to taste
1 egg
2 cups breadcrumbs

Sauce:
1 small clove garlic, minced
2 tablespoons olive oil
1 (16 ounce) can tomatoes,
  crushed
2 (6 ounce) cans tomato paste

1 green pepper, sliced
Pinch of salt
Freshly ground pepper
2 cups water

Balls: Mix all ingredients together, adding more breadcrumbs if mixture is too watery. Shape into medium-sized balls. Refrigerate for at least 3 hours. (It is important to refrigerate so that balls do not fall apart during cooking.) Meanwhile, prepare sauce and drop balls into hot sauce, making sure it is not boiling. Simmer for 1 hour.

Sauce: Sauté garlic in oil over medium heat for 2 minutes. Add remaining ingredients; cover. Reduce heat and simmer for 2 hours before adding balls.

Marie Caldwell - Roxborough, Pa.

SPAGHETTI PIE

Easy
Make Ahead
Freeze

Serves: 8 to 10
Oven Temp: 325°
Baking Time: 30 Minutes

Spaghetti sauce
1 package thin spaghetti
1 egg, slightly beaten
¼ cup grated Parmesan cheese
1 (16 ounce) carton cottage
  cheese
1 small onion, thinly sliced

1 green pepper, sliced
½ pound mushrooms, sliced
½ pound ground beef
1 small ring Italian sausage,
  peeled and chopped
Shredded mozzarella cheese

EGGS, CHEESE, PASTA & RICE

Make your favorite spaghetti sauce. Cook spaghetti according to package directions; drain. Mix with beaten egg and Parmesan cheese. Press into greased 13x9x2 inch pan. Top with cottage cheese. Sauté vegetables, ground beef, sausage until meat is browned. Add to sauce. Spoon over cottage cheese. Sprinkle with mozzarella cheese. Bake at 325° for 30 minutes or until heated through. *May be made ahead of time, prepared in foil pans to freeze. Increase baking time 15 to 20 minutes.*

Mary E. Daly - Spring House, Pa.

SPAGHETTI SAUCE AND MEATBALLS

Moderate
Make Ahead

Serves: 4
Prep Time: 2 Hours

Meatballs:

1 pound ground beef
1 medium onion, finely chopped
1 clove garlic, finely chopped
1 egg

Parsley to taste
Breadcrumbs
Salt
Pepper

Sauce:

2 onions, finely chopped
2 cloves garlic
2 tablespoons oil
3 (28 ounce) cans tomato sauce
1 (18 ounce) can tomato paste

2 cups water
1 bay leaf
Chopped parsley
Salt and pepper to taste

Meatballs: To ground beef add onion, garlic, egg, parsley and enough breadcrumbs to hold mixture together; salt and pepper to taste. Mix well. Shape mixture into balls about 1 inch in diameter. Sauté slowly over low heat until done, turning constantly to retain round shape.

Sauce: Sauté onions and garlic in oil. Remove when clear. In large pot add onions, garlic, tomato sauce and paste, 2 cups water. Stir well to mix. Add bay leaf, chopped parsley, salt and pepper to taste. Bring to boil. Reduce heat to simmer for 1½ hours. Add meatballs and simmer for additional 30 minutes. *Serve with cooked spaghetti, Parmesan cheese, a tossed salad and crusty rolls.*

Dr. Constance E. Clayton, Superintendent, Philadelphia Public Schools

EGGS, CHEESE, PASTA & RICE

BAKED SPAGHETTI

Easy
Make Ahead
Freeze

Serves: 5
Prep Time: 20 Minutes
Oven Temp: 350°
Baking Time: 18 Minutes

2 to 4 slices bacon, diced
2 onions, chopped
1 clove garlic, minced
½ pound lean ground beef
1½ teaspoons salt
Pepper to taste
1 teaspoon chili powder

2 (8 ounce) cans tomato sauce
1 teaspoon Italian seasoning
2½ cups water
½ pound spaghetti, broken into
pieces
1 cup shredded Cheddar cheese

Fry bacon 2 minutes or until crisp. Add onions and garlic. Sauté over medium heat until vegetables are soft. Add ground meat and brown. Add salt, pepper, chili powder, tomato sauce, Italian seasoning and water. Cover and reduce heat; simmer 25 minutes. Layer half uncooked spaghetti, half sauce and half cheese in greased 2 quart casserole. Repeat layers. Bake, covered, at 350° 3 minutes. Uncover and bake 15 minutes until browned and bubbly. May be made ahead but spaghetti should be cooked first.

Betty Jane Whalen - Erdenheim, Pa.

SPAGHETTI ALLA CARBONARA

Easy

Serves: 4
Prep Time: 45 Minutes

3 eggs
3 tablespoons heavy cream
½ cup grated Parmesan cheese
Salt and pepper
3 tablespoons butter or
margarine, melted

¾ pound spaghetti, cooked and
hot
½ pound bacon, cooked and
crumbled
Parsley for garnish

Combine eggs and cream, cheese, a little salt and plenty of pepper. Beat until well blended. Melt butter in a large saucepan. Add the egg mixture; cook over medium heat stirring constantly. Stir until just beginning to thicken. Add the drained spaghetti and bacon. Mix well and serve immediately. Garnish with fresh parsley.

Kas Breslin - Roxborough, Pa.

SOUPER SPAGHETTI CASSEROLE

Easy
Make Ahead

Serves: 4 to 6
Prep Time: 30 Minutes
Oven Temp: 350°
Baking Time: 30 Minutes

1 pound ground beef
½ cup chopped onion
¼ cup chopped green pepper
2 tablespoons butter or
  margarine
1 (10¾ ounce) can cream of
  mushroom soup
1 (10¾ ounce) can tomato soup

1 soup can water
1 clove garlic, minced
1 teaspoon salt
1 tablespoon oil
3 quarts boiling water
8 ounces spaghetti
1 cup shredded sharp process
  cheese

In large skillet cook beef, onion and green pepper in butter until meat is lightly browned and vegetables are tender. Stir often to separate meat. Add soups, water and garlic. Heat and set aside. Add salt and oil to rapidly boiling water. Gradually add spaghetti so that water continues to boil. Cook, uncovered, stirring occasionally, for 8 minutes; drain in colander. In a 3 quart casserole combine spaghetti, meat mixture and ½ cup cheese, top with remaining cheese. Bake at 350° for 30 minutes.

Helen T. Murphy - Feltonville, Pa.

POLENTA

Moderate

Serves: 4
Prep Time: 1 Hour

2 cups corn meal
6 cups water

1 teaspoon salt

Combine corn meal with 2 cups cold water; mix well to eliminate lumps. Bring remaining 4 cups water to a boil in a deep heavy pot. Add salt and corn meal mixture into boiling water, stirring constantly with a wooden spoon. Reduce heat, stirring constantly; cook until thickened. Continue cooking over medium heat for 40 to 50 minutes, stirring occasionally. Pour cooked polenta into a large bowl to shape. Allow to stand for 3 to 5 minutes; flip over onto flat plate, serve with game, chicken cacciatore or veal. To increase or decrease, allow 3 cups water for every 1 cup of corn meal.

Jeanne Roman - Flourtown, Pa.

FOX CHASE

In the 18th century, Fox Chase was filled with tremendous hunting ground, and its name reflects the fox hunts that took place in the beautiful, lush pastures. It was not until World War I that great changes began to take place in this middle-class German Protestant community. With the invention of the automobile, Fox Chase developed into a neighborhood of twin homes, and its inhabitants became a mixture of many ethnic groups.

Although many of the old landmarks are gone, the streets with early family names and a few mansions, such as Knowlton, Ryers, and Stapeley Hall, still remain as reminders of Fox Chase's past. The Old Brauhaus, built in the 17th century as a popular restaurant specializing in German delights, continues its tradition on Oxford Avenue.

The community's Fox Chase Center, better known as Jeannes Hospital, serves as the area's nucleus. Originally these grounds were the home of the rich and influential Jeannes family. In 1907, the Jeannes 5 million dollar estate was bequeathed to the Society of Friends as its Memorial Hospital. Jeannes Hospital has become renowned for its tremendous scientific strides in cancer research.

Breads

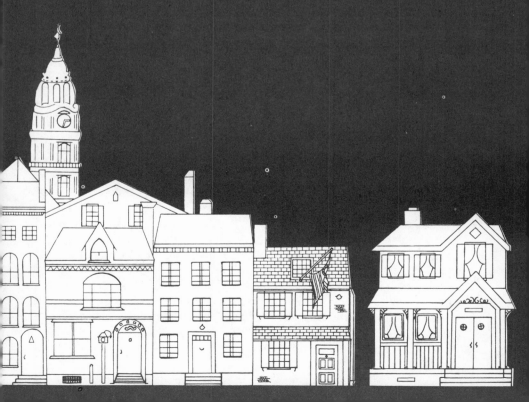

BREADS

PHILADELPHIA STICKY BUNS

Moderate

Yield: 24 Buns or 12 Buns and 1
    Coffee Cake
Prep Time: 45 Minutes
Oven Temp: 375°
Baking Time: 25 Minutes

Sweet Yeast Dough:
½ cup milk
½ cup sugar
1 teaspoon salt
⅔ cup butter or margarine
2 envelopes active dry yeast

½ cup very warm water
4 eggs, at room temperature and
    beaten
4½ cups sifted all-purpose flour

Sticky Buns:
¾ cup firmly packed brown
    sugar
½ cup light corn syrup
¼ cup butter or margarine
½ cup nut halves (optional)
½ recipe Sweet Yeast Dough

2 tablespoons butter or
    margarine, softened
⅓ cup sugar
½ teaspoon cinnamon
½ cup raisins

Sweet Yeast Dough: Combine milk, sugar, salt and butter in saucepan. Heat just until butter is melted; cool to lukewarm. Sprinkle yeast into very warm water in a large bowl. (Very warm water should feel comfortably warm when dropped on wrist.) Add lukewarm milk mixture, beaten eggs and 2 cups flour; beat until smooth. Add just enough of remaining flour to make a soft dough. (May need 2 or more cups flour than recipe calls for; add slowly until of a soft kneading consistency.) Turn out onto lightly floured surface; knead until smooth and elastic, about 5 minutes, using only as much flour as needed to keep dough from sticking. Place in large greased bowl turning to bring greased side up. Cover; let rise in warm place, away from drafts, 1 to 1½ hours or until double in bulk. Punch dough down, knead a few times; let rise 5 minutes. Shape into cinnamon buns or coffee cake. *Yield: 24 buns, 2 coffee cakes or 12 buns, 1 coffee cake.*

Sticky Buns: Combine brown sugar, corn syrup and ¼ cup butter in small saucepan. Simmer 2 minutes. Pour into 9x9x2 inch baking pan or 2 loaf pans; sprinkle with nuts. Roll out yeast dough to a 15x8 inch rectangle on a lightly floured surface. Spread entire surface of dough with soft butter. Combine sugar and cinnamon; sprinkle raisins over dough. Roll up, jelly-roll style beginning with the long end. Pinch to seal seam. Cut into 12 equal slices. Place cut side down in prepared pan. Cover and let rise in warm place about 1 hour or until double in bulk. Bake at 375° for 25 minutes or until golden brown. Turn upside down on plate. Leave pan in place 5 minutes to allow topping to run over buns; lift off pan.

Mary Jean Melissen - Mt. Airy, Pa.

WHOLE WHEAT PIZZA

Easy

Yield: 2 Pizzas
Prep Time: 45 Minutes
Oven Temp: 425°
Baking Time: 20 to 25 Minutes

**1 package dry yeast
1 cup warm water (105° to 115°)
1 teaspoon sugar
1 teaspoon salt
2 tablespoons oil
2½ cups whole wheat flour *or*
  1½ cups whole-wheat, 1 cup
  all-purpose**

**⅔ cup tomato sauce
2 to 2½ cups (8 to 10 ounces)
  shredded Cheddar, Monterey
  Jack or mozzarella cheese
Pepperoni, mushrooms, green
  peppers or your choice of
  toppings**

Dissolve yeast in water. Stir in next 4 ingredients. Beat vigorously for 20 strokes. Allow dough to rest 5 to 10 minutes. With floured hands spread dough evenly in lightly greased pizza pans (2) or baking sheet. Spread tomato sauce over dough. Top with shredded cheese and topping of your choice. Bake at 425° for 20 to 25 minutes. *Children love to help with this.*

Pat Ponzek - Huntingdon Valley, Pa.

BREADS

PUFFY APPLE PANCAKE

Easy

Serves: 2 to 4
Prep Time: 10 Minutes
Oven Temp: 400°, 350°
Baking Time: 10 Minutes, 15
　　Minutes

2 tablespoons butter or
　margarine
3 eggs
¾ cup milk
¾ cup flour

1 cup sliced apples
Cinnamon to taste
Sugar to taste
Nutmeg to taste

Melt butter in ovenproof 10 inch skillet. Beat together eggs, milk and flour; pour into skillet. Bake in skillet, uncovered, at 400° for 10 minutes (pierce large bubbles). Reduce heat to 350° and bake for 15 minutes or until light brown. Sauté apples, cinnamon and sugar until tender (while pancake is baking). Slide pancake onto oval platter, fold in half and pour apple mixture over all.

Ann M. Gray - East Falls, Pa.

WALNUT CHEESE MUFFINS

Easy
Freeze

Yield: 18 to 20 Muffins
Prep Time: 15 Minutes
Oven Temp: 400°
Baking Time: 20 to 25 Minutes

2 eggs
1½ cups milk
6 tablespoons vegetable oil
1½ cups whole-wheat flour
1½ cups unbleached all-
　purpose flour

¼ cup sugar
2 teaspoons baking powder
1 teaspoon salt
¾ cup chopped walnuts
1 cup shredded Cheddar or
　Swiss cheese

Mix eggs, milk and oil together in a small bowl. Stir flours, sugar, baking powder and salt together in large mixing bowl. Add liquid mixture, nuts and cheese, stirring just until flour is moistened. It will still be lumpy. Fill greased muffin tins ⅔ full and bake at 400° for 20 to 25 minutes or until golden brown. Immediately remove from pan and serve hot or let cool and freeze. *Good with simple meal of soup or salad.*

Joan Menocal - Chestnut Hill, Pa.

WHOLE GRAIN BREAD

Moderate
Freeze

Yield: 3 Loaves
Prep Time: 40 Minutes
Oven Temp: 400°, 375°
Baking Time: 40 Minutes

1 package dry yeast
1 tablespoon plus ½ cup sugar, divided
3 cups water, divided
1 beaten egg

¼ cup melted butter or margarine
1½ teaspoons salt
4 cups whole-grain flour
4 cups all-purpose flour

Dissolve yeast in ½ cup water (85°) and 1 tablespoon sugar and allow to stand for 10 minutes. In a large bowl beat the egg, butter, 2½ cups lukewarm water, salt and ½ cup sugar. Add the dissolved yeast. Add mixture of unsifted flours; mix all by hand in the bowl until dough begins to leave sides of bowl. Knead on a lightly floured board for 8 to 10 minutes. Shape dough into a ball, put in a well-buttered bowl and turn to coat on all sides. Cover and let rise in a warm, draft-free place until double in bulk, 1½ to 2 hours. Punch the dough down, knead for 2 or 3 minutes and shape into 3 loaves and place in 9x5 inch pans. Cover pans with a towel and let rise until double in bulk, 1½ to 2 hours. Place loaves in a cold oven. Turn heat to 400° and bake 15 minutes; reduce heat to 375° and bake 25 minutes longer or until the bread sounds hollow when removed from the tins and rapped with the knuckles on the bottom. Cool on racks before slicing.

Joe Lynch - Norristown, Pa.

CORN MEAL PANCAKES

Easy

Serves: 4 to 6
Prep Time: 10 Minutes

1 egg
3 tablespoons oil
1 cup milk, buttermilk or yogurt

¾ cup corn meal
½ cup whole-wheat flour
1 teaspoon baking powder

Beat egg in mixing bowl; add oil and milk blending well. Mix dry ingredients well and add to liquid ingredients. Pour in pancake portions onto preheated greased griddle. Cook until bubbly (about 1 minute) and turn; cook about 1 minute longer. *Serve with butter and maple syrup.*

Pat Ponzek - Huntingdon Valley, Pa.

BREADS

MONKEY BREAD I

Moderate

Yield: 1 Loaf
Prep Time: 35 Minutes
Oven Temp: 375°
Baking Time: 45 Minutes

**5 to 5½ cups all-purpose flour,
    divided
2 packages active dry yeast
⅓ cup sugar
1 teaspoon salt
½ cup water**

**½ cup milk
½ cup butter or margarine
3 large eggs
1 cup or more melted butter or
    margarine for dipping**

In large mixer bowl combine 1½ cups flour, yeast, sugar and salt. In saucepan heat water, milk and butter until warm (120 to 130°), butter need not melt. Add to flour mixture; add eggs. Beat at low speed until moistened. Beat at medium speed for 3 minutes. Add enough remaining flour to make soft dough. Knead on a floured surface for 8 to 10 minutes. Place in a greased bowl turning to grease top of dough. Let rise in a warm place until light and doubled in size about 1 hour. Punch down; turn out onto floured board. Roll out ¼ inch thick. Cut dough into diamonds (with a cookie cutter) or any shape preferred. Dip each piece into melted butter; arrange in a buttered 10 inch tube pan. Cover and let rise again until almost doubled, about 1 hour. Bake at 375° for 45 minutes or until browned and done.

Bill Cosby, "Pride of Philadelphia"

MONKEY BREAD II

Easy

Serves: 6 to 8
Prep Time: 15 Minutes
Oven Temp: 350°
Baking Time: 45 Minutes

4 (10 per package) packages
refrigerator rolls
1¼ cups firmly packed brown
sugar, divided

¾ teaspoon cinnamon
1½ cups butter or margarine
½ cup sugar

Cut each roll into quarters. Roll each piece in mixture of ¾ cup brown sugar and cinnamon. Put half the pieces into a greased bundt or tube pan. Melt together butter and remaining sugars. Pour half mixture over the rolls in pan; add remaining roll pieces. Pour remaining half of butter mixture over top. Bake at 350° for 45 minutes; cool for 5 minutes and remove from pan.

Peggy Zabotney - Roxborough, Pa.

IRISH SODA BREAD

Moderate
Freeze

Yield: 1 Loaf
Serves: About 20
Prep Time: 15 Minutes
Oven Temp: 325°
Baking Time: About 1 Hour, 15
    Minutes

¼ cup butter or margarine
1 cup evaporated milk
1 cup water
4 cups flour
4 teaspoons baking powder

½ teaspoon salt
¾ cup sugar
2 tablespoons caraway seeds
    (optional)
2 cups raisins

Melt butter in a large cast iron skillet. In measuring cup combine milk, water and butter. (Don't wash out skillet.) Pour liquid into dry ingredients which have already been combined in large bowl. Mix until dough forms a ball. Add flour as needed. Add seeds and raisins. Knead 10 times on floured surface. Shape into a round. Make an X ¼ inch deep on bread in center. Bake in prepared skillet at 325° for about 1 to 1¼ hours. Toothpick inserted in center will come out dry when done.

Irene Hurley - Bayonne, N.J.
Father Bruce Ritter - New York, N.Y.

BREADS

IRISH BROWN BREAD

Easy
Make Ahead
Freeze

Yield: 1 Loaf
Prep Time: 10 Minutes
Oven Temp: 375°
Baking Time: 40 Minutes

**3 cups whole-wheat flour
(preferably stone ground)
1 cup all-purpose flour
2 teaspoons salt**

**1 teaspoon baking soda
¾ teaspoon baking powder
1½ to 2 cups buttermilk (or
powdered equivalent)**

Combine dry ingredients and mix thoroughly. Add enough buttermilk to make a soft dough similar to biscuit dough, but firm enough to hold its shape. Knead for a few minutes on a lightly floured board until smooth and velvety. Form into a round loaf and place in a well-buttered 8 inch cake pan or buttered cookie sheet. Cut a cross on top of loaf. Bake at 375° for 35 to 40 minutes or until loaf is nicely browned and sounds hollow when rapped with knuckles. Let loaf cool before slicing very thin. Serve with plenty of sweet butter.

Joan Forde - Chestnut Hill, Pa.

PEPPERONI BREAD

Moderate
Make Ahead

Yield: 2 Loaves
Prep Time: 45 Minutes
Oven Temp: 350°
Baking Time: 30 Minutes

Dough:
**1 cup lukewarm water
1 package dry yeast
1 teaspoon sugar**

**1 teaspoon salt
2 tablespoons vegetable oil
4 cups flour**

Bread:
**4 small sticks of pepperoni,
sliced thin
¼ teaspoon salt
¼ teaspoon pepper**

**¼ teaspoon oregano
½ cup shredded cheese
1 egg yolk, beaten**

Dough: Pour water into a warm bowl, add yeast and stir. After yeast is dissolved add sugar, salt and oil. Mix in flour gradually. When dough becomes stiff, flour your hands and knead it with your fingers. It should be pliable but not sticky. Add a bit more flour if necessary until smooth and elastic. Place in a greased bowl, cover with a clean cloth and set in a warm place for about 1 to 2 hours until almost doubled in bulk. Knead down and divide dough into 2 parts.

Bread: Roll dough in pizza fashion. Spread dough with sliced pepperoni, seasonings and cheese. Roll up jelly-roll style and place seam side down. Spread top of loaves with beaten egg yolk and bake at 350° for 30 minutes.

Barbara Powers - Roxborough, Pa.

SHORT-CUT PEPPERONI BREAD

Easy
Make Ahead
Freeze

Yield: 15 Slices
Prep Time: 5 Minutes
Oven Temp: 350°
Baking Time: 30 Minutes

1 loaf frozen bread dough
½ pound Swiss cheese, sliced
**½ pound pepperoni, thinly
   sliced**

1 egg
Grated Parmesan cheese

Thaw dough according to package directions and let rise. After dough has risen, cut in half; roll out each half as thin as possible. Layer with Swiss cheese and pepperoni. Beat egg and spread thinly over pepperoni and cheese. Sprinkle with Parmesan cheese. Roll into loaves. Bake at 350° for 30 minutes or until golden brown.

Susan Pagliaro - Fox Chase, Pa.
Natalie Wilson - East Falls, Pa.

BREADS

SWEET POTATO BREAD

Moderate

Yield: 1 Loaf
Prep Time: 20 Minutes
Oven Temp: 350°
Baking Time: 1 Hour, 15 Minutes

Stage I:
1 cup sugar
1 cup firmly packed dark brown
   sugar
4 eggs

½ teaspoon salt
1½ cups vegetable oil
1½ cups mashed sweet potato

Stage II:
3 cups all-purpose flour
1 tablespoon baking powder
1 teaspoon baking soda
1 teaspoon cinnamon
1 teaspoon nutmeg

½ teaspoon ground ginger
1 cup chopped walnuts or
   pecans
1 cup golden raisins

Mix all ingredients from Stage I, one at a time beating after each addition. Beat all until very smooth. For Stage II sift dry ingredients together; fold into batter from Stage I and mix well. Add walnuts and raisins. Pour into well-greased square pan. Bake at 350° for about 1 hour and 15 minutes. Test with wooden pick; if still moist bake 15 minutes longer.

Eugenia Zalewski - Mt. Airy, Pa.

UNCLE JACK'S FABULOUS FOOLPROOF BISCUITS

Easy

Yield: 10 to 12
Prep Time: 10 Minutes
Oven Temp: 450°
Baking Time: 8 to 10 Minutes

2 cups biscuit baking mix
½ cup cold water

¼ cup softened butter or
   margarine

Mix all ingredients with 2 forks or pastry blender until soft dough forms. Beat vigorously 20 strokes. Form into balls and drop onto greased cookie sheet. Bake at 450° for 8 to 10 minutes until edges are medium brown. *Always light and buttery and super simple!*

Sharyn Vergare - Chestnut Hill, Pa.

HELEN'S CHEESE BREAD

Easy
Make Ahead

Yield: Lots
Prep Time: 15 Minutes
Oven Temp: 350°
Baking Time: 10 Minutes

6 ounces Swiss cheese,
   shredded
6 ounces Cheddar cheese,
   shredded
1 pound bacon, cooked and
   crumbled
3 (4 ounce) cans chopped
   mushrooms, drained

⅔ cup mayonnaise
2 tablespoons parsley
1 tablespoon oregano
½ teaspoon rosemary
½ teaspoon salt
½ teaspoon pepper
2 loaves French bread

Mix all ingredients except bread together in a bowl; cover and let stand overnight (or at least 6 hours) in refrigerator. Cut French bread in half lengthwise. Spread mixture over bread. Bake open-faced at 350° for 10 minutes and let stand for 5 minutes before slicing.

Sally Beil - Oreland, Pa.

BEER CHEESE CROUTONS

Easy

Yield: 50 Croutons
Prep Time: 15 Minutes
Oven Temp: 400°
Baking Time: 6 Minutes

1 pound Cheddar cheese,
   shredded
¾ cup grated Parmesan cheese
¾ cup beer (your preference)
¼ teaspoon hot pepper sauce
¼ teaspoon garlic powder

1 tablespoon Worcestershire
   sauce
½ teaspoon dry mustard
1 loaf French bread (preferably
   long, slender loaf)

Combine all ingredients except bread in mixing bowl. Using electric mixer, blend slowly until mixture is smooth and all liquid has been incorporated. Slice bread into ¼ inch thick slices; spread each slice approximately ⅛ inch thick with cheese mixture. Arrange on baking pan. Bake at 400° about 6 minutes until cheese is bubbly and lightly browned. Serve immediately.

Krista Milito - Norristown, Pa.

BREADS

BLUEBERRY-BANANA BREAD

Easy
Make Ahead

Yield: 1 Loaf
Prep Time: 25 Minutes
Oven Temp: 350°
Baking Time: About 1 Hour

½ cup vegetable oil
1 cup firmly packed brown sugar
2 large eggs
2 cups all-purpose flour
1½ teaspoons baking soda
Pinch of salt
2 teaspoons cinnamon

About 1½ cups very ripe
 bananas, mashed
½ cup sour cream
1 tablespoon vanilla extract
¾ cup fresh blueberries,
 washed and drained or may
 use frozen

Whisk together oil, sugar and eggs. In separate bowl sift flour, soda, salt and cinnamon. Gradually add flour to oil mixture. Mix in bananas, sour cream and vanilla. Add blueberries and toss gently. Pour mixture into greased loaf pan and bake at 350° about 1 hour or until toothpick comes out clean when inserted in center of loaf. *In an 11x5x3 inch pan, this takes about 45 minutes to bake.*

Evelyn P. Olivieri - Mt. Airy, Pa.

SAVORY BUTTER BREAD

Easy
Make Ahead

Yield: 1 Loaf
Prep Time: 10 Minutes
Oven Temp: 375°
Baking Time: 15 Minutes

1 loaf French or Vienna bread
½ cup butter or margarine,
 softened and seasoned

Slice bread into 1 inch slices about ¾ of the way down. Generously spread with 1 of the Savory Butters. Reshape into loaf and wrap in aluminum foil to bake at 375° for about 15 minutes or until warm. *This may also be warmed on the grill for 10 to 15 minutes. Do not place directly over coals and remember to turn.*

Savory Butters: To the butter add any one or combination of following ingredients:

1 medium clove garlic, crushed or through press
2 tablespoons chopped chives or finely chopped scallions
2 tablespoons finely chopped onion and 2 tablespoons chopped parsley

2 tablespoons finely chopped fresh dill
3 to 4 anchovy fillets, mashed and ½ teaspoon lemon juice
1 teaspoon poppy seed
2 tablespoons Parmesan cheese

Kelly Ann Shaughnessy - Collegeville, Pa.

SURPRISE MUFFINS

Easy

Yield: 12 Medium Muffins
Prep Time: 15 Minutes
Oven Temp: 425°
Baking Time: 20 to 25 Minutes

2 cups flour
1 tablespoon baking powder
½ teaspoon salt
1 to 2 tablespoons sugar *or* 1 tablespoon honey

1 egg
1 cup milk
¼ cup melted butter or margarine

Mix and sift flour, baking powder, salt and sugar. Beat egg until frothy; stir in milk and butter. Make a "well" in the flour mixture; pour in milk mixture all at once. Stir quickly until just mixed but still lumpy. Pour into lightly greased muffin cups and fill ⅔ full. Bake at 425° for 20 to 25 minutes or until cake tester inserted in center comes out clean. Loosen muffins with spatula; tip slightly in pans to prevent steaming until ready to serve. Makes 8 large or 12 medium muffins. *Variations: (1) Sprinkle tops of unbaked muffins with ½ to 1 cup finely chopped apple. Combine ¼ cup sugar and ½ teaspoon cinnamon; shake over apple. Bake as directed. (2) Add ¾ cup raw cranberries, chopped, and ¼ cup sugar to sifted dry ingredients. (3) Add ½ to ¾ cup shredded sharp Cheddar cheese to sifted dry ingredients. (4) Combine ½ cup raisins or dates and ½ cup chopped walnuts; add to sifted dry ingredients. (5) Fill muffin liner with half the batter. Put 1 teaspoon jelly, jam or marmalade into each cup. Add remaining batter. (6) Add 1 cup blueberries to dry ingredients. (7) Experiment with adding about ½ cup oats or bran to dry ingredients.*

Alice Brogan - Ambler, Pa.

BREADS

CRANBERRY-NUT BREAD

Easy
Make Ahead
Freeze

Yield: 1 Loaf
Prep Time: 30 Minutes
Oven Temp: 350°
Baking Time: 1 Hour

¼ cup butter or margarine,
   softened
1 cup sugar
1 egg, beaten
2 cups all-purpose flour
1½ teaspoons baking powder
½ teaspoon baking soda

½ teaspoon salt
½ cup orange juice
Dash of orange extract *or* 1
   tablespoon orange zest
½ cup chopped nuts
1 cup fresh cranberries,
   coarsely chopped

Cream butter in large bowl. Mix in sugar and beat well. Add egg and beat again. Sift dry ingredients together and add alternately with the orange juice to the creamed mixture. Beat until smooth. Add remaining ingredients and mix well. Turn into greased loaf pan (9x5x3 inch) and bake at 350° about 1 hour. Let stand for 5 minutes, then turn out onto a rack to cool. Store overnight before cutting.

Marlene Martin Surrena - Norristown, Pa.

FRED'S FAMOUS FRUITED TOAST

Easy

Serves: 6
Prep Time: 15 Minutes
Oven Temp: 325°
Baking Time: 15 Minutes

2 bananas
2 apples
1 pear
6 slices raisin bread
⅓ cup chopped walnuts

Dash of cinnamon
¼ teaspoon vanilla extract per
   slice of bread
½ teaspoon butter or margarine
   per slice of bread

Peel and slice fruit into small, thin pieces. Lay raisin bread slices on a cookie sheet; sprinkle with walnuts. Cover with assorted fruits so that each piece of bread has all of the fruit types. Sprinkle with cinnamon and vanilla. Place a pat of butter on top. Bake at 325° for 15 minutes. Serve warm with whipped cream or vanilla ice cream or just plain.

Farlino family - Miquon, Pa.

MEXICAN CORN BREAD

Easy

Serves: 6 to 8
Prep Time: 20 Minutes
Oven Temp: 350°
Baking Time: 45 to 50 Minutes

1 cup yellow corn meal
2 eggs, well-beaten
½ teaspoon baking soda
¾ teaspoon salt
1 (16 ounce) can cream-style
   corn
½ cup bacon drippings

1 cup milk
½ pound ground beef
½ pound shredded Longhorn
   Cheddar cheese
1 medium onion, chopped
2 to 4 jalapeño peppers,
   chopped

Mix first 4 ingredients and then the next 3, and combine. Brown ground beef
and drain. Grease iron skillet and preheat in 350° oven. Pour half of corn
meal mixture into heated skillet; top with shredded cheese and then meat,
onion and pepper. Pour remaining corn meal mixture over this and bake at
350° for 45 to 50 minutes.

Lisa Whelchel - Blair, TV program, "Facts of Life"

ZUCCHINI NUT BREAD

Easy - "Children can do"

Yield: 1 Loaf
Prep Time: 20 Minutes
Oven Temp: 350°
Baking Time: 1 Hour

2 cups peeled grated zucchini
3 eggs
1½ cups sugar
¾ cup melted butter
3 cups all-purpose flour
1½ teaspoons salt

1 teaspoon baking soda
¼ teaspoon baking powder
1 tablespoon cinnamon
2 tablespoons vanilla extract
½ cup chopped walnuts

Grate zucchini and set aside to drain. Beat the eggs with the sugar until
pale yellow and thick. Add melted butter and zucchini. Sift flour and dry ingredients; fold into egg mixture. Stir in the vanilla and nuts. Spoon mixture
into a buttered 9x5x3 inch loaf pan. Bake at 350° for 1 hour or until bread
pulls away from the sides of the pan.

Weetzie Lamb - North Hills, Pa.

FRANKFORD

Frankford shows its German influence with the early spelling of its name as "the place at Frankfort in Pennsylvania". It is a strong community built on the modest means of its early settlers.

Most of Frankford's history and romance surround the main street—Frankford Avenue. The Avenue is symbolic of Philadelphia's transformation from a colonial city to a modern one. Along this main route sprung up many fine mansions, historic churches and hotels where elegant personages could be spotted. The stagecoach, the horsecart, the trolley, the bus, and most significantly, "the el" have all travelled along Frankford Avenue.

Philadelphia, the city of rowhouses, owes much to this little community. It was here, at a tavern, that America's first building and loan association was founded.

The Quakers who settled the area had a tremendous influence on Frankford's history by the establishment of the Frankford Friends' School and Friends' Hospital, the nation's oldest private psychiatric hospital. Six of the hospital's 99 acres are covered with brilliant azaleas. Every spring, Friends' Hospital opens its gates to welcome winter-weary Philadelphians to enjoy the spectacular flower display.

Vegetables & Side Dishes

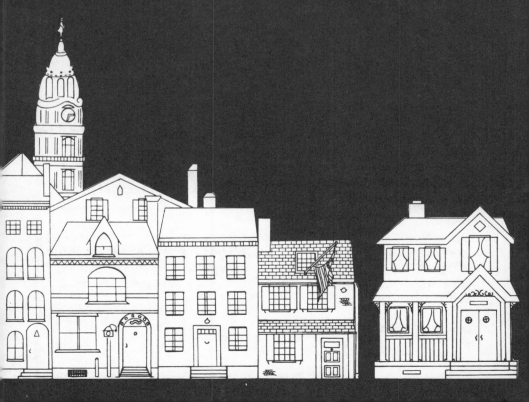

VEGETABLES & SIDE DISHES

SWEET AND SOUR GREEN BEANS

Moderate

Serves: 6
Prep Time: 15 Minutes
Cooking Time: 15 Minutes

1 medium onion, chopped
1 quart green beans (fresh or
   frozen)
½ cup bacon grease, divided

½ cup sugar
½ cup vinegar
8 slices bacon, fried and
   crumbled

Brown onion in small amount of bacon grease. Steam green beans. Combine remaining bacon grease, sugar and vinegar and keep warm. When beans are steamed, crumble the bacon on top and toss with warm dressing. *For company, fry the bacon and prepare the dressing earlier in the day. Reheat and toss as directed just before serving.*

Bonnie A. Shields - Roxborough, Pa.

GOLDEN BROCCOLI CASSEROLE

Easy

Serves: 8
Prep Time: 15 to 20 Minutes
Oven Temp: 350°
Baking Time: 30 Minutes

¼ cup chopped onions
6 tablespoons butter or
   margarine, divided
2 tablespoons flour
½ cup water
2 cups (8 ounces) Cheddar
   cheese, shredded

2 (10 ounce) packages frozen
   chopped broccoli, thawed and
   well-drained
3 eggs, well-beaten
½ cup breadcrumbs
2 tablespoons chopped parsley

Sauté onions in 4 tablespoons butter until soft. Stir in flour and water. Cook over low heat until mixture thickens. Blend in cheese and broccoli; add eggs and mix until blended. Turn into a greased 1½ quart casserole dish, cover with breadcrumbs, parsley and remaining 2 tablespoons butter. Bake at 350° for 30 minutes.

Mary Jo Egoville - Oreland, Pa.

GERMAN RED CABBAGE

Easy

Serves: 6 to 8
Prep Time: 20 Minutes
Cooking Time: 10 Minutes

2½ or 3 pounds red cabbage, shredded
¾ cup boiling water
3 large cooking apples, pared, cored and sliced
3 tablespoons melted butter

¼ cup vinegar
1½ teaspoons flour
¼ cup firmly packed brown sugar
1 teaspoon salt
2 teaspoons pepper

Cook cabbage in boiling water for 10 minutes with apples. Combine remaining ingredients, add to cabbage and mix well.

Marge Solarski - Roxborough, Pa.

GLAZED CARROTS WITH HERBS

Easy

Serves: 4
Prep Time: 10 Minutes
Cooking Time: 10 to 15 Minutes

1 pound carrots, trimmed and sliced ⅓ inch thick on the diagonal
3 tablespoons unsalted butter
⅓ cup chicken broth

¾ teaspoon sugar
Salt and pepper to taste
2 teaspoons minced fresh parsley leaves
2 teaspoons snipped fresh dill

In a saucepan of boiling water cook the carrots for 5 minutes or until just tender. Drain in a colander and refresh them under running cold water. In a skillet toss the carrots with the butter over moderate heat until they are well coated. Add the broth, sugar, salt and pepper to taste. Cook over moderately high heat, tossing the carrots until the liquid is reduced to a glaze. Stir in the parsley and dill.

Brighid Blake - Chestnut Hill, Pa.

VEGETABLES & SIDE DISHES

GREEN BEANS PARMESAN CASSEROLE

Easy

Serves: 6
Prep Time: 10 to 15 Minutes
Oven Temp: 350°
Baking Time: 30 to 40 Minutes

**2 (10 ounce) packages frozen
French-style green beans *or*
fresh beans in season
Milk
¼ cup chopped onion
4 tablespoons butter or
margarine, divided**

**2 tablespoons all-purpose flour
½ teaspoon salt
¼ cup grated Parmesan cheese
1 (5 ounce) can water chestnuts,
drained and sliced
½ cup soft breadcrumbs**

Cook beans according to package directions; drain, reserving the liquid. Add milk to liquid to make 1¼ cups; set aside. In saucepan cook onion in 2 tablespoons butter until tender; blend in flour and salt. Stir in milk mixture all at once. Cook and stir until thickened and bubbly. Stir in half the cheese. Add the cooked beans and water chestnuts reserving a few for topping. Turn into 1 quart casserole. Toss breadcrumbs with remaining cheese and melted butter; sprinkle on top of casserole. Bake, uncovered, at 350° for 30 to 40 minutes or until bubbly. Garnish with reserved water chestnuts.

Barbara Ansel - Jenkintown, Pa.

STRING BEANS AU GRATIN

Easy

Serves: 6
Prep Time: 30 Minutes
Oven Temp: 350°
Baking Time: 25 Minutes

**1½ pounds fresh string beans
White sauce
2 egg yolks, beaten
1½ cups shredded American
cheese**

**Salt and pepper to taste
⅓ cup breadcrumbs
1 teaspoon finely grated lemon
peel**

White Sauce:
**¼ cup butter or margarine
3 tablespoons flour**

2 cups milk

114

Cook string beans until tender. Mix together white sauce, egg yolks and cheese; add beans. Add salt and pepper to taste. Pour into a buttered casserole dish; top with breadcrumbs and lemon peel.

White Sauce: In small saucepan melt butter. Stir in flour; gradually add milk, stirring constantly. Cook until thick.

Betsy Ledwith - Oreland, Pa.

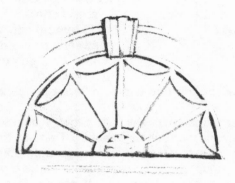

4 BEAN BAKE

Easy

Serves: 8 to 10
Prep Time: 10 Minutes
Oven Temp: 350°
Baking Time: 1 Hour, 30 Minutes

1 (16 ounce) can kidney beans, drained
1 (16 ounce) can green lima beans, drained
1 (16 ounce) can butter beans, drained
1 (16 ounce) can pork and beans, undrained

1 cup firmly packed brown sugar
1 medium onion, chopped
3 tablespoons vinegar
1 teaspoon dry mustard
1 cup lean bacon cubes

Combine all ingredients and place in a heavy covered casserole dish. Bake 1 hour at 350°, uncover and bake ½ hour longer. *At a recent cookout my dear friend spent hours and made her beans from scratch. I arrived with my 10 minute side dish. She swore never to sit up with a pot of beans ever again!*

Jeanne Radocaj - Bridesburg, Pa.

VEGETABLES & SIDE DISHES

ASPARAGUS CASSEROLE

Easy
Make Ahead

Serves: 6 to 8
Prep Time: 25 Minutes
Oven Temp: 350°
Baking Time: 20 Minutes

3 cups bread cubes (French or Italian loaf)
5 or 6 tablespoons butter or margarine, divided
2 tablespoons flour
½ teaspoon salt

1 cup milk
2 cups (½ pound) shredded sharp cheese
1 (15 ounce) can asparagus spears, drained
3 hard-cooked eggs, sliced

To make croutons sauté bread cubes in 3 or 4 tablespoons butter until golden brown; set aside. To make white sauce melt remaining 2 tablespoons butter in saucepan over low heat. Blend in flour and salt. Add milk all at once, stirring until thickened and bubbly. Remove from heat and add cheese. Stir until cheese is melted and sauce is smooth. Layer half the bread cubes, asparagus, egg slices and cheese sauce in a baking dish. Repeat layers of asparagus, egg slices and cheese sauce; top with remaining bread cubes. Bake at 350° for approximately 20 minutes or until thoroughly heated and bubbly.

Mary Bell Cote - Chestnut Hill, Pa.

BROCCOLI DIJON

Easy
Make Ahead (Sauce Only)

Serves: 6
Prep Time: 15 Minutes
Cooking Time: 15 Minutes

2 pounds fresh broccoli
2 tablespoons minced onion
2 tablespoons butter or margarine
2 tablespoons flour
1 cup skim milk

2 tablespoons Dijon mustard
1 teaspoon salt
¼ teaspoon pepper
1 teaspoon sugar
1 tablespoon lemon juice

Wash and trim broccoli. Cook in salted water until tender. Sauté onion in butter; blend in flour. Slowly pour in the milk, stirring constantly. Blend in the mustard, salt, pepper and sugar. Cook and stir until thickened; add lemon juice. Drain broccoli and pour sauce over. *Only 97 calories per serving.*

Virginia McCuen - Flourtown, Pa.

BROCCOLI-ONION DELUXE

Easy

Serves: 6
Prep Time: 20 Minutes
Oven Temp: 350°
Baking Time: 40 to 45 Minutes

1 pound broccoli
2 cups frozen small onions *or* 3
   medium onions, quartered
¼ cup butter, divided
1 tablespoon flour
2 teaspoons salt
Dash of pepper

1 cup milk
1 (3 ounce) package cream
   cheese
½ cup shredded American
   cheese
½ cup breadcrumbs

Cut up broccoli, cook 10 to 15 minutes; drain. Cook onions in boiling salted water until tender; drain. In a saucepan melt half the butter; blend in flour, salt and pepper. Add milk and cook, stirring constantly, until thickened and bubbly. Reduce heat. Blend in cream cheese until smooth. Place vegetables in a 1½ quart casserole. Pour sauce over and mix lightly. Top with shredded cheese. Melt the remaining butter and toss with the breadcrumbs; sprinkle over casserole.

Eugenia Zalewski - Mt. Airy, Pa.

BROCCOLI PUFF

Easy

Serves: 6
Prep Time: 5 Minutes
Oven Temp: 350°
Baking Time: 40 Minutes

2 (10 ounce) packages frozen
   chopped broccoli (thawed) *or*
   6 cups fresh broccoli
1 (10¾ ounce) can cream of
   mushroom soup

1 cup mayonnaise
1 egg
1 cup shredded Cheddar
   cheese, divided
Breadcrumbs

Place broccoli in a casserole dish. Combine the soup, mayonnaise, egg and ¾ cup cheese and pour over broccoli. Top with remaining cheese and breadcrumbs. Bake at 350° for 40 minutes. *If using fresh broccoli, boil in small amount of boiling, salted water for 10 minutes.*

Bob Clarke, Philadelphia Flyers
Judy Verdone - Philadelphia, Pa.

CARROT TART

Moderate

Serves: 8
Prep Time: 45 Minutes
Oven Temp: 350°
Baking Time: 30 Minutes

4 large carrots, very thinly sliced
1 tablespoon butter or
margarine, melted

Filling:
3 cups shredded carrots (about
8 medium)
1 potato, peeled and cubed
2 eggs
¼ cup sour cream
1 teaspoon finely shredded
orange peel

¼ teaspoon salt
⅛ teaspoon turmeric (optional)
⅛ teaspoon ground white
pepper

In saucepan cook sliced carrots in small amount of boiling salted water for 3 to 4 minutes or until tender crisp; drain. Brush an 8 inch round flan or cake pan with melted butter. Beginning in center of pan and working toward outer edges, arrange drained carrot slices in circles, petal fashion, slightly overlapping slices to cover bottom and sides of pan. Set aside while preparing filling.

Filling: Cook shredded carrots and cubed potato in small amount of boiling salted water about 15 minutes or until just tender; drain well. In blender container or food processor bowl place eggs, sour cream, orange peel, salt, turmeric and pepper. Add half the cooked carrots and potato. Cover and blend until smooth. Add remaining cooked vegetables, cover and blend until smooth. Turn into carrot-lined pan; smooth top with spatula. Bake at 350° for 30 to 35 minutes or until set; let stand 5 minutes. With knife carefully loosen carrot slices from sides of pan. Invert tart onto serving plate lifting pan carefully. Serve hot in wedges.

Kay Forde - Chestnut Hill, Pa.

GINGER CARROTS

Easy

Serves: 4
Prep Time: 10 Minutes
Cooking Time: 15 Minutes

5 medium carrots
1 tablespoon sugar
1 teaspoon cornstarch
¼ teaspoon salt

¼ teaspoon ground ginger
¼ cup orange juice
2 tablespoons butter or
margarine

Cut carrots on the bias in 1 inch chunks. Cook, covered, in boiling salted water until just tender, about 10 minutes; drain. In saucepan, mix dry ingredients. Add orange juice; cook and stir constantly until sauce is thick and bubbly. Boil 1 minute. Stir in butter; toss with carrots.

Susann T. Undi - Cheltenham, Pa.

CARROT PUDDING

Easy

Serves: 8 to 10
Prep Time: 15 Minutes
Oven Temp: 350°
Baking Time: 1 Hour

8 cups grated carrots
4 cups flour
2 cups firmly packed brown
sugar
2 teaspoons baking soda

2 cups melted shortening
4 teaspoons baking powder
8 eggs
4 teaspoons salt
4 tablespoons water

Mix all ingredients together well. Pour into a greased pan or ring. Bake at 350° about 1 hour or until set.

Joan Mulroney - Roxborough, Pa.

VEGETABLES & SIDE DISHES

CAULIFLOWER CASSEROLE

Easy

Serves: 4 to 6
Prep Time: 5 Minutes
Oven Temp: 375°
Baking Time: 25 Minutes

1 large fresh cauliflower, cut
1 (10¾ ounce) can cream of
  celery soup
1 (4 ounce) can mushrooms
¼ onion, chopped

½ teaspoon basil
Salt to taste
¼ cup grated Parmesan cheese
½ teaspoon paprika

Cook cauliflower and drain. In a 2 quart casserole dish combine soup, mushrooms, onion, salt and basil. Stir in cauliflower; sprinkle cheese and paprika on top. Bake at 375° for 25 minutes.

Maria Jones - Roxborough, Pa.

CHEESE DILLED CAULIFLOWER

Easy
Make Ahead

Serves: 4 to 6
Prep Time: 5 to 10 Minutes
Oven Temp: Broiler
Baking Time: 10 Minutes

1 medium head cauliflower
¼ cup butter or margarine,
  melted
¼ cup grated Parmesan cheese

1 teaspoon dill weed
1 clove garlic, minced or
  mashed
Salt and pepper to taste

Wash cauliflower and break into small flowerets. Cook in boiling salted water or steam for 6 to 8 minutes until tender. Remove from heat, drain and place in 1 quart baking dish. To melted butter add 2 tablespoons grated cheese, dill and garlic. Mix with hot cauliflower. Season to taste with salt and pepper. Sprinkle remaining cheese on top. Place under broiler, about 6 inches from heat, for about 10 minutes or until top is golden brown. *The first time I made this recipe I turned to ask my husband how he liked it. He replied "not much!" His serving was GONE before I sat down!*

Alice Brogan - Ambler, Pa.

SCALLOPED CORN

Easy
Make Ahead

Serves: 8
Prep Time: 15 Minutes
Oven Temp: 375°
Baking Time: 20 to 25 Minutes

4 cups whole kernel corn
¼ cup slivered almonds
1 (6 ounce) can water chestnuts, sliced
6 to 8 fresh mushrooms, sliced
7 tablespoons butter or margarine, divided

2 tablespoons flour
½ cup half and half cream
1 cup chicken broth
½ cup dry breadcrumbs
½ cup grated Parmesan cheese

Sauté corn, almonds, water chestnuts and mushrooms in 2 tablespoons butter for 5 minutes; set aside. Melt 4 tablespoons butter, stir in flour and cook 1 minute. Add cream and broth and cook until thickened, stirring frequently. In buttered 2 quart casserole combine corn and sauce mixtures. Top with crumbs and cheese and dot with remaining butter. Bake at 375° for 20 to 25 minutes until hot and bubbly.

Claudia Patterson - Mt. Airy, Pa.

CURRIED CORN PUDDING

Easy

Serves: 8
Prep Time: 20 Minutes
Oven Temp: 350°
Baking Time: 45 Minutes

½ cup minced onion
½ cup minced green pepper
3 tablespoons butter or margarine
1 tablespoon curry powder

3 eggs, lightly beaten
2 cups cooked corn
2 cups light cream
1 teaspoon salt
½ teaspoon sugar

In a skillet sauté onion and green pepper in butter until soft. Stir in curry powder and transfer mixture to a bowl. Add eggs, corn, cream, salt and sugar. Pour mixture into a well-buttered 1¼ quart soufflé dish and bake at 350° for 45 minutes until puffed and golden. *Garnish with parsley if desired.*

Bea Wilson - Mt. Airy, Pa.

EGGPLANT PARMESAN

Moderate
Make Ahead
Freeze

Serves: 10
Prep Time: 45 Minutes
Oven Temp: 350°
Baking Time: 45 Minutes

3 or 4 medium eggplants, pared and sliced ¼ inch thick
11 or 12 eggs, divided
3 tablespoons water
Salt and pepper
Breadcrumbs
Vegetable oil or shortening

Spaghetti sauce (your own recipe)
1 pound sliced mozzarella cheese
½ cup grated Parmesan cheese
Grated Parmesan cheese for topping

Dip eggplant slices in mixture of 3 eggs, water and salt and pepper. Then dip in breadcrumbs to coat. Fry eggplant slices in deep fat until golden brown. Place on paper toweling to drain. Cover bottom of 9x13x2 inch baking pan with spaghetti sauce. Arrange eggplant slices over sauce. Place several slices of mozzarella cheese over eggplant. Spread with spaghetti sauce. Mix together remaining eggs and ½ cup grated Parmesan cheese; spread ⅓ over mixture in pan. Repeat layers, beginning with eggplant, 2 more times; sprinkle top with Parmesan cheese. Bake at 350° for 45 minutes. Let stand about 10 minutes before serving. Cut into large squares for serving.

Mrs. Armand Vozzo - Flourtown, Pa.

COOKING TIP

Root vegetables grow beneath the ground and should be started in cold water to cook, covered with a lid. Green vegetables grow above the ground and should be started in boiling water, uncovered. Don't overcook them.

Jeanne Roman - Flourtown, Pa.

CRUNCHY SEASONED POTATOES

Easy

Serves: 4
Prep Time: 10 to 15 Minutes
Oven Temp: 400°
Baking Time: 1 Hour, plus
　　additional 10 Minutes

6 medium potatoes
⅓ cup oil
1 tablespoon fresh parsley,
**　minced**

1 clove garlic, minced
½ teaspoon salt or to taste
⅛ teaspoon pepper

Bake the potatoes for 1 hour at 400°. While potatoes are baking, combine remaining ingredients and let stand to blend flavors. Remove potatoes from oven and cut into bite-size or larger pieces. Spread on a baking sheet and broil until crispy about 10 minutes. Turn to brown all sides. Toss in seasoned oil. *My children love the crunchy texture of these potatoes.*

Elaine Cellini - Miquon, Pa.

POTATO CROQUETTES

Easy
Make Ahead

Serves: 6
Prep Time: 20 Minutes
Cooking Time: 10 Minutes

2½ pounds potatoes
3 tablespoons (1½ ounces)
**　butter or margarine**
3 ounces grated Parmesan
**　cheese**
1 ounce shredded Gruyère
**　cheese**

2 eggs, divided
1 tablespoon grated onion
Salt and pepper to taste
¼ teaspoon nutmeg
Breadcrumbs
Butter or margarine

Boil potatoes until soft; peel and mash well. Stir in butter, cheeses and 1 beaten egg, onion and seasoning. Form into croquettes, roll in remaining beaten egg and breadcrumbs and fry in butter until golden brown about 10 minutes.

Pru Rawson - Wyndmoor, Pa.

VEGETABLES & SIDE DISHES

MARINATED VEGETABLES

Red onions
Cherry tomatoes
Scallions
Mushrooms
Cauliflower

Broccoli
Green peppers
Cucumbers
Carrots

Cut all vegetables into pieces.

Marinade:
¾ cup cider vinegar
¼ cup water
1 cup oil
1 tablespoon salt

1 tablespoon pepper
1 tablespoon garlic powder
1 tablespoon dill weed

Combine ingredients and toss together with vegetables; marinate overnight.

Regina Cassidy - Olney, Pa.

MUSHROOMS BERKELEY

Easy

Serves: 4 to 6
Prep Time: 20 Minutes
Cooking Time: 55 Minutes

1 pound fresh mushrooms
2 medium green peppers

1 large onion
½ cup butter or margarine

Sauce:
2 tablespoons Dijon mustard
2 tablespoons Worcestershire
** sauce**
1 tablespoon firmly packed
** brown sugar**

¾ cup mellow red table wine
Freshly ground pepper
Seasoned salt

Wash mushrooms and cut in half. Wash and seed peppers and cut into 1 inch squares. Peel and chop onion. Melt butter in a large saucepan and sauté onion until transparent. When onion is clear, add mushrooms and peppers and sauté a few minutes, stirring often. As mushrooms brown and reduce in size, add wine sauce. Simmer for 45 minutes until sauce is thickened. *Delicious served over noodles or rice.*

Sauce: Mix together mustard, brown sugar, and Worcestershire until blended into a very smooth paste. Add wine and season with lots of pepper and a little seasoned salt; stir well.

Brenda Aslin - Mt. Airy, Pa.

GRATIN OF POTATOES

Moderate
Food Processor

Serves: 4 to 6
Prep Time: 20 Minutes
Oven Temp: 325°
Baking Time: 20 Minutes

1 large clove of garlic, peeled
1 large Spanish onion (10 ounce), peeled and quartered
3 tablespoons unsalted butter
3 (16 ounce) baking potatoes
¾ cup plus 1 tablespoon heavy cream, divided

½ cup plus 2 tablespoons milk
1 teaspoon salt
Freshly ground pepper to taste
Freshly grated nutmeg to taste

In a food processor process garlic with metal blade until minced. Leaving the garlic in the bowl, remove metal blade and insert the slicing disc. Slice onion using moderate pressure. In a heavy 2 quart saucepan melt the butter over moderate heat. Add garlic and onion and cook for 5 minutes until soft but not brown. While the garlic and onions are cooking, slice the potatoes using firm pressure. Put them in the pan with garlic and onions. Add ½ cup plus 2 tablespoons cream, milk, salt, pepper and nutmeg. Cook over moderately low heat, stirring frequently, for 25 minutes until the vegetables are almost tender and the mixture is thick. Butter a 9 or 10 inch baking dish. Transfer the contents of the saucepan to the gratin dish. Smooth the surface with a spatula. Spoon the remaining 3 tablespoons of cream over the top. Bake at 325° for 20 minutes. Place the gratin dish under the broiler, 6 inches from heat and broil for 5 minutes or until the top is lightly browned.

Rita Hughes - East Falls, Pa.

LOQUESTO'S RATATOUILLE

Moderate
Make Ahead

Serves: 6
Prep Time: 20 Minutes
Cooking Time: 60 Minutes

⅓ cup oil (approximately)
3 cloves garlic, crushed
1 large onion, chopped
1 eggplant (about 1¼ pounds)
½ cup flour
2 yellow squash (about ½
   pound)

4 small zucchini (about 1 pound)
2 medium green peppers
1 (32 ounce) jar Newman's Own
   Marinara Sauce With
   Mushrooms
1 cup white wine
½ cup stuffed olives, sliced

Heat oil and sauté garlic and onion until glazed. Cut stem from eggplant and cut into 1 inch cubes or wedges. Toss with flour and add to pan. Sauté 10 minutes. Trim stems from squash and zucchini and cut into ½ inch wedges, about 1½ inches long. Add to pan and cook 10 minutes. Cut green peppers into strips and add to pan, toss lightly, and cook 10 minutes. Add marinara sauce and white wine and cook about 20 minutes until vegetables are tender and sauce slightly reduced. Add sliced olives. Let cool at room temperature. *Keeps well in refrigerator. Serve hot or at room temperature.*

P. Loquesto Newman - Westport, Ct.

SPINACH AND BACON TART

Moderate

Serves: 6
Prep Time: 40 Minutes
Oven Temp: 300°
Baking Time: 45 to 50 Minutes

6 slices bacon, diced
4 tablespoons butter or
   margarine, divided
½ cup chopped onion
1½ to 2 pounds fresh cooked
   spinach, drained, cooled and
   squeezed dry

3 tablespoons sour cream
1½ teaspoons dill weed
2 eggs
¼ pound feta cheese, crumbled
½ pound puff pastry dough *or* 4
   frozen pastry shells

Sauté bacon until crisp; drain. Melt 2 tablespoons butter in a small skillet over medium heat. Add onion and sauté until golden. Combine spinach, onion, sour cream, dill weed and eggs in blender and puree. Transfer to bowl and stir in bacon and feta cheese. Grease an 8 inch round baking dish. Divide puff pastry into 4 equal parts and roll each into an 8 inch round. (If using frozen shells, roll them into 8 inch rounds.) Set 1 round in bottom of prepared dish. Brush with remaining melted butter. Top with another pastry round. Spread spinach mixture to within 1 inch of edges on all sides. Paint pastry rim with water. Top with another pastry round, brush with butter and add final pastry round. Press all edges of pastry together. Roll out scraps, if any, and cut into leaves for decoration. Moisten them with water and press gently onto top. Bake 45 to 50 minutes at 300°.

Susan Miller - Philadelphia, Pa.

MONEGASQUE TILLANS

Chopped onions
Olive oil
Minced meat (half veal and half
  pork)
1 clove garlic, minced
Chopped parsley
Basil
Grated Parmesan cheese

Breadcrumbs
2 eggs
Salt and pepper to taste
Tomatoes
Large whole onions
Squash
Eggplant

In a saucepan sauté chopped onions in small amount of olive oil then add minced meat, garlic, parsley and basil. Stir in some Parmesan cheese, breadcrumbs and eggs. Season to taste with salt and pepper. Cut the tomatoes in half and place on an oiled and salted baking sheet. Bake at 325° for 15 minutes. Stuff the tomatoes and top with some breadcrumbs and grated cheese and a dash of olive oil. Return to oven and heat thoroughly. Serve warm. For onions and squash: cut in half and boil until tender; as for tomatoes scoop out and stuff. For eggplant: cut in half and fry; scoop out and proceed as for the tomatoes.

Prince Rainier of Monaco

VEGETABLES & SIDE DISHES

SPINACH ITALIANO

Easy

Serves: 2 to 4
Prep Time: 10 Minutes
Cooking Time: 10 Minutes

1 pound fresh spinach,
** thoroughly rinsed**
¼ cup water
2 small cloves garlic, crushed
¼ cup vegetable oil

Salt and pepper to taste
2 tablespoons grated cheese
** (optional)**
Dash of nutmeg (optional)

Cook spinach in a small amount of boiling water until limp. Drain well. Meanwhile, sauté garlic in oil for 1 minute and add spinach. Cook over low to medium heat for 2 or 3 minutes. Season to taste with salt and pepper. Sprinkle with cheese and nutmeg if desired. *The second time you make this, you'll want to double the amount.*

Anna Maria Haines - Chestnut Hill, Pa.

SPINACH CASSEROLE

Easy
Make Ahead

Serves: 8
Prep Time: 15 Minutes
Oven Temp: 350°
Baking Time: 35 to 40 Minutes

2 (10 ounce) packages frozen
** chopped spinach**
2 cups cream-style cottage
** cheese**
¼ cup butter or margarine, cut
** into pieces**

1½ cups American cheese,
** cubed**
3 eggs, beaten
¼ cup flour
1 tablespoon salt

Defrost spinach but do not cook. Mix together by hand all remaining ingredients. Add to spinach and mix thoroughly. Pour into a greased casserole. Bake at 350° for 35 to 40 minutes.

Marie Goldkamp - Blue Bell, Pa.

TIP FOR PEELING TOMATOES

Drop tomatoes into boiling water, remove pan from heat, and let stand for 15 seconds. Drain. Skin will slide off easily.

Marie King Wolfe - Chestnut Hill, Pa.

LES TOMATOES À LA PARISIENNE

Moderate
Make Ahead

Serves: 8
Prep Time: 30 Minutes

Mayonnaise:
2 fresh egg yolks
½ teaspoon salt
**¼ teaspoon dry mustard or ½
teaspoon prepared mustard**

**½ to 1 tablespoon wine or
tarragon vinegar; or lemon
juice**
Approximately 1¼ cups olive oil

Tomato Cups:
8 tomatoes
Salt
**6 ounces crabmeat, lobster or
prawns**

3 tablespoons thick mayonnaise
Ground pepper

Mayonnaise: All ingredients must be at room temperature. Put egg yolks, salt, mustard and few drops of vinegar or lemon juice in blender and blend thoroughly before adding any oil. Add oil 1 drop at a time to mixture beating constantly. When mayonnaise thickens, add ½ teaspoon vinegar or lemon juice and increase flow of oil to thin stream, beating continuously, until all oil is added. Add remaining vinegar or lemon juice if desired. (Consistency should be thick and jelly-like.)

Tomato Cups: Slice off stem end of each tomato, scoop out pulp and sprinkle cavities with salt. Turn upside down to drain. Chop crabmeat, lobster or prawns coarsely and mix with 3 tablespoons mayonnaise. Fill tomatoes; replace tops.

Pru Rawson - Wyndmoor, Pa.

VEGETABLES & SIDE DISHES

STUFFED TOMATOES

Easy

Serves: 6
Prep Time: 30 Minutes

6 medium tomatoes
Salt
½ cup minced scallions
½ cup minced green and black olives
4 anchovy fillets, minced

½ cup cornichons (gherkins), diced
¼ cup mayonnaise
1 tablespoon Dijon mustard
1 tablespoon minced parsley
6 whole olives

Peel and slice top off each tomato; scoop out interior. Sprinkle cavity with salt and turn upside down on a rack to drain about 20 minutes. Combine remaining ingredients except whole olives. Wipe out tomato shells with paper towel; fill and top each with olive. Serve on lettuce leaf.

Jean Hamara - Sunbury, Pa.

BAKED TOMATOES WITH VEGETABLE FILLING

Easy

Prep Time: 15 Minutes
Oven Temp: 325°
Baking Time: 10 Minutes

1 tomato per serving
¾ cup shredded raw zucchini per serving
1 clove garlic, minced

Olive oil
Salt, pepper, basil to taste
1 tablespoon freshly grated Parmesan cheese per serving

Peel tomatoes. Scoop out insides leaving ¼ to ½ inch shell (depending on size of tomato). (May use the tomato meat for part of stuffing or in something else.) Remove all seeds. Invert tomatoes on a plate and set aside. (If more than 15 to 20 minutes, cover and refrigerate; may need to allow more baking time if cold.) Sauté garlic and zucchini in oil until *al dente*. Season as desired with salt, pepper and basil. Add grated cheese and cook for 1 minute more. Place tomatoes in a flat baking dish that has been lightly oiled. (You may need to trim a very thin slice from bottom of tomatoes so that they sit flat.) Season with salt and pepper. Add zucchini mixture. Bake about 10 minutes at 325° or until heated through but still firm.

VEGETABLES & SIDE DISHES

Variations: Prepare tomatoes same way. Use frozen creamed spinach or frozen spinach soufflé and prepare as package directs. Bake unfilled tomatoes for 5 to 7 minutes. Fill with spinach mixture. This is also a great filling for large sautéed mushroom caps.

Cheryl Young - Chestnut Hill, Pa.

ZUCCHINI PROVENÇALE

Easy

Serves: 6
Prep Time: 20 Minutes
Cooking Time: 30 Minutes

Provençale Sauce:
1½ tablespoons lightly salted butter
1½ tablespoons olive oil
3 tablespoons chopped onion
1 clove garlic, crushed
1½ cups peeled, seeded and chopped tomatoes

1½ tablespoons finely chopped parsley
1½ tablespoons basil
1½ teaspoons kosher salt
1½ teaspoons freshly ground pepper

Zucchini:
2½ pounds zucchini, sliced into 2 inch julienne

2 tablespoons olive oil
Kosher salt and pepper to taste

Provençale Sauce: In a heavy saucepan heat butter and oil. Add onion and cook, stirring for 1 minute until limp. Add garlic and cook 1 minute longer. Add tomatoes and cook until thick, stirring often. Add parsley, basil and salt and pepper; set sauce aside.

Zucchini: Sauté julienned zucchini in oil for 3 minutes, stir in sauce. Season with salt and pepper to taste.

Pru Rawson - Wyndmoor, Pa.

COOKING TIP

To preserve the freshness of basil into the winter months, tear off leaves and place in ice cube trays with water. After water freezes completely, remove cubes, place in plastic bags and freeze. Use in stews, soups and sauces.

Betsy Gullan - Mt. Airy, Pa.

VEGETABLES & SIDE DISHES

MRS. PENACOLI'S ZUCCHINI SURPRISE

Easy

Serves: 6
Prep Time: 10 Minutes
Cooking Time: 20 Minutes

1 tablespoon butter or
  margarine
1 medium onion, chopped
2 pounds ground chuck
5 or 6 large (10 or 12 small)
  zucchini, washed and cut into
  bite-sized chunks
1 (15 ounce) can tomato puree
  (or your own tomato sauce)

Fresh garlic or garlic powder
Salt and pepper to taste
Sweet basil to taste
Parsley flakes to taste
Grated Parmesan or Romano
  cheese

In a large Dutch oven, melt butter and sauté onion and ground chuck until brown. Add the zucchini, purée and seasonings; simmer until zucchini is cooked (not too soft). Sprinkle with cheese. *This will serve 6 generously. For a variation add a cut-up eggplant to the zucchini.*

Jerry Penacoli - KYW-TV3, Philadelphia, Pa.

ZUCCHINI LASAGNA

Moderate
Make Ahead

Serves: 6
Prep Time: 10 Minutes
Oven Temp: 350°
Baking Time: 25 to 30 Minutes

1 recipe of Mrs. Penacoli's
  Zucchini Surprise
Ricotta cheese

Sliced mozzarella cheese
Grated Parmesan cheese

Take the leftovers from Mrs. Penacoli's Zucchini Surprise or make a new batch and put a layer of it in the bottom of a casserole or rectangular baking dish. Spread a layer of ricotta cheese over the zucchini. Top with a layer of sliced mozzarella cheese. Repeat layers of zucchini and mozzarella; top with Parmesan cheese. Bake at 350° for 25 to 30 minutes or until cheese is melted and bubbly.

Jerry Penacoli - KYW-TV3, Philadelphia, Pa.

ZUCCHINI D'ESTE

Easy

Serves: 6
Prep Time: 20 Minutes
Cooking Time: 20 to 30 Minutes

1 medium onion, chopped
1 green pepper, chopped
1 clove garlic, minced
2 tablespoons butter or
  margarine
4 medium zucchini, thinly sliced
1 teaspoon celery seed

½ teaspoon salt
¼ teaspoon pepper
¼ teaspoon paprika
2 large firm tomatoes, thinly
  sliced
1 cup shredded Cheddar cheese

Cook onion, pepper and garlic in butter until soft. Add zucchini and seasonings. Cover and cook over low heat 10 to 15 minutes or until barely soft. Add tomatoes. Cover and cook until tomatoes soften (5 to 10 minutes). Add cheese and cook until it melts. Stir and serve.

Kathy Brescia - Roxborough, Pa.

ZUCCHINI RICE PIE

Easy
Make Ahead

Serves: 6
Prep Time: 15 Minutes
Oven Temp: 350°
Baking Time: 25 to 30 Minutes

1 large onion, finely chopped
1 cup chopped fresh
  mushrooms
1 medium zucchini, chopped
½ teaspoon dried basil
½ teaspoon dried oregano
2 tablespoons butter or
  margarine

1½ cups cooked rice
5 eggs, well-beaten
⅓ cup milk
⅓ cup grated Parmesan cheese,
  divided

Cook onion, mushrooms, zucchini, basil and oregano in butter until vegetables are tender. Stir in rice, eggs, milk and 2 tablespoons cheese. Turn into well-greased 9 inch pie pan. Sprinkle with remaining Parmesan. Bake at 350° for 25 to 30 minutes or until set. Let stand 10 minutes before serving. *Serve as a side dish with meats, poultry and fish.*

Mary McBride - Rydal, Pa.

VEGETABLES & SIDE DISHES

MUSHROOMS MAGNIFIQUE

Moderate

Yield: 12 Caps
Prep Time: 25 Minutes
Oven Temp: 350°
Baking Time: 20 Minutes

12 large mushrooms, cleaned
2 tablespoons butter or
margarine
½ clove garlic, minced
¼ teaspoon salt

⅛ teaspoon thyme
½ cup finely chopped pecans
1½ teaspoons chopped parsley
½ cup heavy cream

Remove stems from mushrooms; finely chop enough stems to make ¼ cup. Salt caps lightly. Mix butter with garlic, salt, thyme, pecans, parsley and chopped mushroom stems until well blended. Heap mixture into mushroom caps and place in a shallow baking dish. Pour cream over all. Bake at 350° for 20 minutes or until mushrooms are tender, basting several times during baking.

Eugenia Zalewski - Mt. Airy, Pa.

ROCKY MOUNTAIN BAKED BEANS

Easy
Make Ahead

Serves: 20
Prep Time: 20 Minutes
Oven Temp: 325°
Baking Time: 3 Hours, 30 Minutes

2 (29 ounce) cans pork and
beans
1 pound lean bacon, cut into
pieces
2 medium onions, cut into
chunks

2 large green peppers, cut into
chunks
2 teaspoons Worcestershire
sauce
1 cup catsup
1 cup firmly packed brown sugar

Combine all ingredients and put in a large casserole dish. Bake covered at 325° for 3 hours, stirring occasionally. Uncover the last 30 minutes of baking time. *Serves 20. Great for picnics, parties, etc.*

Mary Monahan - Doylestown, Pa.

INDIAN GREEN CHUTNEY

Moderate
Make Ahead
Food Processor

3 tablespoons brown sugar (or
   Indian jaggery)
3 tablespoons coconut
2 tablespoons sesame seed
1 tablespoon coriander
1 tablespoon cumin powder
2 teaspoons cumin seed
½ tablespoon salt
1 teaspoon turmeric
½ teaspoon hing (asafoetide
   powder) (optional)

¼ cup unsalted peanuts
1 small piece fresh ginger,
   peeled
2 or 3 hot chili peppers, seeded
1 bunch scallions (some green)
2 bunches parsley, no stems
2 tablespoons lemon juice (or
   mango powder)

Place all the dry ingredients in a food processor or blender; blend very well. Add the greens and blend until very smooth. Add more lemon, brown sugar and green chilies as desired. *May be stored in refrigerator for long period of time. This works best in a food processor and with great difficulty in a blender.*

Arlen Specter - U.S. Senate, Pa.

CLASSIC BREAKFAST APPLES

Easy

Serves: 4
Prep Time: 10 Minutes
Cooking Time: 20 Minutes

1 cup sugar
1 teaspoon cinnamon
¼ teaspoon nutmeg

4 or 5 large cooking apples
3 teaspoons water
¼ cup butter or margarine

Combine sugar, cinnamon and nutmeg. Pare apples and slice or chop into small pieces. Put about 4 cups of apples in a bowl and toss with the spice mixture. In a saucepan combine apples, water and butter. Cover and cook over low to medium heat about 20 minutes, stirring occasionally. *Serve with eggs, bacon and biscuits.*

Marshae Murrell - Laverock, Pa.

VEGETABLES & SIDE DISHES

GLAZED SPICED ORANGE SLICES

Easy
Make Ahead

Yield: 1 Quart
Prep Time: 10 Minutes
Cooking Time: 1 Hour, 30 Minutes

4 seedless oranges
2 cups sugar
½ cup cider

¼ cup water
5 whole cloves
1 (3 inch) stick cinnamon

Slice the oranges ¼ inch thick. Simmer in just enough water to cover them for 30 minutes. Drain, rinse and return slices to pan. Add all remaining ingredients to the pan and simmer for 1 hour. The slices should be tender and well glazed. Allow the slices to stand 2 weeks in the refrigerator or pack them into sterilized jars. *This makes a lovely pork accompaniment or dessert.*

Louise Daft - Lafayette Hill, Pa.

BAKED PINEAPPLE CASSEROLE

Easy
Make Ahead

Serves: 6 to 8
Prep Time: 10 Minutes
Oven Temp: 350°
Baking Time: 45 Minutes

½ cup butter or margarine
1 cup sugar
4 eggs, well-beaten

1 (15½ ounce) can crushed
    pineapple, drained
5 slices white bread, cubed

Grease a 1½ quart casserole; set aside. Cream butter and sugar; add eggs. Stir in pineapple and bread cubes. Pour into prepared dish; bake at 350° for 45 minutes until lightly browned. Serve hot or cold. *This may be prepared the day before and refrigerated. If so, allow a little more time for baking. Very good as an accompaniment to baked ham.*

Patricia Calhoun - Penllyn, Pa.
Mary McBride - Rydal, Pa.

CURRIED FRUIT

Easy

Serves: 6
Prep Time: 10 Minutes
Oven Temp: 350°
Baking Time: 1 Hour

⅓ cup butter or margarine,
softened
¾ cup firmly packed brown
sugar
1 tablespoon curry powder
1 (29 ounce) can peach halves,
drained

1 (29 ounce) can pear halves,
drained
1 (20 ounce) can pineapple
chunks, drained

Combine all ingredients in baking dish and bake at 350° for 1 hour. *Great with ham.*

Patricia Calhoun - Penllyn, Pa.

GRANDMA FRENCH'S YORKSHIRE PUDDING

Moderate

Serves: 12
Prep Time: 15 Minutes
Oven Temp: 450°
Baking Time: 1 Hour

4 eggs
3 cups milk
3 cups all-purpose flour

Salt to taste
Drippings from a standing rib
roast

Mix the eggs and milk well then add the flour and season with salt. Cook a standing rib roast with a small piece of suet in the pan with the roast. When the roast is finished, remove only the roast from the pan. Keep the drippings over low heat and add the flour mixture. Place in the oven and bake at 450° for 1 hour.

Mary Ann Kerlin - Lafayette Hill, Pa.

GERMANTOWN

Germantown was founded in 1683 by thirteen families from the Rhineland who wanted to try William Penn's "Holy Experiment". Thus, it became one of Philadelphia's oldest outlying neighborhoods with its own stores, businesses and even its own German newspaper.

Germantown has always been steeped in history. It was here that the Battle of Germantown was fought against the British, and battle scars of cannon-ball and bullet holes can be seen in its many historic houses. In 1793, it was the nation's capitol during the yellow fever epidemic when President George Washington and his wife, Martha, moved to the Deshler-Morris House.

Germantown Avenue, its main road and designated historic thoroughfare, is lined with many gray mansions that attest to the wealth once found here. The historic buildings include the colonial homes of Cliveden, Wyck and Stenton. In the Walnut Lane area, there are some fine examples of Victorian Suburban houses, including the Ebenezer Maxwell Mansion. Beautiful and scenic Wissahickon Drive, another of its wide thoroughfares, is a natural wilderness area within the city.

Recently celebrating its tri-centennial, Germantown has marched through Philadelphia's development as a community of good transportation, good homes and good values.

Poultry
& Game

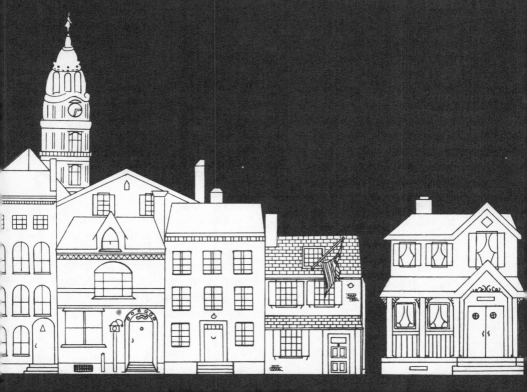

POULTRY & GAME

CHICKEN BREASTS WITH TOMATO-TARRAGON CREAM SAUCE

Easy

Serves: 4
Prep Time: About 15 Minutes
Cooking Time: 15 Minutes

4 small whole chicken breasts, skinned, boned and butterflied
¼ cup flour seasoned with salt, pepper and cayenne
4 tablespoons butter or margarine
1½ tablespoons chopped shallots

¾ cup dry white wine
1 cup coarsely chopped tomatoes
1½ teaspoons lemon juice
¾ cup heavy cream
2 teaspoons chopped fresh tarragon
Salt and pepper to taste

Dredge chicken pieces in the seasoned flour. Heat the butter until it stops sputtering in a large sauté pan. Put the chicken in the pan (don't crowd) and sauté until golden. Turn and brown other side. Add shallots and continue to cook 1 or 2 minutes, stirring constantly. Add the wine. Stir to dissolve the browned particles in the bottom of the pan. Add the tomatoes and lemon juice. Cook, while stirring, a few minutes. Add the cream; bring to a boil and cook until cream is reduced and coats the chicken. Add the tarragon, salt and pepper to taste. Serve at once.

Paul Roller, Roller's Restaurant - Chestnut Hill, Pa.

CHICKEN STROGANOFF

Easy

Serves: 4
Prep Time: 30 Minutes
Cooking Time: 15 Minutes

4 chicken breasts, skinned, boned and cut into bite-sized pieces
6 tablespoons safflower oil, divided
1 small onion, diced
½ cup flour
Pinch of thyme
Pinch of nutmeg

½ teaspoon salt
¼ teaspoon white pepper
2 teaspoons fresh lemon juice
1 cup chicken broth
1 cup sour cream
Hot, buttered spinach noodles, cooked and drained
Minced parsley for garnish

Heat 2 tablespoons oil in large skillet. Sauté onion until transparent. Remove onion and set aside. Combine flour, thyme, nutmeg, salt and pepper in a bag and dredge chicken pieces. Add remaining 4 tablespoons oil to pan. Add chicken; brown over medium heat until light golden in color. Return onion to pan. Mix in lemon juice and broth. Simmer 10 minutes; reduce heat to low. Stir 2 tablespoons hot chicken broth into sour cream. Add to pan, stirring constantly, and heat gently to serving temperature. Do not boil or sauce will curdle. Spoon over hot, buttered spinach noodles and garnish with parsley.

Terri Lambert - Roxborough, Pa.

CHICKEN WAIKIKI

Moderate
Make Ahead
Freeze

Serves: 6
Prep Time: 20 Minutes
Oven Temp: 350°
Baking Time: 1 Hour

**6 chicken breasts, skinned,
  boned and cut into chunks
½ cup flour**

**⅓ cup oil
1 teaspoon salt
¼ teaspoon pepper**

**Sauce:
1 (8 ounce) can sliced pineapple
Water
1 cup sugar
2 teaspoons cornstarch
¾ cup cider vinegar**

**1 tablespoon soy sauce
¼ teaspoon ground ginger
1 chicken bouillon cube
1 large green pepper, cut into
  rings**

Wash chicken, coat with flour and cook in hot oil in skillet for 10 minutes until browned; turn and brown other side. Arrange chicken in baking dish, skin side up. Sprinkle with salt and pepper; set aside.

Sauce: Drain pineapple juice into a pan. Add enough water to equal 1¼ cups liquid; set pineapple aside. Combine juice and all other ingredients except green pepper and pineapple. Boil for 2 minutes. Pour over chicken. Bake, uncovered, for 30 minutes at 350°. Add pepper and pineapple; bake an additional 30 minutes. *Good for a buffet dinner.*

Farlino Family - Miquon, Pa.

POULTRY & GAME

CHICKEN AND NOODLES IN CREAM SAUCE

Moderate

Serves: 4 to 6
Prep Time: 30 Minutes
Oven Temp: 450°
Baking Time: 10 Minutes

1 (8 ounce) package noodles
3 tablespoons butter or
    margarine, divided
1 cup chopped mushrooms
2 tablespoons minced shallots
3 tablespoons flour

2 cups chicken broth
½ cup heavy cream
Salt and pepper to taste
2 to 3 cups cooked chicken,
    cubed
2 tablespoons shredded cheese

Cook noodles slightly less than package directions. Toss with 1 tablespoon butter and keep warm. Melt remaining butter in saucepan. Add mushrooms and shallots. Cook until liquid evaporates. Add flour; stir until blended. Add broth, stirring rapidly until thickened and smooth. Simmer 5 minutes. Add cream to broth mixture with salt and pepper to taste; simmer briefly. Add chicken. Spread noodles in buttered 12x8x2 inch baking dish. Next add a layer of chicken in sauce; sprinkle with cheese. Bake at 450° for 10 minutes or until brown and heated through.

Marie King Wolfe - Chestnut Hill, Pa.

CHICKEN PAPRIKASH

Easy

Serves: 4
Prep Time: 15 Minutes
Cooking Time: 45 Minutes

3 tablespoons flour
2 pounds chicken parts, cut into
    bite-sized chunks
3 tablespoons shortening
1 (10½ ounce) can chicken gravy

⅓ cup sour cream
1 cup sliced onion
1 clove garlic, minced
2 teaspoons paprika
½ teaspoon salt

Flour chicken chunks and brown in hot shortening; drain fat. Stir in remaining ingredients. Cover and simmer, stirring occasionally, for 45 minutes or until tender. Serve over noodles.

Susann T. Undi - Cheltenham, Pa.

HOT CHICKEN SALAD

Easy
Make Ahead

Serves: 6
Prep Time: 30 Minutes
Oven Temp: 350°
Baking Time: 30 Minutes

3 cups cooked chicken, diced
2 cups thinly sliced celery
½ cup slivered almonds, toasted
½ cup water chestnuts, sliced
   very thin

¼ cup pimento, cut into thin
   strips (optional)

Sauce:
1 cup mayonnaise
4 hard-cooked eggs, sliced
3 tablespoons lemon juice
2 tablespoons grated onion

1 teaspoon salt
¼ teaspoon pepper
½ cup sour cream

Topping:
1 cup crushed potato chips
½ cup shredded American
   cheese

Combine first 5 ingredients; toss until well blended.

Sauce: Mix in next 7 ingredients until well blended. Turn into shallow baking dish.

Topping: Mix cheese and chips together. Sprinkle over salad. Bake at 350° for 30 minutes or until thoroughly heated. Serve hot.

Barbara M. O'Neill - Norristown, Pa.

POULTRY & GAME

SING LING CHICKEN

Moderate
Make Ahead

Serves: 6
Prep Time: 10 Minutes
Cooking Time: 20 Minutes

4 chicken breasts
1 large onion, sliced
5 teaspoons soy sauce
1 tablespoon cornstarch
1 tablespoon oil

Garlic slices
Several ginger slices, about ½
inch in diameter
5 teaspoons oyster sauce

Marinate chicken and onions with soy sauce and cornstarch. Refrigerate about 4 hours before cooking. Heat oil in frying pan. Sauté garlic and ginger. Add onions, chicken and oyster sauce. Stir. Cook until chicken is tender. Remove garlic and ginger pieces before serving. *Serve with rice.*

Susan Pagliaro - Fox Chase, Pa.

ORIENTAL CHICKEN SALAD

Easy
Make Ahead

Serves: 4
Prep Time: 30 Minutes

1½ pounds boneless chicken
breast, cooked and cut into
bite-sized pieces
1 bunch or less fresh broccoli
flowerets

2 scallions, cut into 1 inch
pieces
3 ounces chopped walnuts
3 tablespoons toasted sesame
seeds

Marinade Sauce:
1 cup soy bean oil
1 tablespoon dry mustard

1 tablespoon lemon juice
½ cup soy sauce

Combine chicken, broccoli, scallions, walnuts and sesame seeds in mixing bowl. Add sauce; toss until chicken is coated. Cover and refrigerate 4 hours before serving cold over endive.

Marinade Sauce: Combine all ingredients in blender and mix well.

O'Hara's Dining Saloon - West Philadelphia, Pa.

144

CHICKEN WRAPPED WITH BACON

Easy

Serves: 8
Prep Time: 10 Minutes
Oven Temp: 275°
Baking Time: 3 Hours

4 chicken breasts, split and
   boned
8 strips bacon
¼ pound chipped beef

1 (10¾ ounce) can cream of
   mushroom soup
2 cups sour cream

Wrap chicken with bacon. Place chipped beef in greased 12x8x2 inch casserole, top with chicken. Combine soup and sour cream; pour over chicken. Bake, uncovered, at 275° for 3 hours. *Serve with wild rice or rice pilaf.*

Bonnie Courtney - Holmesburg, Pa.

WILD CHICKEN

Easy

Serves: 4
Prep Time: 5 Minutes
Oven Temp: 475°
Baking Time: 50 Minutes

1 (7 ounce) package long grain
   and wild rice, not quick-
   cooking
¼ cup butter or margarine,
   melted
1 cup water
⅔ cup white wine
4 split chicken breasts

Seasoned salt
1 (4 ounce) can sliced
   mushrooms
1 (8 ounce) can water chestnuts,
   sliced
1 (8 ounce) package slivered
   almonds

Combine rice with butter, water and wine. Pour into a 13x9x2 inch baking dish. Lay seasoned chicken breasts over rice. Sprinkle chicken with rice seasoning packet. Sprinkle mushrooms, water chestnuts and almonds on top. Bake, covered, at 475° for 40 minutes, uncovered for 10 minutes.

Bonnie Shields - Roxborough, Pa.

POULTRY & GAME

CHEESE STUFFED CHICKEN BREASTS

Moderate

Serves: 6 Large or 12 Small
Prep Time: 30 Minutes
Oven Temp: 350°
Baking Time: 1 Hour

1 large onion, chopped
1 (10 ounce) can mushrooms
1 large rib of celery, chopped
2 tablespoons oil
2 eggs, slightly beaten
1 tablespoon chopped parsley
4 tablespoons breadcrumbs
1 tablespoon Parmesan cheese

1 cup shredded mozzarella
  cheese
Salt to taste
Pepper to taste
6 chicken breasts, boned
2 (10¾ ounce) cans tomato soup
1 teaspoon basil

Lightly sauté onion, mushrooms, and celery in oil. Add eggs, parsley, breadcrumbs, cheeses, salt and pepper. Fill breast parts with mixture. Roll up and secure with toothpicks. Arrange in 13x9x2 inch baking dish. Prepare tomato soup according to directions on can; add basil; pour over chicken. Bake at 350° for 1 hour. *Good with rice or Noodles Alfredo.*

Judy Verdone - East Falls, Pa.

SESAME CHICKEN

Moderate

Serves: 1
Prep Time: 10 Minutes
Cooking Time: 15 Minutes

Flour
1 (8 ounce) chicken breast,
  skinned, boned and lightly
  pounded
2 tablespoons sesame oil

½ cup white wine
1 scallion, diced
2 teaspoons sesame seeds,
  toasted

Lightly flour chicken breast. Sauté in moderately hot sesame oil for 3 minutes or until brown. Turn and cook another 2 minutes. Add wine and scallions. Cook until liquid is reduced by half. To serve, place chicken on plate, breast side down, pour over remaining sauce in pan then sprinkle with toasted sesame seeds. *Serve with broccoli and rice.*

Chef Seth Lowenstein, Blue Willow - New York, N.Y.

CHICKEN IN WINE SAUCE

Easy

Serves: 6
Prep Time: 15 Minutes
Cooking Time: 20 Minutes

½ cup oil
3 split chicken breasts
Garlic salt
Seasoned breadcrumbs
1 (8 ounce) can mushrooms,
  sliced

Salt and pepper
½ cup dry vermouth
Parsley

Heat oil in skillet until hot. Brown chicken breasts which have been sprinkled on both sides with garlic salt and seasoned breadcrumbs. Lower heat, cover chicken with mushrooms, salt and pepper to taste and vermouth. Simmer slowly for 20 minutes. Add more vermouth and 2 to 4 tablespoons water if necessary to keep moist and make gravy. Sprinkle with parsley before serving.

Barbara Forde - Chestnut Hill, Pa.

CHICKEN CASSEROLE

Easy
Freeze

Serves: 8
Prep Time: 15 Minutes
Oven Temp: 350°
Baking Time: 30 Minutes

4 whole chicken breasts, boiled
  and cubed
2 cups sour cream
1 (10¾ ounce) can cream of
  mushroom soup
1 (10 ounce) can sliced
  mushrooms

1 cup chicken broth
2 tablespoons butter or
  margarine
1 (16 ounce) package herb
  seasoned stuffing mix

Combine first 4 ingredients. Place in greased 12x8x2 inch baking dish. Heat broth and butter and pour over stuffing. Spread stuffing over chicken. Bake at 350° for 30 minutes. *If frozen, bake double time.*

Nancy Arena Carbine - Glenside, Pa.
Joan DeNofa - Philadelphia, Pa.

CHICKEN TETRAZZINI

Easy
Make Ahead

Serves: 5
Prep Time: 40 Minutes
Oven Temp: 350°
Baking Time: 30 Minutes

12 ounces spaghetti
½ cup butter or margarine
½ cup flour
1 teaspoon salt
½ teaspoon pepper

2 cups chicken broth
2 cups heavy cream
4 cups cooked chicken, cubed
8 ounces sliced mushrooms
Grated Parmesan cheese

Cook spaghetti according to package directions; drain. Melt butter in saucepan over low heat. Blend in flour and seasoning. Cook, stirring constantly, until mixture is smooth and bubbly. Remove from heat. Stir in chicken broth and cream. Bring to a boil, stirring constantly. Boil 1 minute. Add spaghetti, chicken and mushrooms. Pour into greased 9x13 inch pan or greased 3 quart casserole. Sprinkle with Parmesan cheese. Bake at 350° for 30 minutes.

Mary D'Angelo - Roxborough, Pa.

HONEY CHICKEN

Easy

Serves: 4 to 6
Prep Time: 10 Minutes
Oven Temp: 350°
Baking Time: 45 Minutes

½ cup butter or margarine
½ cup honey
¼ cup brown mustard
½ teaspoon curry powder or to
taste

4 boneless chicken breasts,
halved

Melt butter in a saucepan; stir in honey, mustard and curry. Remove from heat. Dip chicken pieces in mixture and place in 13x9x2 inch baking dish. Pour remaining sauce over chicken. Bake, uncovered, at 350° for 45 minutes. Should be slightly brown. If not, turn up heat for a few minutes to brown. Serve with rice.

Gay Simpson - Mt. Airy, Pa.

CHICKEN WITH BLUE CHEESE DRESSING

Moderate

Serves: 4 to 6
Prep Time: 30 Minutes
Cooking Time: 20 Minutes

24 chicken wings
Salt (optional)
Freshly ground pepper
4 cups peanut, vegetable, or corn oil

4 tablespoons butter
3 to 5 tablespoons hot pepper sauce
1 tablespoon white vinegar
Celery sticks

Blue Cheese Dressing:
1 cup mayonnaise
2 tablespoons finely chopped onion
1 teaspoon finely minced garlic
¼ cup finely chopped parsley
½ cup sour cream

1 tablespoon lemon juice
1 tablespoon white vinegar
¼ cup crumbled blue cheese
Salt to taste
Freshly ground pepper to taste
Cayenne pepper to taste

Cut off and discard the small tip of each wing. Cut the main wing bone and second wing bone at the joint. Sprinkle the wings with salt if desired and pepper to taste. Heat the oil in a deep-fat fryer to 375°. Add half the wings and cook about 10 minutes, stirring occasionally. When the chicken wings are golden brown and crisp, remove them and drain well. Add remaining wings and cook about 10 minutes or until golden brown and crisp; drain well. Melt the butter in a saucepan and add 2 to 5 tablespoons hot sauce and vinegar. Put the chicken wings on a warm serving platter and pour the butter mixture over them. Serve with blue cheese dressing and celery sticks.

Blue Cheese Dressing: Combine all ingredients in a mixing bowl; mix well. Chill for 1 hour or longer. Yield: about 2½ cups.

Don Polec, WPVI-TV Action News
Dave Roberts, WPVI-TV Action News

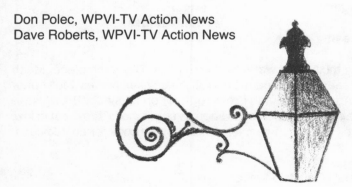

POULTRY & GAME

CHICKEN WITH ROSEMARY AND FENNEL

Easy

Serves: 4
Prep Time: 25 to 30 Minutes
Cooking Time: 15 Minutes

**2 chicken breasts, skinned,
  boned and split**
2 tablespoons flour
**2 tablespoons butter or
  margarine**

2 tablespoons corn oil
Dried rosemary
**Fresh fennel stalks or leaves,
  cut up**

Lightly flour chicken breasts and sauté in hot butter or oil. Shake pan constantly so that flour crusts but does not color. Sprinkle each breast with rosemary and to skillet add about 10 to 12 cut up pieces of fennel. Cover and poach in the butter and oil, turning meat occasionally, over low heat 10 to 15 minutes. Remove from heat and allow to stand, covered, about 10 minutes more.

Ann Wiser - Fort Washington, Pa.

PUERTO RICAN SWEET AND SOUR CHICKEN

Moderate
Make Ahead
Freeze

Serves: 4 to 6
Prep Time: 15 Minutes
Cooking Time: 1 Hour, 15 Minutes

1 (3½ pound) fryer, cut up
2 cups water
Juice of 1 lime
1 garlic clove
1 teaspoon oregano
Pepper
2¼ teaspoons salt

¼ cup butter or margarine
**1 pound Italian sweet or hot
  sausage, sliced**
**1 cup firmly packed light brown
  sugar**
¼ cup vinegar

Wash chicken in mixture of water and lime juice. Dry each piece. Mash garlic with other seasonings and rub into all the chicken pieces. Melt butter in large skillet. Add chicken and brown quickly on all sides. Brown sausages. Add remaining ingredients. As soon as sugar melts, turn heat to low. Cover skillet; cook for 30 minutes, turn chicken then cook for an additional 30 minutes until tender.

Charlotte Rodgers - Country Craft Shoppe - Flourtown, Pa.

SESAME PECAN CHICKEN

Moderate
Make Ahead

Serves: 4
Prep Time: 30 Minutes
Cooking Time: 10 Minutes

2 large cloves garlic
1 teaspoon salt
1 cup buttermilk
2 chicken breasts, boned,
  skinned and split
¾ cup pecans
¾ cup walnuts
½ cup natural sesame seeds
¼ cup flour

Salt and pepper to taste
1 teaspoon paprika
1 tablespoon butter or
  margarine
1 tablespoon corn oil
¾ cup heavy cream
1 rounded teaspoon Dijon
  mustard

Crush peeled garlic with 1 teaspoon salt; add to buttermilk. Pour over chicken; marinate in mixture for at least 2 hours or overnight. Combine nuts, sesame seeds, flour, salt and pepper to taste and paprika in a food processor; turn on and off until mixture is blended but not too fine. (This amount of breading should be sufficient for several additional breasts, depending on size.) Wipe most of the marinade off the chicken. Bread pieces with nut mixture; pat lightly and refrigerate for several hours putting waxed paper under, over and between layers of chicken. Melt butter and oil in frying pan until almost smoking. Turn heat down to low. Cook chicken until brown. Turn; remove from pan when other side is brown and chicken is firm to touch. (This takes 3 or 4 minutes per side.) Drain fat from pan. Add cream, mustard, a few grinds of pepper and salt if desired. Whisk occasionally until mixture thickens. Pour sauce over chicken and serve. (The sauce need not cover chicken entirely.) *When chicken breasts are boned, skinned and split, with your fingers break the membrane under the filet and fold it out to the far side. Pound the filet with the side of your palm to flatten it.*

Under The Blue Moon - Chestnut Hill, Pa.

MARCO POLO LO MEIN

Easy

Serves: 2 to 3
Prep Time: 30 Minutes
Cooking Time: 10 Minutes

¾ pound chicken breasts, skinned, boned and cut into ¼ inch strips
1 clove garlic, minced
2 tablespoons vegetable oil
1 bunch scallions, coarsely chopped
1 cup sliced mushrooms
1 medium red or green pepper, cut into ¼ inch strips
1½ ribs celery, cut into ¼ inch pieces

1 (8 ounce) can sliced water chestnuts
2 tablespoons soy sauce
2 tablespoons dry sherry or water (do not use cooking sherry)
1 tablespoon cornstarch
4 ounces thin spaghetti, break into halves, cook and drain
½ cup homestyle spaghetti sauce

Stir-fry first 3 ingredients until chicken is tender. Remove from wok or frying pan and set aside. Stir-fry scallions and mushrooms until mushrooms are just tender; do not overcook. Add pepper, celery and water chestnuts; toss. Combine soy sauce, sherry and cornstarch in small bowl. Add to wok and toss. Add spaghetti and sauce; toss. Return chicken to wok and toss once again. Cover and let cook just long enough to heat spaghetti through. *This dish may be served as a main or side dish.*

Diane R. Dobbins - North Wales, Pa.

RIESLING CHICKEN

ˈEasy

Serves: 6 to 8
Prep Time: 35 Minutes
Cooking Time: 45 Minutes to 1 Hour

2 chickens
¼ cup butter or margarine
4 shallots, chopped
1½ cups flowery white wine, preferably Riesling
1½ cups chicken stock

1 bunch parsley
½ pound grapes, peeled, halved, seeded
2 tablespoons flour
2 tablespoons cream

Joint each chicken into 8 pieces. Melt butter in large sauté pan. Brown chicken pieces all over; remove from pan. Sauté shallots slowly in same pan until tender. Return chicken to pan. Add wine, stock and parsley. Cover, bring to a boil. Reduce heat and simmer about 40 minutes until chicken is tender. Arrange chicken on hot serving dish. Scatter grapes over top; keep covered. Boil stock rapidly until reduced to 1½ cups; skim off fat. Mix 2 tablespoons of the fat with the flour then stir it back into the hot stock and bring to a boil. Check seasoning; simmer for 5 minutes. Add cream and pour over chicken.

Prudence Leith, Leith's School of Food and Wine - London, England

SWISS CHICKEN KAY

Moderate
Make Ahead

Serves: 6
Prep Time: 30 Minutes
Oven Temp: 350°
Baking Time: 25 Minutes

6 tablespoons butter or
  margarine, divided
2 tablespoons oil
6 chicken breasts, skinned,
  boned and halved
¾ pound large white
  mushrooms, washed, dried
  and stems removed
1 large bunch fresh broccoli,
  cooked

Lemon pepper
2 tablespoons flour
½ cup chicken stock
½ cup white wine
2 cups shredded Swiss cheese,
  divided
Salt and pepper

Melt 2 tablespoons butter with oil in skillet. Add chicken and cook for 10 minutes. Remove chicken to platter; set aside. Melt 2 more tablespoons butter in skillet. Add mushrooms and sauté 5 minutes or until tender. Arrange cooked broccoli in bottom of buttered 13x9x2 inch baking dish. Season chicken with lemon pepper; arrange over broccoli. Melt remaining 2 tablespoons butter in 1 quart saucepan over low heat. Whisk in flour, cook, stirring constantly, 3 minutes. Pour in chicken stock and wine, whisk until blended. Cook until thickened. Add 1½ cups cheese and stir until melted. Season with salt and pepper. Pour sauce over chicken. Arrange mushrooms on top; sprinkle with remaining ½ cup Swiss cheese if desired. Broil 5 minutes or bake at 350° for 20 minutes until heated through.

Marilyn Anderson - Roxborough, Pa.

POULTRY & GAME

CRUNCHY CHICKEN

Easy
Make Ahead

Serves: 6
Prep Time: 10 Minutes
Oven Temp: 350°
Baking Time: 45 Minutes

1 cup sour cream
2 tablespoons lemon juice
2 teaspoons Worcestershire
  sauce
1 teaspoon celery salt or celery
  seed
1 teaspoon paprika
½ teaspoon garlic salt or
  powder

½ teaspoon salt
⅛ teaspoon pepper
3 chicken breasts, boned,
  skinned and split
1 (16 ounce) package herb
  seasoned stuffing mix
¾ cup butter or margarine

Mix first 8 ingredients. Dip chicken breasts in sour cream mixture, then in
stuffing mix. Roll breasts in pinwheel fashion and place in baking pan (may
do ahead to this point). Melt butter and drizzle over chicken rolls. Bake at
350° for 45 minutes and serve. *Great for entertaining!*

Janie Nolen - Lafayette Hill, Pa.

CHICKEN BREASTS IN MARSALA
CREAM SAUCE

Easy

Serves: 4 to 6
Prep Time: 25 Minutes
Oven Temp: 400°
Baking Time: 15 to 20 Minutes

Juice of ½ lemon
6 chicken breasts, boned
¼ teaspoon salt

¼ teaspoon pepper
6 tablespoons butter or
  margarine

Marsala Cream Sauce:
¼ cup beef stock or bouillon
  cube
¼ cup Marsala wine
1 cup heavy cream

½ teaspoon tarragon
Salt and pepper to taste
Lemon juice to taste
Chopped parsley

Squeeze juice from lemon over chicken breasts. Sprinkle lightly with salt and pepper. Place in a 13x9x2 inch casserole. Top each breast with 1 tablespoon butter. Bake at 400° for 15 to 20 minutes or until chicken feels springy to touch, do not overcook. Remove to serving dish; keep warm while making sauce.

Marsala Cream Sauce: Pour ¼ cup each of beef stock and Marsala wine into casserole with remaining cooking liquid. Boil down rapidly until liquid is syrupy. Add heavy cream; boil until slightly thickened. Add tarragon, seasonings and lemon juice to taste. Pour over chicken. Sprinkle with parsley and serve.

Sis Milito - Norristown, Pa.

SINGING CHICKEN IN A CASSEROLE

Moderate
Make Ahead

Serves: 2
Prep Time: 30 Minutes
Cooking Time: 15 Minutes

2 pounds chicken, skinned, boned, and cut into 1 inch squares
1½ tablespoons cornstarch
3 tablespoons soy sauce
1½ cups plus 1½ tablespoons oil, divided
1 cup sliced onion
½ red pepper, seeded and sliced
2 tablespoons chopped green onion
1 tablespoon fresh ginger root, skinned and chopped

1 teaspoon finely chopped garlic
1 teaspoon salt
1½ tablespoons oyster-flavored sauce
1½ teaspoons sesame oil
⅛ teaspoon white pepper
¼ to ½ cup seasoned chicken broth
2 tablespoons dry red wine (optional)

Marinate chicken with cornstarch and soy sauce for 1 hour. Heat 1½ cups oil to 350°. Fry chicken for 4 minutes; drain on paper towels. In a pan, heat 1½ tablespoons oil; sauté onions, red pepper, green onion, ginger root, garlic and salt until vegetables are soft. Add chicken, oyster-flavored sauce, sesame oil, pepper, broth and wine. Cook over high heat for 1 minute. Pour into a 2½ to 3 quart casserole dish or Chinese earthenware pot. Cook, covered, over medium high heat for 8 minutes. Serve directly and bubbling from the casserole dish.

Ginger Chang-Vancouver, British Columbia

POULTRY & GAME

CHICKEN CORDON BLEU

Moderate
Make Ahead
Freeze

Serves: 8
Prep Time: 30 Minutes
Oven Temp: 425°
Baking Time: 30 Minutes

**1 (7 ounce) package chicken
flavored rice-macaroni mix
8 boneless chicken breasts
Salt and pepper to taste
¾ pound deli ham, sliced thin
10 ounces sharp Cheddar
cheese, thinly sliced**

**1 (10¾ ounce) can cream of
chicken soup
½ soup can mayonnaise or
salad dressing
Paprika and parsley (optional)**

Cook rice-macaroni mix as directed on package. Flatten chicken breasts; salt and pepper to taste. Place rolled ham in center of chicken breast. Place a piece of cheese on each side of ham. Roll chicken breasts and fasten with toothpicks. Mix soup and mayonnaise. Put rice-macaroni mixture in greased 13x9x2 inch baking dish. Place rolled breasts on top of rice. Spoon mayonnaise and soup mixture over chicken. Sprinkle with paprika and parsley for garnish. Bake at 425° for 30 minutes or until done.

Deborah Carroll - Roxborough, Pa.

CHICKEN ARLÉSIENNE

Moderate
Make Ahead

Serves: 4
Prep Time: 30 Minutes
Oven Temp: 400°
Baking Time: 7 to 8 Minutes

**2 whole chicken breasts, boned,
skinned and split
Salt
Flour
9 tablespoons unsalted butter or
margarine, divided
3 medium onions, chopped**

**3 large garlic cloves, minced
2 large tomatoes, peeled,
seeded and diced
3 Granny Smith apples, halved,
cored, unpeeled
8 tablespoons shredded
Cheddar cheese**

Cut each chicken breast half into 2 thin layers, butterfly fashion. Put each piece between 2 sheets of waxed paper and pound lightly to flatten. Sprinkle each lightly with salt and flour. Heat 3 tablespoons butter until sizzling; sauté chicken escallops, 30 seconds per side, or until just barely done. Remove from heat and transfer to wire rack to cool. Sauté the onion in 3 more tablespoons butter for 5 minutes. Add garlic, sauté 2 to 3 minutes. Add tomato and ½ teaspoon salt, cook 3 minutes longer; remove from heat. Cut each apple half into 6 slices. Sauté apples in 3 tablespoons remaining butter for 5 to 7 minutes, until just barely tender. Arrange cooled chicken escallops in oven-proof serving dish. Generously top each with amount of onion-tomato mixture. On each escallop arrange 4 to 5 apple slices in parallel formation over onion-tomato mixture. (At this point, dish may be covered and refrigerated overnight if desired. If so, allow to come to room temperature before proceeding.) Sprinkle 1 tablespoon shredded cheese over apples. Bake at 400° for 7 to 8 minutes until heated through.

Brighid Blake - Chestnut Hill, Pa.

CHOWNING'S TAVERN BRUNSWICK STEW

Moderate
Make Ahead

Serves: 8 to 10
Prep Time: 30 Minutes
Cooking Time: 2 Hours, 15 Minutes

1 (6 pound) stewing hen or 2
   broiler-fryers (3 pounds each)
3 quarts water
2 large onions, sliced
2 cups okra, cut (optional)
4 cups fresh or 2 (16 ounce)
   cans tomatoes
2 cups lima beans

3 medium potatoes, diced
4 cups corn, cut from cob or 2
   (16 ounce) cans whole kernel
   corn
1 tablespoon salt
1 teaspoon pepper
1 tablespoon sugar

Cut chicken into pieces and simmer in 3 quarts water for a thin stew, 2 quarts for thick stew, until meat can easily be removed from bones about 2 hours, 15 minutes. Add raw vegetables to broth and simmer, uncovered, until beans and potatoes are tender. Stir occasionally to prevent scorching. Add chicken, boned and diced if desired, and seasonings. *Brunswick stew benefits from long, slow cooking. The flavor improves if made the night before and reheated.*

Linda McAndrew - Norristown, Pa.

POULTRY & GAME

CHICKEN PUFF CORDON BLEU

Moderate
Make Ahead

Serves: 8
Prep Time: 25 Minutes
Oven Temp: 350°
Baking Time: 35 Minutes

2 sheets frozen puff pastry
8 whole chicken breasts, boned,
  skinned and split
Salt and pepper to taste

3 tablespoons butter or
  margarine
8 slices Swiss cheese
8 slices boiled ham

Thaw pastry sheets about 20 minutes. Season chicken breasts with salt and pepper. Sauté in butter about 1 minute on each side; drain and set aside to cool. Unfold thawed pastry sheets. Cut pastry into 4 squares. On a lightly floured board, roll out each pastry square large enough to enclose chicken breast. Place chicken in center of each square. Top with cheese and ham slice. Wrap pastry around chicken with ham and cheese. Bake at 350° for 35 minutes.

Barbara Forde - Chestnut Hill, Pa.

CHICKEN CURRY-NAVY STYLE

Moderate
Make Ahead
Freeze

Serves: 10
Prep Time: 45 Minutes to 1 Hour
Cooking Time: 1 Hour, 15 Minutes

2 (3½ pound) chickens
1 teaspoon salt
2 tablespoons lemon juice

¼ cup butter or margarine
Pepper to taste

Curry Sauce:
2 yellow onions, sliced
1 large carrot, sliced
1 green apple, sliced
2 ribs celery, sliced
½ cup vegetable oil
4 tablespoons curry powder
4 tablespoons flour
1 teaspoon tomato paste
2½ cups chicken stock
2 tablespoons lemon juice

1 tablespoon shredded coconut
1 tablespoon honey
1 small stick cinnamon
1 small piece of ginger
1 large clove garlic, minced
1 clove
½ teaspoon dry mustard
Salt and cayenne pepper to
  taste

Cook chicken in water with salt, lemon juice, butter and pepper. Bone and set aside.

Curry Sauce: Sauté vegetables and apple in oil for 5 minutes. Add curry powder and cook 5 minutes. Add flour and cook another 5 minutes, stirring constantly. Prepare sauce by combining all other ingredients. Add chicken and simmer at least 1 hour. Sauce may be prepared and frozen. *Chicken is best prepared 1 to 2 days before serving. Serve with wild rice and any combination of condiments such as raisins, grated coconut, finely chopped nuts, chopped hard-cooked eggs, finely chopped tomatoes, chopped cooked bacon, finely chopped onion, chutney.*

Anne Madden - Paoli, Pa.

MERRY MOROCCAN CHICKEN

Easy

Serves: 4
Prep Time: 25 Minutes
Oven Temp: 450°
Baking Time: 1 Hour

1 (2½ to 3 pound) fryer with
 giblets
¼ cup oil
¼ cup butter or margarine
1 medium onion, finely chopped
3 cloves garlic, crushed
2 to 3 tablespoons fresh ginger,
 chopped
Salt to taste

Pepper to taste
¼ teaspoon saffron
1½ teaspoons ground coriander
½ teaspoon turmeric
2 lemons, quartered
1 cup white wine
1 cup water
½ to ¾ (4 ounce) can olives

Put whole chicken, breast side down, in range-to-oven pot with lid. Add oil, butter, onion, garlic, fresh ginger, parsley, salt and pepper to taste, saffron, ground coriander and turmeric. Add giblets and lemon quarters (give a squeeze as you drop them in). Add white wine and water. Bring to boil on top of range. Immediately turn chicken right side up. Stir liquid; baste chicken thoroughly. Roast at 450° for 1 hour, basting frequently with pan juices, spices and onions. Remove from oven. Put chicken on serving platter. Over medium high heat cook pan juices several minutes to reduce juices slightly. Add olives and heat through. Remove giblets and pour sauce over chicken (lemons and all). Serve with rice pilaf.

Lawrence Coughlin, U. S. Representative - Pa.

POULTRY & GAME

DEVILED CHICKEN LEGS

Easy
Make Ahead

Serves: 4
Prep Time: 15 Minutes
Oven Temp: Broil
Baking Time: 20 to 25 Minutes

8 chicken legs
1 tablespoon dry mustard
1 tablespoon Dijon mustard
1 tablespoon Worcestershire
sauce

½ teaspoon cayenne pepper
½ teaspoon salt
½ cup butter or margarine,
melted
1 cup dry white breadcrumbs

Heat the broiler. Score chicken legs deeply with a pointed knife. In shallow dish combine mustards, Worcestershire, cayenne and salt. Mix until well blended. Coat legs with seasoning working it well into the slits. Dip legs in melted butter then roll them in breadcrumbs. Broil until browned and tender, 10 to 12 minutes per side. Brush legs with melted butter while broiling so they stay moist. *The chicken legs may be made a day ahead and kept wrapped and refrigerated. Reheat at 350° for 15 minutes or serve cold.*

Ecole de Cuisine LaVarenne - Paris, France

LEMON CHICKEN BREASTS

Easy
Make Ahead

Serves: 6
Prep Time: 30 Minutes

3 whole chicken breasts,
skinned, boned and halved
Salt and freshly ground pepper
Flour for dredging
2 eggs, beaten
1 cup fine fresh breadcrumbs

½ cup olive oil
2 cloves garlic
Lemon zest
2 tablespoons lemon juice
6 lemon slices
Chopped parsley

Place chicken breasts between sheets of waxed paper and pound until thin. Sprinkle both sides with salt and pepper. Dredge with flour and dip in beaten eggs. Coat with breadcrumbs; tap lightly with the flat edge of knife to make the crumbs stick. Refrigerate 1 hour or more so crumbs will adhere. In a skillet heat the oil with finely chopped garlic and lemon zest. Add chicken and cook until golden brown on both sides. During cooking sprinkle with lemon juice. Garnish with lemon slices and parsley.

Rena Rowan, Vice-President Design, Jones New York

FRENCH CHICKEN

Easy

Serves: 4
Prep Time: 10 Minutes
Oven Temp: 325°
Baking Time: 1 Hour, 25 Minutes

**2 whole chicken breasts,
  skinned
1 to 2 cups water
1 cup vermouth or white wine**

**1 (8 ounce) bottle French salad
  dressing
1 (1 ounce) package dried onion
  soup mix**

Lay chicken breasts in 9x13x2 inch casserole dish. Add 1 to 2 cups water, vermouth or wine, salad dressing and onion soup mix. Cover and bake at 325° for about 55 minutes, remove lid for last 20 or 30 minutes to brown. *Great served over wild rice.*

Paula Murphy - Glenside, Pa.

CHICKEN DELICIOUS

Easy

Serves: 4
Prep Time: 45 Minutes
Oven Temp: 350°
Baking Time: About 45 Minutes

**4 cups cooked, cubed chicken
1 (10¾ ounce) can cream of
  mushroom soup, undiluted
1 (5 ounce) can water chestnuts
1 cup mayonnaise**

**1 cup chopped celery
¼ cup green pepper, chopped
1 (6 ounce) package corn bread
  stuffing mix
¾ cup butter or margarine**

In a large bowl combine chicken and next 5 ingredients. Spread mixture in greased 13x9x2 inch baking dish. Mix corn bread stuffing mix with butter; sprinkle on top of casserole. Bake at 350° for 45 minutes.

Evelyn Gorman - Fort Washington, Pa.
Marianne Leahy - Roxborough, Pa.

POULTRY & GAME

CHICKEN CACCIATORE AND NOODLES

Moderate

Serves: 6
Prep Time: 15 Minutes
Cooking Time: 45 Minutes

2 (3 pound) chickens, cut up
½ cup olive oil
½ cup butter or margarine
2 cups finely chopped onions
1 green pepper, chopped
4 garlic cloves
½ teaspoon basil

1 teaspoon salt
Freshly ground pepper
1 cup canned tomatoes
¼ cup dry red wine
8 ounces noodles, cooked and
   drained

Sauté chicken in combined oil and butter for 10 minutes or until golden brown. Add onions, green pepper, garlic, basil, salt and pepper. Simmer for 5 minutes. Add tomatoes; bring to a boil. Reduce heat, cover and simmer for 20 minutes, stirring occasionally. Add wine and simmer for 10 minutes. Put noodles in warm casserole or serving dish. Serve chicken and sauce over the noodles.

Guiseppina Malatesta - Mt. Airy, Pa.

CHICKEN AND BROCCOLI ALMONDINE

Easy

Serves: 5 to 6
Prep Time: 20 Minutes
Oven Temp: 350°
Baking Time: 60 to 65 Minutes

1 (10 ounce) package frozen
   chopped broccoli
1 (4.75 ounce) package julienne
   potato mix
2 cups cooked chicken, cubed
½ cup slivered almonds

¼ cup chopped onion
1 teaspoon salt
¼ teaspoon pepper
2 cups milk
½ cup water
1 cup shredded Cheddar cheese

Rinse frozen broccoli under running cold water to separate; drain. Mix broccoli and mix remaining ingredients except cheese; spread in greased 2 quart casserole dish. Bake, uncovered, at 350° for 60 to 65 minutes until potatoes are tender. Sprinkle with cheese; bake until cheese is melted, about 1 minute longer.

Betty Jane Whalen - Erdenheim, Pa.

BARBECUE CHICKEN

Easy

Serves: 6 to 8
Prep Time: 15 Minutes
Oven Temp: 300°
Baking Time: 1 Hour, 30 Minutes

4 pounds chicken breasts
3 cups catsup
¼ cup sugar
¼ cup vinegar
1 clove garlic, minced

¾ teaspoon dry mustard
⅛ teaspoon thyme
1 tablespoon Worcestershire
  sauce
1 chicken bouillon cube

Broil chicken for 20 minutes until light brown. Combine remaining ingredients to make basting sauce. Turn and baste chicken every 10 minutes. Bake at 300° for 45 to 60 minutes or until done.

Muriel Graci - Roxborough, Pa.

ROAST DUCK WITH ORANGE SAUCE

Moderate

Serves: 4
Prep Time: 25 Minutes
Oven Temp: 400°
Baking Time: 15 to 20 Minutes

2 medium oranges
2 ducks, fresh or frozen
  (thawed)
⅓ cup sugar
2 cups clear beef stock (or
  canned broth)
⅓ cup red wine vinegar

1 tablespoon lemon juice
2 teaspoons red currant jelly
Orange juice to taste
2 tablespoons Grand Marnier
2 tablespoons unsalted butter, in
  pieces

Julienne the skin of the oranges into 1 inch extra fine strips, blanch and reserve. Dry the ducks and roast at 400° 15 to 20 minutes on each side; pour off excess fat. Carmelize the sugar by cooking in stock over medium heat until browned. Add vinegar, lemon juice, jelly and orange juice. Before serving add Grand Marnier and orange strips. Remove from heat and swirl in butter.

Brighid Blake - Chestnut Hill, Pa.

MANAYUNK

The Lenni Lenape Indians are responsible for giving the name of "Mana-yunk" to this Philadelphia hamlet along the Schuylkill River and adjacent industrial Canal.

Manayunk means "our drinking place". It was first settled as a textile town and still has that look. Its now-silent mills of solid stone recall the industrial architecture of Manchester in England. Strikingly different from the flat terrain of most of Philadelphia, Manayunk's steep streets are reminiscent of another city, San Francisco.

Today the empty lofts and storefronts of these mills are being filled with newcomers (many young professionals) who enjoy this stable village setting. Housing is not in ample supply since most of the established inhabitants are reluctant to sell their home and move elsewhere. Manayunk still remains the enclave of Italians, Irish, Polish, Germans and, of course, a mixture of these ethnic heritages.

The founding of Manayunk is marked each year in May by Canal Day. Residents and community groups participate in parades and events along Main Street which make this a day of celebration.

Meats

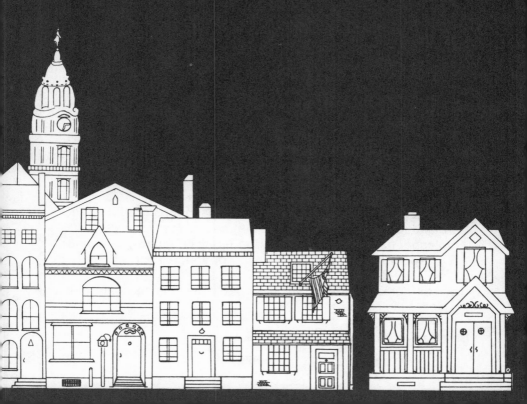

MEATS

MARINATED LONDON BROIL

Easy
Make Ahead

Serves: 4 to 6
Prep Time: 10 Minutes
Oven Temp: Broil
Baking Time: Depends on
    Thickness

1 London Broil cut of beef,
   approximately 1½ pounds
1 small onion, chopped
2 tablespoons vinegar
¼ cup water

2 tablespoons catsup
1 tablespoon brown sugar
2 tablespoons vegetable oil
1 teaspoon salt
½ teaspoon hot pepper sauce

Place London Broil and chopped onion in shallow glass baking dish. Combine remaining ingredients, mixing thoroughly. Pour over beef, turn and marinate, covered, in refrigerator 24 hours. Turn meat occasionally. Remove from marinade and place on rack in preheated broiler. Broil 10 minutes on each side, depending on thickness. Brush with marinade during broiling time. Serve sliced diagonally into very thin slices. *Good enough for company-great cooked on grill.*

Virginia McCuen - Flourtown, Pa.

TERIYAKI MARINADE

Easy
Make Ahead

Yield: 1½ Cups
Prep Time: 5 Minutes

¼ cup soy sauce
3 tablespoons honey
2 tablespoons vinegar
1½ teaspoons garlic powder

1½ teaspoons ground ginger
¾ cup oil (safflower is best)
1 finely chopped green onion
   (optional)

Blend all ingredients, pour over steak or chicken, marinate 4 to 48 hours-
the longer, the better.

Dorothea J. Duncan - Toms River, N.J.

FIREPLACE SIRLOIN

Easy

Serves: 6
Cooking Time: 20 Minutes (Rare)

**2½ inch thick sirloin steak
(about 3 to 4 pounds)**

Salt

The fireplace should have been in use about 2 or 3 hours providing a deep, hot bed of wood ashes. When ready to cook the steak, remove some of the hot embers from the burning logs and place the logs to the side of the fire (for removal of the remaining embers to cook the second side of the steak). Pour salt over one side of the steak until it is completely covered. Place steak, salt side down, on the hot embers. Cook about 25 minutes. Remove from the embers and brush off the remaining salt. Stir embers and add remaining embers from the logs that have been set aside. Salt the uncooked side of the steak and place, salt side down, on the embers. Cook about 20 minutes if you like it rare. Remove steak from embers, brush off remaining salt, place on platter and carve in thin slices. *Dip in melted butter and place on bread. Serve with salad. A great way to entertain 6 people informally.*

George P. Shultz, Secretary of State, Reagan Administration

RADNOR HUNT MEAT CHOWDER

Easy
Make Ahead

Serves: 8
Prep Time: 30 Minutes
Cooking Time: 1 Hour, 20 Minutes

**1 pound sausage
4 cups water
2 (16 ounce) cans kidney beans,
   drained
1 (29 ounce) can stewed
   tomatoes
1 onion, chopped
1 bay leaf**

**¼ teaspoon garlic powder
½ tablespoon thyme
2 teaspoons salt
⅛ teaspoon pepper
⅛ teaspoon caraway seed
Pinch of red pepper
1 cup diced raw potatoes
½ cup chopped green pepper**

Brown sausage in skillet; drain. In kettle combine sausage with water, beans, tomatoes, onions, bay leaf, and seasoning; simmer for 1 hour. Add potatoes and green pepper and simmer for 20 minutes longer.

Trish Lynch - Norristown, Pa.

MEATS

POT ROAST INDIENNE

Moderate

Serves: 6 to 8
Prep Time: About 45 Minutes
Cooking Time: 3 Hours, 30 Minutes

4 pounds beef chuck or round
1 teaspoon salt
2 tablespoons lemon juice
3 slices bacon
1 clove garlic, minced
⅔ cup chopped onion
¼ cup chopped parsley

4 whole cloves
½ teaspoon cinnamon
1 bay leaf
1 cup canned tomatoes
1 teaspoon sugar
1 cup orange juice

Season meat with salt and lemon juice. Cook bacon until crisp, remove from pan. Add meat to bacon drippings, brown on all sides. Combine next 8 ingredients and add to beef. Crumble bacon over meat, bring to a boil then reduce heat. Cover and simmer 10 minutes; add orange juice and simmer, covered, about 3 hours or until tender. If necessary add water to keep moist.

Helen T. Murphy - Feltonville, Pa.

TOURNEDOS WITH SHALLOT BUTTER AND PÂTÉ

Moderate

Serves: 6
Prep Time: 10 Minutes
Cooking Time: 8 Minutes

1 (2 to 3 pound) filet of beef
2 tablespoons butter or
    margarine
2 cloves garlic, crushed
1 teaspoon pepper

Shallot butter (see below)
6 slices white bread
1 (4¾ ounce) can liver paté,
    chilled

Shallot Butter:
½ cup butter or margarine
2 tablespoons shallots, chopped
1 tablespoon chopped parsley
¼ teaspoon salt

⅛ teaspoon white pepper
½ clove garlic, chopped
¼ cup dry white or red wine

With a sharp knife, cut filet crosswise into 6 steaks each about ½ inch thick. Brush all over with a mixture of melted butter and garlic. Sprinkle with pepper; set aside. Make shallot butter (see below). Toast bread slices. Trim to same size as steaks. Slice liver paté into 6 round slices. (It must be well chilled or it will be difficult to slice.) Place steaks on rack of broiler pan. Broil 4 inches from heat for 4 minutes. Turn and broil 3 or 4 minutes longer for rare doneness. Place each steak on a toast round, then top with a slice of liver paté and a generous spoonful of shallot butter. Serve at once. *This is an excellent main dish for a small dinner party.*

Shallot Butter: Beat butter until creamy; add shallots, parsley, salt, pepper and garlic; blend in wine. Chill.

Billy and Sondra Cunningham, Coach, Philadelphia 76'ers - Philadelphia, Pa.

ENCHILADA CASSEROLE

Moderate

Serves: 6 to 8
Prep Time: 20 Minutes
Oven Temp: 350°
Baking Time: 20 Minutes

2 tablespoons vegetable oil
1 onion, finely chopped
2 pounds ground beef
1 (10 ounce) can enchilada
  sauce
1 (8 ounce) can tomato sauce
1 cup canned whole kernel corn,
  drained

2 teaspoons salt
½ teaspoon pepper
¼ teaspoon rosemary, crumbled
¼ teaspoon oregano, crumbled
12 flour tortillas
3 cups shredded sharp Cheddar
  cheese (or more if desired)

Heat oil in large skillet over medium heat. Add onion and sauté until soft, about 3 to 5 minutes. Add beef and cook until browned, stirring frequently. Drain off excess fat. Combine enchilada and tomato sauces in small bowl. Pour half into meat mixture. Blend in corn, salt, pepper, rosemary and oregano and bring to a boil; reduce heat and simmer 5 minutes. Arrange 6 tortillas in bottom of a greased 9x13 inch baking dish. Add meat mixture spreading evenly. Sprinkle with half of cheese. Arrange remaining tortillas over top. Cover with remaining sauce and cheese. Bake at 350° about 15 to 20 minutes until heated through.

Joan Mulroney - Roxborough, Pa.

MEATS

SUPER BURGERS

Moderate
Make Ahead

Serves: 4
Prep Time: 10 Minutes
Cooking Time: 40 Minutes

2 pounds lean ground beef
¼ cup diced green pepper
¼ cup sliced scallions
½ cup sliced mushrooms
2 cloves garlic, crushed
Salt, pepper, basil (optional)
1 tablespoon butter or margarine

1 peeled tomato, seeded and chopped
⅔ cup shredded Swiss, Cheddar or other cheese (optional)
8 strips bacon, at room temperature

Make 8 very large, flat patties from beef. Season with salt and pepper if desired. Sauté next 5 ingredients in butter. Season as desired. Place 1 tablespoon vegetable mixture and small amount of tomato and cheese, if using, on 4 of the patties. Top each with 1 of remaining patties and crimp edges together; press together so they form a flattened ball. Wrap 2 strips bacon in an "X" around each burger; secure with toothpicks or small skewers. Grill far from coals for about 40 minutes. *These are huge!*

Cheryl Young - Chestnut Hill, Pa.

BEEF AND POTATO MOUSSAKA

Moderate
Make Ahead
Freeze

Serves: 6 to 8
Prep Time: 30 Minutes
Oven Temp: 400°
Baking Time: About 60 Minutes

7 medium potatoes
1 tablespoon olive oil
1 large onion, chopped
1 clove garlic, minced
1½ pounds ground beef
1 (6 ounce) can tomato paste

1 (6 ounce) can water
¼ cup chopped parsley
½ teaspoon cinnamon
1 teaspoon salt
¼ teaspoon pepper

Sauce:
4 large eggs
¼ cup butter or margarine
¼ cup flour
2 cups milk

½ teaspoon salt
Dash of pepper
½ cup grated Parmesan cheese

Peel potatoes; slice ⅛ inch thick. Place in a bowl of cold water. Heat oil in saucepan; sauté onion and garlic. Add meat and brown until pink is gone; drain off fat. Add tomato paste, water, spices, salt and pepper; simmer for 5 minutes. Drain potatoes. Arrange half the slices in bottom of a buttered 3 quart baking dish. Sprinkle lightly with salt and pepper. Pour half of sauce over potatoes. Spread meat mixture over sauce. Layer remaining potatoes over meat. Sprinkle with salt and pepper. Pour remaining sauce over all. Bake at 400° for 1 hour or until potatoes are tender and top is browned. Cut into squares. Serve with salad and a vegetable; freeze in foil.

Sauce: Beat eggs until slightly frothy. Melt butter in heavy saucepan. Stir in flour until absorbed; remove from heat. Gradually stir in milk. Cook over medium heat, stirring constantly until mixture thickens and comes to a boil; remove from heat. Stir in small amount of beaten eggs a little at a time. Blend in salt, pepper and cheese. May add layers of eggplant or zucchini.

Stacy Bezanis - Willow Grove, Pa.

PEPPER STEAK WITH RICE

Moderate

Serves: 6
Prep Time: 15 Minutes
Cooking Time: 40 Minutes

1 pound lean beef round steak
  (½ inch thick)
1 tablespoon paprika
2 tablespoons butter or
  margarine
2 cloves garlic, crushed
1½ cups beef broth
1 cup sliced green onions,
  including tops

2 green peppers, cut into strips
2 tablespoons cornstarch
¼ cup water
¼ cup soy sauce
2 large fresh tomatoes, cut into
  eighths
3 cups hot cooked rice

Pound steak to ¼ inch thickness. Cut into ¼ inch wide strips. Sprinkle meat with paprika and allow to stand while preparing other ingredients. In a large skillet brown meat in butter; add garlic and broth. Cover and simmer 30 minutes. Stir in onions and green peppers. Cover and cook 5 minutes more. Blend cornstarch, water and soy sauce; stir into meat mixture. Cook, stirring constantly, until clear and thickened about 2 minutes. Add tomatoes and stir gently. Serve over hot rice.

Carlotta Cage - Mt. Airy, Pa.
Jean Stewart-Bratton - Norristown, Pa.

MEATS

GERMAN BAKED BRISKET

Easy
Make Ahead

Serves: 6 to 8
Prep Time: 20 Minutes
Oven Temp: 325°
Baking Time: 3 Hours

3½ to 4 pounds fresh beef
  brisket
¼ cup catsup
1 tablespoon lemon juice
¾ teaspoon salt
2 tablespoons Worcestershire
  sauce

2 tablespoons dark brown sugar
⅛ teaspoon hot pepper sauce
1 tablespoon cornstarch
1 tablespoon cold water

Place meat in large casserole or baking pan. In very hot oven (450°) brown well, about 10 minutes on each side. Combine remaining ingredients and mix well. Reduce oven to 325°. Pour mixture over meat; cover and bake 3 hours or until tender, basting occasionally. Remove meat to platter or carving board. Skim fat from pan juices. If desired, thicken pan juices with cornstarch mixed with cold water. *Even better served next day.*

Flossie Narducci - Blue Bell, Pa.

MEXICAN CHILI

Moderate
Make Ahead
May Freeze

Serves: Buffet
Prep Time: 1 Hour
Cooking Time: 2 Hours, 15 Minutes

2 pounds dried pinto beans
3 (16 ounce) cans whole peeled
  tomatoes (Italian Pomodori)
2 ounces powdered cumin
2 tablespoons fresh basil
2 tablespoons oregano
Chili powder to taste
5 pounds ground beef round
Olive oil
Salt and coarse ground pepper
  to taste
12 spicy Italian sausages

4 green bell peppers, seeded
  and finely diced
4 onions, peeled and finely
  diced
4 red onions, peeled and finely
  diced
4 squares unsweetened
  chocolate
1 small bunch parsley
2 garlic cloves
Juice of 2 lemons

Soak beans in water overnight then boil until *al dente*. Pour off excess water-until water level is at the top of the beans. Allow to simmer slowly on a back burner in a pot large enough to hold remaining ingredients. Gently puree the tomatoes in a blender leaving small chunks if possible; add to beans and continue to simmer. Add seasonings to pot. Put the beef in a fry pan with a little olive oil and sauté adding salt and coarse ground pepper. Add to the bean pot and stir. Remove the skin from the sausage and separate the meat into small chunks. Put in the fry pan and sauté adding coarse ground pepper; add to the bean pot and stir. Sauté green pepper in olive oil adding salt and pepper. Add to the bean pot and stir. Reserve half the onions to sprinkle on top of chili when you serve it. Sauté the other half in olive oil with pepper; add to bean pot; stir. Melt the chocolate in a small quantity of water over low heat; add to bean pot; stir some more. Chop only the leaves of the parsley and add to the bean pot; stir. Crush and add garlic to the bean pot (*only* if you like garlic). Chili will taste as good without it. Add lemon juice and stir. Allow chili to simmer for 2 hours covered. If there is too much juice or water in the chili, simmer without the cover. Leftovers may be refrigerated or frozen.

William Wilson, U.S. Ambassador to Holy See

CHILI CON CARNE AND TOMATOES

Moderate

Serves: 4 to 5
Prep Time: 30 Minutes
Cooking Time: 2 Hours

1 pound ground beef
1 cup chopped onion
1 cup chopped green pepper
1 (28 ounce) can tomatoes
1 (8 ounce) can tomato sauce
2 teaspoons chili powder or to
   taste

1 teaspoon salt
⅛ teaspoon cayenne red pepper
⅛ teaspoon paprika
1 (15½ ounce) can kidney beans

In large skillet cook and stir meat, onion and green pepper until meat is brown; drain off fat. Stir in tomatoes with liquid and rest of ingredients except kidney beans. Heat to boiling, reduce heat, cover and simmer 2 hours, stirring occasionally. Stir in kidney beans, heat through. Serve with salad and warm bread.

Kathy McNally - Chestnut Hill, Pa.

SHEPHERD'S PIE

Moderate

Serves: 6
Prep Time: 1 Hour
Oven Temp: 350°
Baking Time: 25 Minutes

1 medium onion, chopped
1 small green pepper, chopped
3 tablespoons butter or
   margarine, divided
1½ pounds ground beef
5 or 6 potatoes

¼ cup milk
1 teaspoon salt
Pepper to taste
Seasoned salt
Pinch of nutmeg
¼ cup grated Parmesan cheese

In skillet sauté onion and green pepper in 2 tablespoons butter until onion is transparent. Remove from skillet; add ground beef and brown. Drain off fat and place ground beef on paper towels and blot. Boil potatoes and mash with remaining butter, milk, salt and pepper to taste. Add a dash of seasoned salt, nutmeg and Parmesan cheese. Mix ground beef with onions and peppers and pour into greased casserole. Top with mashed potatoes; brush with melted butter. Bake at 350° for 25 minutes or until potatoes are lightly browned.

Rinda McGoldrick - Oreland, Pa.

SUPER BEEF CASSEROLE

Easy
Make Ahead

Serves: 6 to 8
Prep Time: 25 Minutes
Oven Temp: 350°
Baking Time: 1 Hour and 20 to 25
   Minutes

2 pounds beef cubes
Salt and pepper to taste
2 onions, chopped
2 tablespoons olive oil
1 (4 ounce) can mushroom
   pieces, drained and liquid
   reserved
¾ cup milk
1 (10¾ ounce) can cream of
   mushroom soup

¾ cup sour cream
1 teaspoon salt
¼ teaspoon pepper
4 medium potatoes, pared and
   sliced
2 cups shredded sharp cheese
⅓ cup cracker crumbs

The day before serving: Season beef cubes with salt and pepper and brown in a skillet with onions in oil. Drain mushrooms and add enough water to mushroom liquid to make 1 cup. Add this and mushrooms to beef. Bring to a boil then simmer, covered, 2 hours. Add more water if mixture starts to dry out. Cook beef until tender; refrigerate. Mix milk, soup, sour cream, salt and pepper in small bowl. Place beef mixture in a 9x13 inch pan. Top with sliced potatoes. Pour milk mixture over potatoes. Put cheese over the top. Bake, uncovered, at 350° for 1 hour. Sprinkle cracker crumbs over top and bake an additional 20 to 25 minutes.

Mary Bell Cote - Chestnut Hill, Pa.

STEAK AU POIVRE

Easy

Serves: 4
Prep Time: 10 Minutes
Cooking Time: 15 Minutes

4 tablespoons peppercorns
4 boneless shell or sirloin steaks, each ¾ inch thick
Salt
7 tablespoons butter or margarine, divided
2 tablespoons vegetable oil

1 tablespoon minced shallots or green onions
½ cup dry white wine
1 cup heavy cream
1 tablespoon flour
¼ cup brandy
1 tablespoon chopped parsley

Crush peppercorns coarsely by pressing firmly with bottom of a skillet. Trim excess fat from the steaks; pat dry. Sprinkle with salt. Press pepper firmly into each side of steaks. Heat 2 tablespoons butter and oil in large skillet over medium heat. Sauté steaks 2 to 3 minutes per side for medium rare. Regulate heat so meat won't scorch. If steaks are too large, cook in 2 batches. Remove to a warm platter. Pour fat from skillet. Add shallots or green onions and wine to skillet. Cook 1 minute. Add cream and bring to a boil. Blend 1 tablespoon melted butter and flour. Stir into sauce until smooth. Add brandy. Season with salt. Remove from heat, add remaining butter, 1 tablespoon at a time, rotating skillet until butter is melted. Pour around steaks or in sauceboat. Sprinkle steaks with parsley.

Bernie Parent, Philadelphia Flyers - Philadelphia, Pa.

MEATS

LOBSTER-STUFFED TENDERLOIN OF BEEF

Easy

Serves: 8
Prep Time: 30 Minutes
Oven Temp: 425°
Baking Time: 50 Minutes

3 to 4 pound whole beef
   tenderloin
2 (4 ounce) frozen lobster tails
Boiling water
1 tablespoon pesto sauce
1 tablespoon lemon juice

9 tablespoons butter or
   margarine, divided
½ cup sliced green onion
½ cup dry white wine
1 small clove of garlic, crushed

Cut beef tenderloin lengthwise to within ½ inch of bottom to butterfly. Place frozen lobster tails in boiling salted water to cover. Return to boiling; reduce heat and simmer 5 or 6 minutes. Carefully remove lobster from shells. Cut in half lengthwise. Coat lobster with pesto sauce and lemon juice; place lobster end to end inside beef. Drizzle 1 tablespoon melted butter on lobster. Close meat around lobster; tie together securely with string at intervals of 1 inch. Place on rack in shallow roasting pan. Roast at 425° for 45 to 50 minutes for rare. In a saucepan cook green onion and garlic in remaining butter over very low heat until tender, stirring frequently. Add wine and heat through. To serve slice roast, spoon on wine sauce.

Cathy Schock - Lafayette Hill, Pa.

BOEUF BOURGUIGNONNE

Moderate
Make Ahead
Freeze

Serves: 6 to 8
Prep Time: 45 Minutes
Cooking Time: 2 Hours, 45 Minutes

3 pounds top round beef, cut
   into 2 inch cubes
1 small onion, sliced
2 cups red wine
1 bay leaf
4 sprigs parsley
Pinch of thyme
2 tablespoons vegetable oil
½ teaspoon salt
Pepper to taste

1 small carrot, sliced
1 clove garlic, crushed
3 tablespoons butter or
   margarine, divided
1 tablespoon flour
½ cup consommé
¼ pound salt pork, diced
24 small white onions
1 cup fresh mushrooms, sliced

In a deep bowl combine meat, sliced onion, wine, bay leaf, parsley, thyme, oil, salt, pepper, carrot and garlic. Let stand for 4 hours, turning meat occasionally. Remove meat and pat dry with paper towels. Strain marinade and set aside for later use. In a Dutch oven or large, heavy saucepan, heat 2 tablespoons butter. Add the meat and cook until well browned on all sides. Add flour and cook for 3 minutes, stirring constantly. Stir in consommé and marinade. Bring to a boil. Cover and simmer for 2 hours. Meanwhile in a small saucepan, heat remaining butter. Add salt pork and onions and cook over medium heat for 10 minutes or until pork and onions are golden brown. Add them to the pan in which meat is cooking. Add mushrooms; bring to a boil. Cover and simmer for 45 minutes or until meat is fork tender. Serve hot.

Mary Bradley - Mt. Airy, Pa.

SAUERBRATEN

Easy

Serves: 6 to 8
Prep Time: 20 Minutes
Cooking Time: 4 Hours, 15 Minutes

1 cup light beer
1½ cups wine vinegar
3 onions, chopped
3 bay leaves
8 peppercorns
2 tablespoons pickling spices
½ cup water

4 pounds chuck roast
2 tablespoons flour
1½ teaspoons salt
3 tablespoons butter or
** margarine**
12 gingersnap cookies

Mix first 7 ingredients together in large bowl; add meat and refrigerate 2 days, turning frequently. Remove meat and reserve marinade. Dredge meat with flour and salt. Heat butter in Dutch oven and brown meat. Add 1 cup strained marinade; bring to a boil. Reduce heat to simmer, cover and cook at least 4 hours. Add more marinade if necessary to keep moist. Place meat on heated platter. Stir 2 cups strained marinade into pot. Blend crumbled gingersnaps and cook stirring constantly. *Serve with noodles, mashed potatoes, red cabbage, potato pancakes.*

Alice Brogan - Ambler, Pa.

MEATS

FRITTO MISTO (MIXED FRY)

Moderate

Serves: 6 to 8
Prep Time: 30 Minutes
Cooking Time: Varies

**Any variety or combination of
meat, fish, fruit, cheese or
vegetables, cut in small
pieces**

Batter:
2 cups sifted flour
1 teaspoon salt
¼ teaspoon white pepper
⅓ cup olive oil

1½ cups lukewarm water
**3 egg whites, at room
temperature**
Fat for deep frying

Sift together flour, salt and pepper. Add oil and gradually blend in water, beating steadily with wire whisk until smooth and thick like heavy cream. Let stand at room temperature for 2 hours or more. Just before using, whip the egg whites until stiff but not dry and fold into the batter. Dip selected ingredients into the batter, and fry in hot fat a few at a time until golden brown. Drain and keep warm in a very low oven until all is prepared.

Elaine Cellini - Miquon, Pa.

ELEPHANT STEW

Easy
Make Ahead

Serves: 400
Prep Time: 2 Months
Baking Time: 5 Weeks

1 elephant
Salt and pepper

2 rabbits (optional)

Cut elephant into bite-sized pieces. This takes about 2 months. Add enough gravy to cover (about 500 gallons). Cook over kerosene fire for 5 weeks. *This will serve 400 people. If more are expected add rabbits, but only if necessary as most people do not like "hare" in their stew.*

Joan Rivers, Celebrity

SHERRIED BEEF

Easy

Serves: 6 to 8
Prep Time: 30 Minutes
Oven Temp: 325°
Baking Time: 3 Hours

1 small onion, chopped
1 medium clove garlic, minced
¼ cup butter or margarine
2 (10¾ ounce) cans condensed golden mushroom soup

¾ cup sherry
½ cup water
3 to 4 pounds chuck roast, cubed

In a skillet sauté onion and garlic in butter until transparent. Add soup, sherry and water and simmer for 1 minute. Put cubed beef in lightly greased large baking dish and pour soup mixture on top. Cover and bake at 325° for 3 hours. Serve over rice or noodles. *Great for company. They'll never know how easy it was.*

The Dansbys - Mt. Airy, Pa.

GRANDPA WONG'S KABOBS

Easy

Serves: 4
Prep Time: 15 Minutes
Oven Temp: Broil
Baking Time: 10 Minutes

3 tablespoons sugar
3 tablespoons soy sauce
⅛ teaspoon ground ginger or fresh grated

1 small clove garlic, minced
⅛ teaspoon Chinese five spices
1 pound boneless sirloin, cut into 1 inch cubes

Combine sugar, soy sauce, ginger, garlic and Chinese five spices. Add sirloin cubes and marinate overnight. Place on skewers and broil 5 minutes on each side. May cook on grill.

Maureen W. Britt - Plymouth Meeting, Pa.

MEATS

HAM AND POTATOES

Easy
Make Ahead

Serves: 6
Prep Time: 20 Minutes
Oven Temp: 375°
Baking Time: 1 Hour

**4 cups thinly sliced raw
  potatoes
2 pounds or 10 to 12 thin slices
  ham
2 tablespoons flour
1 teaspoon salt**

**⅛ teaspoon pepper
1 teaspoon dry mustard
3 tablespoons butter or
  margarine
2 cups milk, scalded
½ cup shredded sharp cheese**

Layer ⅓ of potatoes and ham in a buttered 8 cup baking dish. Combine flour, salt, pepper and dry mustard. Sprinkle half over the potatoes and ham. Repeat layers, ending with potato slices on top. Dot with butter; pour milk over top. Bake, covered, at 375° for 45 minutes. Uncover, sprinkle with cheese evenly over top and bake 15 minutes longer. *If casserole is to stand for a while before serving, pour an additional ½ cup scalded milk over just before adding cheese and baking for the last 15 minutes.*

Sister Elizabeth Ferguson - Harrisburg, Pa.

LAMB-VEGETABLE RAGOUT

Moderate

Serves: 6 to 8
Prep Time: 30 Minutes
Cooking Time: 2 Hours

**3 pound lamb shoulder
1 tablespoon butter or
  margarine
2 onions, diced
4 carrots, cut into 2 inch sticks
4 ribs celery, cut into 1 inch
  pieces
¼ teaspoon thyme
1 bay leaf**

**4 cups chicken stock or bouillon
Salt and pepper to taste
5 potatoes, divided
3 cloves garlic, finely chopped
12 small white whole onions,
  peeled
¼ cup red wine
4 slices bacon
Chopped fresh parsley**

Bone lamb; remove excess fat and cube. Melt butter in heavy kettle; add diced onion and cook until soft. Add meat, stir and brown evenly. Add carrots, celery, thyme and bay leaf; stir well. Add chicken stock, bring to a boil; lower heat to simmer. Add salt and pepper. Cover and simmer ½ hour. Stir in 2 grated and peeled potatoes and garlic. Cover and simmer 15 minutes. Add whole onions and wine, simmer 15 minutes. Add cubed remaining potatoes and simmer, covered, until all vegetables and meat are tender, about 1 hour. Cook bacon, drain and crumble. Use as garnish with parsley when ready to serve.

Kathy Brescia - Roxborough, Pa.

SEASONED RACK OF LAMB

Moderate

Serves: 4
Prep Time: 15 Minutes
Oven Temp: Broil
Baking Time: 30 Minutes

Rack of lamb
Salt and pepper

Dijon mustard
Topping

Topping:
4 slices white bread, French or Italian
2 to 3 ounces butter

2 cloves fresh crushed garlic
Chopped parsley

Season back of rack of lamb with salt and pepper and spread with mustard. Broil for 15 minutes. Turn and season again with salt and pepper and mustard. Broil for 10 minutes. Remove from oven and pat the topping on the lamb with fingers and return to broiler for about 4 or 5 minutes until topping is golden brown. Watch closely so topping doesn't burn. *Sensational!*

Topping: Trim crusts from bread and crumble bread with fingers until fine. Melt butter and add garlic and chopped parsley. Pour butter mixture over the crumbled bread; blend well. Put on lamb.

Maureen W. Britt - Plymouth Meeting, Pa.

SPANISH STYLE LIVER

Easy

Serves: 4
Prep Time: 15 Minutes
Cooking Time: 15 Minutes

1 medium onion, peeled and
    sliced
½ green pepper, seeded and
    thinly sliced
½ red pepper, seeded and thinly
    sliced
1 clove garlic, peeled and
    crushed
1 tablespoon oil
1 tablespoon butter or
    margarine

1 pound calf liver, rinsed and cut
    into strips
1 cup beef stock or bouillon
    cube
3 tablespoons red wine
2 level tablespoons tomato
    paste
½ cup canned pimentos, sliced
Salt and pepper to taste

Sauté onion, green and red peppers and garlic in oil and butter for 5 minutes or until softened. Push to the side of the skillet and add the liver. Turn liver when color changes and cook 5 minutes longer. Pour in the stock and wine. Add tomato paste and pimentos and seasoning to taste. Stir together well and simmer over gentle heat for about 5 minutes. Check seasoning before serving. *Even my children enjoy this!*

Christine Robinson - Lansdale, Pa.

LAMB AND EGGPLANT CASSEROLE

Easy
Make Ahead
Freeze

Serves: 4
Prep Time: 30 to 45 Minutes
Oven Temp: 375°
Baking Time: 20 Minutes

1 eggplant, peeled and sliced
    into ½ inch rounds
1 large onion, chopped
1 large clove garlic, minced
Vegetable oil
1 pound lean ground lamb
1 teaspoon salt
¼ teaspoon black pepper

¼ teaspoon ground cinnamon
½ teaspoon dried oregano
½ teaspoon dried thyme
1 (16 ounce) can tomatoes,
    drained and chopped
1½ cups shredded cheese,
    mozzarella and Parmesan
    combined

Salt the eggplant slices on both sides. Place in single layer on a cookie sheet; cover with another cookie sheet and a heavy lid. (This drains excess water and bitterness from eggplant.) Sauté the onion and garlic in small amount of oil. When slightly golden, remove from heat and put in shallow 8x12x2 inch baking dish. Brown the lamb in same frying pan; drain fat. Add lamb to onions with spices, tomatoes and mix. Dry the eggplant slices with paper towels and sauté, a few at a time, in a little oil until both sides are nicely browned. Arrange eggplant on top of lamb, overlapping slightly if necessary. Sprinkle with cheese. Bake at 375° about 20 minutes or until golden and bubbly. (Bake longer if frozen.)

Joan Menocal - Chestnut Hill, Pa.

LIVER IN SOUR CREAM SAUCE

Easy

Serves: 3 to 4
Prep Time: 5 Minutes
Cooking Time: 15 Minutes

½ cup thinly sliced onions
Butter or chicken fat
1 pound chicken livers or calf
  liver
1½ teaspoons salt
2 teaspoons Worcestershire
  sauce

⅛ teaspoon rosemary
1 tablespoon cornstarch
¼ cup white wine or water
1 cup sour cream or yogurt

Sauté onions in butter or chicken fat. Add livers, salt, Worcestershire, and rosemary. Cook 15 minutes. Add cornstarch and white wine or water. Add sour cream or yogurt; warm and serve immediately.

Alice Brogan - Ambler, Pa.

MEATS

PORK ROAST WITH TANGY SAUCE

Easy

Serves: 6
Prep Time: 30 Minutes
Oven Temp: 325°
Baking Time: About 2 Hours

½ teaspoon salt
½ teaspoon garlic salt
1 teaspoon chili powder, divided
4 pounds boneless pork loin

1 cup apply jelly
1 cup catsup
2 tablespoons cider vinegar

Combine salt, garlic salt and ½ teaspoon chili powder; rub on roast. Place fat side up in shallow roasting pan. (May use cooking bag.) Bake at 325° about 2 hours until pork reaches 170° on meat thermometer. Combine jelly, catsup, ½ teaspoon chili powder and vinegar. Bring to a boil; simmer 2 minutes uncovered; set aside. Brush with sauce 15 minutes before roast is done. Heat remaining sauce and serve with meat.

Lois Wilson - Chestnut Hill, Pa.

TERRINE OF PORK, VEAL AND HAM

Moderate
Make Ahead

Serves: 8 to 10
Prep Time: 30 Minutes
Oven Temp: 350°
Baking Time: 1 Hour, 30 Minutes

1 (6 ounce) slice filet of veal, ½ inch thick, cut into ¼ inch strips
2 tablespoons brandy
Salt and pepper
4 ounces thin unsmoked bacon
1 (6 ounce) slice lean cooked ham, cut into ¼ inch strips
1 tablespoon butter or margarine
3 tablespoons finely chopped onion

6 tablespoons madeira, port or brandy
1 pound fresh pork, finely minced
12 ounces lean veal, minced
2 small eggs
Large pinch allspice
¼ teaspoon dried thyme
½ clove garlic, crushed
1 bay leaf

Marinate veal strips in brandy and a little salt and pepper while preparing other ingredients. Line a 5 cup terrine with bacon, reserving some for top layer. Prepare farce mixture: melt butter and sauté onion gently until soft, add wine and quickly reduce by half; add minced pork and veal, beaten eggs, salt and pepper, allspice, thyme, garlic and brandy drained from veal. Beat well until mixed. Spread ⅓ mixture into lined terrine and lay drained veal strips on top. Cover with farce and strips of ham and final layer of farce. Put bay leaf and remainder of bacon on top. Cover with foil and let stand in hot water in baking dish. Bake at 350° for 1½ hours. Remove and weight with brick or heavy object. Leave to mature 3 days in refrigerator. *For a special game paté: replace veal and ham with raw, skinless strips of pheasant, duck, hare, rabbit or other game.*

Pru Rawson - Wyndmoor, Pa.

ED'S LOIN OF PORK

Easy

Serves: 6 to 8
Prep Time: 10 Minutes
Oven Temp: 350°
Baking Time: 2 to 3 Hours

1 pork loin
Vegetable oil
Onion slices

Parsley
Garlic cloves, minced
Grand Marnier

Wipe pork with vegetable oil. Alternately place onion slices and parsley on top (using skewers). Make a few slits with knife and put minced garlic in each slit. Roast in normal fashion. During last 45 minutes of cooking, baste frequently with Grand Marnier. This adds a delightful flavor to the pork and makes an incredibly good gravy. *Serve with scalloped apples and corn pudding.*

Ed McMahon, Tonight Show - Burbank, Ca.

MEATS

BARBECUE BASTING SAUCE

Easy
Make Ahead
Freeze

Yield: 2 cups

3 tablespoons butter or
  margarine
1 medium onion, chopped
1 cup catsup
1 cup water
3 tablespoons Worcestershire
  sauce
3 tablespoons liquid smoke

2 tablespoons brown sugar
4 tablespoons vinegar
1 tablespoon prepared mustard
1 chicken bouillon cube
Pinch of dried red pepper
Dash of hot pepper sauce
Dash of celery salt
Salt and pepper to taste

In large saucepan melt butter, brown onions. Add remaining ingredients and simmer for 15 minutes. Baste meat every 15 minutes until cooked. *This is great for beef, pork or chicken.*

Willie Monroe - KYW-TV - Philadelphia, Pa.

PORK AND SAUERKRAUT

Easy

Serves: 6 to 8
Prep Time: 20 Minutes
Oven Temp: 325°
Baking Time: 3 to 3½ Hours

2 tablespoons chopped onions
1 tablespoon butter or
  margarine
12 peppercorns
2 (32 ounce) packages
  sauerkraut
4 bay leaves

12 whole allspice
2 cups water
1 cup white wine
3 pound pork roast
1 stick of kielbasa, sliced
  (optional)

In Dutch oven sauté onions in butter. Add peppercorns and brown. Add sauerkraut, bay leaves, allspice, water and wine. Make a well in center of sauerkraut and place pork roast. Cover and bake at 325° for 3 to 3½ hours. Remove spices before serving. If desired add kielbasa about 40 minutes before finished cooking.

Gingie Hayes - East Falls. Pa.

BUTTERFLY PORK

Easy

Serves: 8 to 10
Prep Time: 5 Minutes
Oven Temp: 350°
Baking Time: 1 Hour, 15 Minutes

1 (6 or 7 pound) pork loin, boned
2 medium cloves garlic, mashed
½ teaspoon salt
1 teaspoon rosemary, finely
  crushed

½ teaspoon thyme
⅛ teaspoon allspice

Place pork loin, flat-side down, in baking pan. Mix remaining ingredients to form a marinade. Spread on pork and marinate overnight or at least 8 hours. Bake at 350° for 1 hour, basting continually. Place flat side up and score fat. (Scoring is cutting several diagonal lines across meat about ¼ inch deep.) Place under broiler for 10 to 15 minutes.

Pat Castelli - Glenside, Pa.

BARBECUED SPARE RIBS

Easy

Serves: 3 to 4
Prep Time: 15 Minutes
Oven Temp: Broil
Cooking Time: 1 Hour

5 pounds spare ribs
1 piece crushed ginger

Water

Sauce:
1 cup firmly packed brown sugar
¾ cup soy sauce

1 cup catsup
⅓ cup oyster sauce

Place ribs, ginger and water to cover in a large pot. Bring to a boil and simmer for 45 to 60 minutes.

Sauce: Combine all ingredients for sauce and marinate ribs 3 or 4 hours. Cook on grill or oven broil 5 minutes per side.

Maureen W. Britt - Plymouth Meeting, Pa.

MEATS

BARBECUED RIBS

Moderate

Serves: 4
Prep Time: 15 Minutes
Oven Temp: 350°, 375°
Baking Time: 2 Hours

2 to 3 pounds country ribs
2 tablespoons butter or
   margarine
1 tablespoon all-purpose flour
1 cup water
½ cup sugar
1 onion, chopped
½ teaspoon salt

¼ teaspoon ground ginger
¼ teaspoon nutmeg
¼ teaspoon paprika
1 cup tomatoes
1 cup catsup
3 tablespoons Worcestershire
   sauce

Arrange ribs in shallow roasting pan. Roast in oven at 350° for 30 minutes. Pour off excess fat and continue to roast 30 minutes longer. Meanwhile, melt butter in saucepan. Add flour, stirring until smooth. Gradually add water, stirring constantly. Add remaining ingredients. Remove ribs from oven and pour off fat. Cover ribs with sauce. Bake 1 hour longer at 375°. Baste and turn ribs occasionally. *Last minute company?-Just add hot dogs for the last 30 or 40 minutes-You won't taste better!*

N. Minehan - Wyndmoor, Pa.

VEAL BIANCO

Easy

Serves: 6
Prep Time: 15 Minutes
Cooking Time: 10 Minutes

1 small clove of garlic, minced
½ cup mushrooms, sliced
2 tablespoons olive oil
6 medallions of veal, pounded
   lightly
Flour

2 tablespoons cognac
½ cup heavy cream
½ cup veal stock or chicken
   stock
Parsley for garnish

Sauté garlic and mushrooms in oil for a few minutes. Dredge veal in flour, shaking off excess. Brown veal in pan, adding a little more oil if necessary. Add remaining ingredients and cook for 5 minutes or until sauce thickens slightly. Garnish with parsley.

Chef Carlo Sena, La Famiglia Restaurant - Philadelphia, Pa.

SAUSAGE SUPPER

Easy
Make Ahead

Serves: 4 to 6
Prep Time: 10 Minutes
Oven Temp: 350°
Baking Time: 1 Hour

1 pound bulk sausage
1 large purple onion, sliced
1 (16 ounce) can niblet corn,
drained
2 large potatoes, peeled, sliced
and parboiled

Salt and pepper, to taste
1 (10¾ ounce) can condensed
tomato soup

Shape sausage into approximately 25 balls. Brown in skillet. Place balls and drippings into casserole dish. Layer onions on top; then the corn; then the potatoes and salt and pepper. Pour soup over top and bake at 350° for 1 hour. "This recipe is from my German grandmother."

Diane Allen, KYW-TV News, Channel 3

PEPPERONATA

Moderate
Make Ahead
Freeze

Serves: 6 to 8
Prep Time: 30 Minutes
Cooking Time: 1 Hour, 10 Minutes

½ cup olive oil
2 pounds lean cubed veal
2 crushed garlic cloves
1 cup dry white wine
4 large ripe tomatoes, peeled
and seeded

2 bay leaves
2 onions, finely sliced
1 teaspoon dried rosemary
Salt and pepper
6 red, yellow and green peppers,
sliced lengthwise and seeded

Heat the oil in a pan and sauté the meat with the garlic until brown. Discard garlic; add wine and cook until reduced. Add tomatoes, bay leaves, onions, rosemary, salt and pepper and peppers; bring to a boil. Cover and simmer gently for 1 hour, stirring occasionally. Add stock if necessary. Serve with rice. Also good without the meat. Remove bay leaves before serving.

Pru Rawson - Wyndmoor, Pa.

MEATS

COOKING TIP

For whole ginger root: Cut into 3 or 4 pieces. Wrap each piece in freezer paper and secure with rubber band. When needed, take out ginger root and grate while frozen; return unused portion to freezer.

Evelyn P. Olivieri - Mt. Airy, Pa.

TORTA RUSTICA

Moderate
Make Ahead

Serves: 14 to 16
Prep Time: 1 Hour, 15 Minutes
Oven Temp: 400°, Middle Rack
Baking Time: 50 to 60 Minutes

Pizza Dough:
1 package active dry yeast
⅔ cup warm water
3 cups all-purpose flour

¾ teaspoon salt
1 tablespoon olive oil

Filling:
1 pound good quality Italian
** sausage**
1 pound mozzarella cheese,
** sliced**
½ cup tomato sauce
½ teaspoon oregano
¼ pound button mushrooms,
** sautéed**
1 (10 ounce) package frozen
** spinach, thawed and**
** squeezed dry**

1 egg, beaten
¼ pound grated Parmesan
** cheese**
1 (7 ounce) jar whole pimentos,
** drained thoroughly**
¼ pound pepperoni, sliced thin
About 12 large pimento-stuffed
** green olives, cut in half**
** lengthwise**
1 egg, beaten (eggwash)

Pizza Dough: Combine yeast and warm water in a large bowl; let stand 5 minutes. Add flour, salt and olive oil. Work mixture into a dough, adding additional flour to form a ball. Knead for 5 to 10 minutes or until smooth. Cover with a damp towel and let rise in a warm place about 1 hour or until doubled in size. Punch down.

Filling: While dough is rising, cook sausage thoroughly, drain and thinly slice. Grease an 11x5x3 inch loaf pan. Roll out ¾ of prepared dough and line the bottom and sides of pan. Make sure dough is not too thin or this will cause the juices to seep out during baking. Place ⅓ of mozzarella cheese in bottom of pan and top with sausages. Spoon tomato sauce over this and sprinkle with oregano and sautéed mushrooms. Combine spinach, 1 beaten egg and Parmesan cheese and layer in pan. Add pimentos in a layer and then remaining mozzarella. Arrange pepperoni slices on cheese and top with olives. Roll out remaining ¼ dough and cover filling, moistening edges with a little water. Crimp edges to seal completely. Brush with remaining beaten egg and make several air holes in top to allow steam to escape. Bake at 400° for 50 to 60 minutes or until crust is browned. Cool before slicing. *It may be easier to turn out of pan directly onto a cutting board and slice upside down if top crust is too crisp. This makes a great picnic luncheon served with a salad.*

Evelyn P. Olivieri - Mt. Airy, Pa.

HEARTY WINTER STEW

Easy
Make Ahead

Serves: 10 to 14
Prep Time: 40 Minutes
Cooking Time: 4 Hours, 45 Minutes

2 cups navy beans
2 cups dried peas
3 to 4 slices crisp bacon
1 teaspoon salt
Freshly ground pepper
1 whole bay leaf or 2 fresh
  leaves
½ teaspoon thyme
3 quarts chicken or beef broth
2 cups canned tomatoes

2 cups chopped onions
1 cup chopped celery
2 cloves garlic, minced
1 (10 ounce) package frozen
  spinach
1 pound smoked sausage,
  sliced
2 boneless chicken breasts,
  uncooked and cubed

Wash beans and peas. In large pot combine first 8 ingredients and simmer for 3 hours. Add vegetables and garlic and simmer, uncovered, for 1 additional hour or until slightly thickened. Add spinach, sausage, chicken and simmer additional 45 minutes. *Best if made a day or 2 ahead. Wonderful served with rice, salad and crusty bread.*

Judith Buten - Chestnut Hill, Pa.

191

VEAL ROLLANTINE

Moderate
Make Ahead

Serves: 6 to 10
Prep Time: 30 to 40 Minutes
Oven Temp: 350°
Baking Time: 1 Hour

2½ pounds escallops of veal,
  pounded very thin
½ pound prosciutto, sliced very
  thin
½ pound salami, sliced thin
½ pound mortadella, sliced thin
¼ cup Parmesan cheese, grated
¼ cup fine dry breadcrumbs

2 tablespoons chopped parsley
1 tablespoon fresh basil or 1
  teaspoon dried basil
6 hard-cooked eggs
Freshly ground pepper to taste
About 10 strips bacon.
2 cups tomato sauce

Place cutlets side by side, slightly overlapping, to form a rectangle about 14 inches wide. Gently pound pieces together to make rolling easier. Cover with prosciutto; then a layer of salami; then a layer of mortadella. Sprinkle with cheese and breadcrumbs, parsley and basil. Place whole eggs down the center in a line. Sprinkle top with oil and pepper and begin tightly rolling edge of veal, jelly-roll style, rolling lengthwise. Tie the meat in a few places if you think necessary. Place in baking pan or roasting pan, top with bacon strips and cover with tomato sauce. Bake at 350° for 1 hour. Remove to large platter, remove string (if used) and slice. Serve warm or cold.

Herb Olivieri - Mt. Airy, Pa.

OSSO BUCCO MILANESE

Moderate

Serves: 8
Prep Time: 20 Minutes
Cooking Time: 2 Hours

8 to 12 veal shanks
Salt and pepper
Flour
2 ounces oil
2 ounces clarified butter

1 cup white wine
1 (16 ounce) can peeled
  tomatoes
2 cups veal stock

Gremolata:
2 cloves garlic, minced
1 lemon rind, grated

8 sprigs parsley, chopped
4 chopped anchovy fillets

Season veal shanks with salt and pepper and roll in flour. Sauté in oil and clarified butter on both sides until brown. Combine wine, tomatoes and veal stock and pour over shanks, cover and cook over low heat about 2 hours until meat is so tender it almost falls off the bones. If necessary, extra stock may be added during cooking.

Gremolata (an essential part of the Osso Bucco): Mix the garlic, lemon rind, chopped parsley and anchovies together; place over veal shanks and stir to distribute the flavor of the Gremolata evenly. *An important part of this dish is the marrow from the bones; you will need a small marrow fork to dig the marrow out of the bone. Serve with Risotto Milanese.*

Vincent J. Alberici, Bellevue Stratford Hotel - Philadelphia, Pa.

VEAL IN LEMON AND BUTTER

Serves: 6
Prep Time: 15 Minutes
Oven Temp: 350°
Cooking Time: 20 Minutes

½ cup flour
½ cup breadcrumbs
1 teaspoon salt
¼ teaspoon pepper
¼ teaspoon paprika
1 teaspoon oregano
1 teaspoon basil
1 teaspoon parsley flakes

½ teaspoon onion powder
2 pounds veal, cut Italian style
6 tablespoons olive oil, divided
5 tablespoons butter or
   margarine, divided
½ pound fresh mushrooms,
   sliced
3 lemons, divided

Mix together flour, breadcrumbs and seasonings on a large piece of waxed paper. Dredge veal well in this mixture. Heat 1 tablespoon oil and 1 tablespoon butter in large skillet; sauté meat until brown on both sides, 1 to 2 minutes per side. Transfer meat to flat baking dish when browned. Use more oil and butter to finish browning. Melt remaining butter and oil and sauté mushrooms over high heat for 1 minute. Cut 2 lemons in half and juice. Add juice to butter sauce. Garnish veal with remaining lemon, thinly sliced. Pour sauce over meat. Bake at 350° for 15 minutes; serve immediately.

Julius and Turquoise Erving - Philadelphia 76'ers

MEATS

VEAL PICANTE

Moderate

Serves: 4
Prep Time: 15 Minutes
Cooking Time: 15 Minutes

1 pound veal medallions,
  pounded thin
Salt
Pepper
Flour
¼ cup butter or margarine

6 shallots, chopped
2 teaspoons fresh parsley
½ cup chicken broth
½ cup white wine
Juice of 2 lemons

Season veal with salt, pepper and flour. Melt butter in large skillet; add veal and brown. Remove meat from pan and set aside. Sauté shallots and parsley in butter in pan. Add chicken broth and wine; cook over high heat for 2 minutes, stirring constantly. Lower heat and return veal to pan. Squeeze juice of lemons on veal and heat for another minute. Arrange veal on hot platter and cover with sauce from pan. Garnish with thin lemon slices.

Donna J. Bartynski - Maple Glen, Pa.

VEAL MARSALA SCALLOPINI

Easy

Serves: 4
Prep Time: 10 Minutes
Cooking Time: 5 Minutes

1 pound thin veal cutlets
⅓ cup grated Parmesan cheese
1 clove garlic
¼ cup butter

4 or 5 mushrooms, thinly sliced
Dash of cayenne pepper
¼ cup chicken broth
¼ cup marsala wine

Flatten veal and coat with cheese. Sauté meat and garlic in butter until golden brown. Add butter as needed; remove meat and garlic and set aside. In same butter sauté mushrooms and set aside on top of veal. To the butter, add pepper, broth and wine; stir until all brown. Add veal and mushrooms to pan; cook 1 minute over high heat. Serve at once.

Barbara Carolan - Ambler, Pa.

VITELLO TONNATO

Moderate
Make Ahead

Serves: 6 to 8
Prep Time: 30 Minutes
Cooking Time: 1 Hour

2½ **pound veal roast**
Water
½ **onion**
½ **carrot**

1 **rib celery**
1 **bay leaf**
2 **tablespoons vinegar**

Sauce:
1 (6½ **ounce) can white tuna in**
    oil
Juice of 2 lemons
1 (2 **ounce) can anchovy fillets**

3 **hard-cooked eggs**
½ **cup olive oil**
2 **tablespoons capers in vinegar**

Tie the roast with cord so it keeps a good shape. Bring just enough water to cover roast to a boil in a heavy pan. Add onion, carrot, celery, bay leaf and vinegar. Cover and simmer gently until meat is done, about 1 hour. Let cool in broth then wrap in foil and refrigerate until time to slice it.

Sauce: Drain and break up tuna in a bowl. Squeeze lemon juice and leave for an hour. Dry anchovy fillets. In food processor add tuna, anchovies, eggs and capers. When blended, add oil gradually. Slice meat finely, serve on platter covered with sauce and garnish with lemon slices and capers.

Pru Rawson - Wyndmoor, Pa.

RITTENHOUSE SQUARE

Once a fashionable residential neighborhood begun in the 19th century, Rittenhouse Square was noted for its nannies who strolled the beautiful walkways which were secluded from the industrialization of the rest of the city. Several mansions remain on the Square, typical of the many that once surrounded it. A 20th century addition are the modern highrise apartment buildings which overlook the park area. South of the Square are blocks of fine 19th century brownstones and Victorian rowhouses.

Originally, Rittenhouse Square was one of four public parks set aside in William Penn's plan for Philadelphia. It was named after David Rittenhouse, a prominent Philadelphian and our country's first astronomer.

Today, it is an enjoyable and heavily-used area, featuring a variety of events. In May, thousands flock to Rittenhouse Square to buy flowers and other goodies at the Flower Market. The Art Alliance sponsors a "Clothes-line" exhibit in June, affording artists the opportunity to display their creative abilities. The Square also provides a place to do what many residents like best—watch other Philadelphians.

Seafood

SEAFOOD

BLUEFISH BAKED IN WINE

Easy

Serves: 4 to 6
Prep Time: 10 to 15 Minutes
Oven Temp: 350°
Baking Time: 15 to 20 Minutes

2 pounds bluefish fillets
Salt, pepper and paprika to taste
¼ cup butter or margarine,
melted

¼ cup dry white wine
1 tablespoon soy sauce
Seasoned breadcrumbs

Cut fillets into serving pieces and place in well-buttered baking dish. Sprinkle fish with salt, pepper and paprika to taste. Combine melted butter with wine and soy sauce; pour over fish. Sprinkle with seasoned breadcrumbs. Bake at 350° for 15 to 20 minutes until fish flakes easily. Serve with remaining sauce in pan.

Rose Marie Zaro - Norristown, Pa.

BAKED BLUEFISH COMMODORE BENEDICT

Easy

Serves: 6
Prep Time: 20 Minutes
Oven Temp: 350°
Baking Time: 20 to 35 Minutes

3 to 3½ pounds bluefish fillets
¼ cup butter or margarine
3 egg yolks
2 tablespoons onion, coarsely
chopped
2 tablespoons capers
2 tablespoons sweet and sour
gherkins, coarsely chopped

2 tablespoons strained lemon
juice
1 tablespoon tarragon vinegar
Salt and paprika to taste
Lemon and parsley for garnish

Place fish in a well-buttered baking dish. Bake at 350° for 15 to 25 minutes basting frequently with melted butter. Cream ¼ cup butter and beat in egg yolks. Add rest of ingredients; spread fish with egg mixture. Return fish to oven for 5 to 10 minutes more or until fish is tender. Garnish with lemon and parsley. *May also be baked in electric skillet or on the grill.*

Alice Brogan - Ambler, Pa.

PETITES ST. JACQUES ET HOMARD EN COURT BOUILLON

Difficult
Make Ahead

Serves: 4 for Entree
Prep Time: 1 Hour
Oven Temp: 350°-400°
Baking Time: 1 Minute

4 (1 pound) lobsters
3 quarts water
1 head of red snapper
1 medium onion, sliced very thin
1 leek, sliced very thin
4 ounces carrots, peeled and
　sliced
1 rib of celery, sliced
Salt and pepper to taste

8 ounces Long Island scallops
1 small bunch parsley, coarsely
　chopped
1 small bunch dill, coarsely
　chopped
1 tomato, peeled and diced
4 ounces Perce Pierre or
　zucchini skins cut into
　julienne

Cook lobster in 3 quarts water for 3 minutes, no salt and pepper. Reserve half the lobster water. Cut head of snapper into 4 pieces and soak in cold water for 15 minutes. Cook head of snapper in lobster water for 30 minutes. Skim and reduce by half. Drain fish stock and add onion, leek, carrots and celery. Cook for 30 minutes over low heat. Add salt and pepper to taste. While vegetables are being cooked, shell lobster and remove bones from claws. Blanch Perce Pierre for 20 seconds and drain. Cut lobster body in tiny slices; do not cut claws. Place lobster meat in a soup plate with scallops and put in the oven for 30 seconds at 350 to 400°. Pour hot bouillon on top of the lobster and scallops. Add parsley, dill, diced tomatoes, Perce Pierre and lobster claws on top. Return to oven for 30 seconds and serve immediately.

Alain Sailhac, Chef, Le Cirque Inn - New York, N.Y.

SEAFOOD

CRABMEAT MORNAY

Easy

Serves: 4
Prep Time: 20 Minutes
Cooking Time: 25 to 30 Minutes

1 cup finely chopped green
  onion
½ cup finely chopped parsley
1 cup butter or margarine
2 tablespoons flour
2 cups light cream

3 or 4 cups shredded Swiss
  cheese
Salt, garlic salt, pepper to taste
1 pound crabmeat
1 tablespoon dry sherry
Hot pepper sauce to taste

Sauté onion and parsley in butter until tender but not brown. Add flour; cook, stirring constantly, until flour is blended. Add cream, cheese, and seasonings. Cook over low heat until mixture begins to thicken. Add crabmeat, sherry and hot sauce. Simmer for 15 to 20 minutes. (The mixture may be thinned if necessary with butter, milk or cream.) Serve hot with large pieces of fresh Italian, French bread or white melba rounds.

Terri Lambert - Roxborough, Pa.

CRAB STUFFED FLOUNDER

Moderate

Serves: 8
Prep Time: 45 Minutes
Oven Temp: 400°
Baking Time: 35 Minutes

¼ cup chopped onion
¼ cup plus 3 tablespoons butter
  or margarine, divided
1 (4 ounce) can chopped
  mushrooms, drained and
  liquid reserved
1 (7½ ounce) can crabmeat,
  drained and cartilage removed
½ cup coarse saltine cracker
  crumbs

2 tablespoons snipped parsley
¾ teaspoon salt, divided
Dash of pepper
2 pounds (8) flounder fillets
3 tablespoons flour
Milk
⅓ cup dry white wine
1 cup (4 ounces) Swiss cheese,
  shredded
½ teaspoon paprika

In skillet, sauté onion in ¼ cup butter until tender but not brown. Stir drained mushrooms into skillet with flaked crabmeat, cracker crumbs, parsley, ½ teaspoon salt and a dash of pepper. Spread mixture over flounder fillets. Roll fillets and place seam-side down in baking dish. In saucepan melt remaining 3 tablespoons butter. Blend in flour and ¼ teaspoon salt. Add enough milk to reserved mushroom liquid to make 1½ cups. Add with wine to saucepan. Cook and stir until mixture thickens and bubbles. Pour over fillets. Bake at 400° for 25 minutes. Sprinkle with cheese and paprika. Return to oven for 10 minutes or until fish flakes.

Brenda Aslin - Mt. Airy, Pa.

CRABMEAT CASSEROLE

Easy
Make Ahead
Freeze

Serves: 4
Prep Time: 20 Minutes
Oven Temp: 400°
Baking Time: 10 to 15 Minutes

2 (6 ounce) packages frozen lump king crabmeat
3 tablespoons butter or margarine
3 tablespoons flour
1 cup milk
½ cup light cream
½ cup chicken broth
¾ cup shredded sharp Cheddar cheese

1 (4 ounce) can whole mushroom caps
2 tablespoons grated onion
1 teaspoon salt
¼ teaspoon paprika
2 tablespons white wine
¼ cup fine breadcrumbs

Defrost crabmeat and drain. Melt butter; mix with milk and flour until smooth. Stir in cream and broth. Cook, stirring constantly, until it thickens over low heat. Add cheese, mushrooms, onion, salt, paprika and wine. Stir until cheese melts; stir in crab. Pour into a greased 1¼ quart casserole and sprinkle with breadcrumbs. Bake at 400° for 10 to 15 minutes.

Phyllis Mastrangelo - Plymouth Meeting, Pa.

SEAFOOD

BAKED FISH NAPOLETANO

Moderate

Serves: 4
Prep Time: 10 Minutes
Oven Temp: 375°
Baking Time: 25 Minutes

**4 portions white fish, skinned
   and boned
2 tablespoons olive oil
1 medium onion, chopped
1 (8 ounce) can peeled tomatoes
2 cloves garlic, whole
1 teaspoon salt**

**½ teaspoon pepper
8 pitted green olives, chopped
1 tablespoon capers, drained
1 tablespoon chopped parsley
1 small rib celery, very finely
   chopped**

Arrange fish in single layer in an oiled, shallow, oven-proof dish. Heat the olive oil in a fry pan and sauté the onion gently until soft and golden. Add the canned tomatoes with juice, garlic, salt and pepper. Cook over moderate heat, stirring frequently, for 5 minutes. Stir in olives, capers, parsley and celery and spoon sauce evenly over the fish. Cover and bake at 375° for 25 minutes. Serve hot.

Bishop L. DeSimone - Philadelphia, Pa.

LOBSTER POMPADOUR

Easy

Serves: 6
Prep Time: 15 Minutes
Cooking Time: 10 Minutes

**3 ounces sliced fresh
   mushrooms
1 cup thinly sliced celery
½ teaspoon chervil, crushed
¼ cup butter or margarine
1 (10 ounce) can frozen
   condensed cream of shrimp
   soup, thawed**

**1 cup light cream
1 cup whole tomatoes, drained
   and quartered
3 cups cubed cooked lobster
6 frozen patty shells, baked**

In saucepan brown mushrooms and cook celery with chervil in butter until tender. Add soup, cream, tomatoes and lobster. Heat, stirring occasionally. Serve in patty shells.

Patricia Boris - Roxborough, Pa.

TUNA EN CROUTE

Moderate
Make Ahead

Serves: 4 to 6
Prep Time: 15 Minutes
Oven Temp: 350°
Baking Time: 15 to 20 Minutes

1 (6½ ounce) can tuna, drained
1 teaspoon vinegar
2 to 3 tablespoons mayonnaise
1 teaspoon onion, finely
  chopped

1 small tomato, chopped
Salt and pepper to taste
Pie pastry
1 green olive
Parsley for garnish

Flake tuna and mix with next 5 ingredients. Form into a fish shape on a cookie sheet (preferably without edges). Place pie pastry over tuna shape. Cut excess pastry and use to make fins and tail. Cut scale shape into pastry by snipping lightly with scissors. Cut out a hole for eye. Brush pastry with milk; bake at 350° for 15 to 20 minutes or until lightly browned. Slide fish onto platter and place olive in eye hole and garnish with parsley.

Sister Loretto Carmel - Flourtown, Pa.

FLOUNDER SAUTÉED WITH BANANAS AND ALMONDS

Moderate

Serves: 4
Prep Time: 15 Minutes
Cooking Time: About 20 Minutes

1½ to 2 pounds flounder fillets
½ cup flour seasoned with
  nutmeg, salt and pepper
1 large banana
¾ cup sliced or slivered
  almonds

2 tablespoons oil
1 tablespoon butter or
  margarine
¼ cup almond liqueur
Juice of ½ lemon

Coat flounder with seasoned flour. Peel banana and cut into ⅛ inch slices. Heat combined oil and butter until a light haze forms. Sauté almonds until golden. Remove and reserve almonds. Keep heat moderate, but do not allow oil to brown. Sauté fillets until lightly browned. Turn and brown second side. Add banana to cook when you turn the fillets. Remove fillets to serving plate. Add almond liqueur and lemon to sauce in pan. Add almonds and stir until smooth. Pour sauce over fillets.

Virginia McCuen - Flourtown, Pa.

SEAFOOD

COQUILLES ST. JACQUES AUX HERBES

Easy

Serves: 6
Prep Time: 5 Minutes
Oven Temp: Broiler
Baking Time: 6 Minutes

¼ cup vegetable oil
3 tablespoons lemon juice
1 teaspoon crushed basil leaves
½ teaspoon salt
¼ teaspoon crushed rosemary
   leaves

¼ teaspoon garlic powder
⅛ teaspoon ground red pepper
⅛ teaspoon grated lemon peel
2 pounds bay scallops

In a medium bowl combine oil, lemon juice, seasonings and lemon peel. Add scallops; toss to coat evenly. Cover and refrigerate for 1 hour. Strain scallops, reserving marinade. Preheat broiler to hot. Place scallops on foil-lined broiler pan. Broil 2 inches from heat source until scallops are cooked just through, about 6 minutes, turning and brushing with reserved marinade twice.

Leonard Tose, Philadelphia Eagles - Philadelphia, Pa.

BAKED MONKFISH WITH BUERRE BLANC SAUCE

Moderate
Partial Make Ahead

Serves: 2
Prep Time: 40 Minutes
Oven Temp: 325°
Baking Time: 10 to 20 Minutes

Fish:
1 pound monkfish, cut into 1
   inch slices
Mayonnaise

Breadcrumbs

Sauce:
1 ounce minced shallots
½ tablespoon crushed dried
   whole peppercorns
2 ounces white wine

½ ounce white vinegar
4 ounces heavy cream
½ cup unsalted butter or
   margarine

Fish: Place monkfish slices in buttered oven-proof pan. Coat top with mayonnaise. Sprinkle with breadcrumbs. Bake at 325° for 10 to 20 minutes until fish is tender and breadcrumbs are brown.

Sauce: Reduce to near dry the shallots, peppercorns, wine and vinegar. (If shallots are too dry, they will darken and discolor sauce.) Add heavy cream, reduce by at least half. Cut softened butter into 8 pieces; gently whisk into shallot mixture. Strain through chinoise (china cap). Pour over baked fish. Will hold in bain marie for several hours.

D. Alan Armstrong, Tiffany Dining Saloon - Centre Square, Pa.

SHRIMP ROCKEFELLER

Moderate
Make Ahead

Serves: 8
Prep Time: 25 Minutes
Oven Temp: 400°
Baking Time: 15 Minutes

2 (10 ounce) packages frozen
  chopped spinach
¼ cup water
½ cup grated onion
¾ teaspoon salt
3 slices white bread, crusts
  removed and cubed
½ cup butter or margarine
1½ teaspoons Worcestershire
  sauce

¼ teaspoon hot pepper sauce
1 teaspoon celery salt
½ teaspoon garlic powder
2 (10 ounce) packages frozen
  cooked shrimp, thawed
8 scallop shells (puff pastry)
½ cup dry breadcrumbs
2 tablespoons melted butter or
  margarine
¼ cup grated Parmesan cheese

Cook spinach with water, onion and salt just until spinach separates. To undrained spinach add bread, butter, Worcestershire, hot pepper sauce, celery salt, and garlic powder. Simmer 10 minutes. Reserve 8 shrimp for garnish. Divide remaining shrimp among 8 puff pastry shells; cover with spinach mixture. Moisten breadcrumbs with butter; sprinkle over spinach. Top with 8 shrimp and Parmesan cheese. Bake at 400° for 15 minutes or until lightly browned. Great for first course or appetizer!

Robbyn O'Neill - Oreland, Pa.

SEAFOOD

SEAFOOD CASSEROLE

Easy
Make Ahead

Serves: 10 to 12
Prep Time: 30 Minutes
Oven Temp: 325°
Baking Time: 45 Minutes

1 pound scallops
1 pint oysters
1 pound fresh mushrooms
2 (10¾ ounce) cans cream of
   mushroom soup
¼ cup sherry

Dash of salt, pepper and paprika
3 pounds fresh cooked shrimp
Breadcrumbs
2 tablespoons butter or
   margarine
Cooked rice

Cover scallops with cold water, bring to a boil, drain and cut in half. Boil oysters in own liquid 2 or 3 minutes, drain, reserving liquid. Cut mushrooms into thirds, sauté 5 minutes in butter. Mix ¾ cup oyster liquid into mushroom soup. Add sherry, salt, pepper and paprika to taste. Combine seafood, including shrimp, and mushrooms and pour into a large, buttered baking dish. Pour soup over all, top with breadcrumbs, and dot with additional butter. Bake at 325° for 45 minutes. Serve over steamed rice.

Mildred L. Hager - Jenkintown, Pa.

FILET OF SALMON NOILLY

Moderate

Serves: 4
Prep Time: 30 to 35 Minutes
Oven Temp: 400°
Baking Time: 20 Minutes

6 medium shallots
4 (¾ pound each) pieces of filet
   of salmon
Salt and pepper
Bouquet garni (bay leaf, parsley
   sprig, thyme and celery stalk
   tied in cheesecloth)
2 cups dry white wine
1 cup heavy cream, divided

½ cup Noilly Prat vermouth
½ cup water
2 tablespoons lemon juice
4 big white mushrooms
3 ounces salmon caviar
8 small potatoes, boiled with
   pinch of salt
4 fleurons
Parsley for garnish

Grease a flat rectangular pan with butter and put shallots on bottom. Arrange pieces of salmon on top, season with salt and pepper and bouquet garni. Add white wine and half of cream and bake 20 minutes at 400°. When it is cooked, take salmon out of pan and keep in a warm place. Pour cooking juice into a saucepan; bring to a boil. Add remaining cream and reduce to half, about 5 minutes. Add Noilly and boil for 2 minutes longer; mix well. In a small saucepan bring water with pinch of salt and lemon juice to a boil. Score mushroom caps with knife, place in boiling water for 5 minutes, remove from heat and keep warm. On platter place 4 pieces of salmon in the middle, cover with sauce. On each piece of salmon put 1 teaspoon salmon caviar and 1 mushroom. Arrange potatoes and fleurons around the edge of platter and garnish with parsley.

Inn at Phillips Mill - New Hope, Pa.

FRUITS DE MER AUX PETITS LÉGUMES

Moderate

Serves: 6

24 ounces bay scallops
24 ounces shrimp
2 ribs celery
2 carrots
1 bunch scallions
6 ounces snow peas or green
  beans
10 tablespoons butter or
  margarine, divided

2 chopped shallots
3 tablespoons fresh fines
  herbes
3 leeks (white part only)
Salt and pepper
1½ cups dry vermouth
Dash of lemon juice

Clean bay scallops, clean and devein the shrimp leaving tails on. Cut celery, carrots and scallions in julienne strips. Clean snow peas and cut off ends. If beans are used, julienne. Cook vegetables separately in boiling water. Cook carrots for 2 minutes; celery and beans (if used) for 1 minute; snow peas for 15 seconds. Remove from heat immediately and run under cold water to stop the cooking and maintain color. Heat 4 tablespoons butter in sauté pan. Add shallots and sauté 1 minute. Add shrimp then bay scallops. When shrimp turn slightly pink, after 2 or 3 minutes, add fines herbes. Add remaining vegetables, salt, pepper and wine. Add remaining butter in small dots; bring to a boil. Remove vegetables and shellfish. Set aside and keep warm. Reduce the sauce by half; add a dash of lemon juice. Check seasoning. Pour sauce over vegetables and shellfish and serve.

Alouette - Center City - Philadelphia, Pa.

SAUTÉED SCALLOPS WITH TARRAGON AND SUN-DRIED TOMATOES

Easy

Serves: 4
Prep Time: 5 Minutes
Cooking Time: 15 to 20 Minutes

1 clove garlic, mashed
6 tablespoons unsalted butter or
  margarine
1½ pounds scallops
Salt and pepper
¾ cup dry white wine

2 tablespoons fresh tarragon or
  1 tablespoon dried
2 teaspoons lemon juice
3 tablespoons sun-dried
  tomatoes in olive oil (about 3
  tomatoes), finely chopped

Sauté the garlic in the butter over medium-high heat for 1 to 2 minutes. Remove the garlic and add the scallops and a little salt and pepper. Cook the scallops until they turn white; remove from pan with slotted spoon and reserve; keep warm. Add the wine, tarragon and lemon juice to the pan and simmer with the scallop juice for a few minutes. Add any scallop juice, that has drained in the bowl that contains the scallops, to the sauté pan. Add the sun-dried tomatoes to the pan and simmer until reduced. Return the scallops to the pan and cook just enough to heat; do not overcook! Correct seasonings; serve immediately. *Great served on a bed of fresh linguini.*

John D. Ingersoll, The Chestnut Hill Cheese Shop - Chestnut Hill, Pa.

BAR ROOM SHRIMP

Easy
Make Ahead

Serves: 10
Prep Time: 10 Minutes
Cooking Time: 5 to 10 Minutes

5 pounds shrimp, unpeeled
3 tablespoons salt
1 tablespoon red pepper

1 tablespoon pepper
1 tablespoon whole allspice
2 quarts beer

Place shrimp in a large stock pot and add remaining ingredients with enough water to cover shrimp. Rapidly bring shrimp to a boil. When the shrimp become pink and curl, test for doneness (they should be firm but tender). Cooking time depends on size of shrimp. Remove shrimp to a colander to drain and strain cooking liquid through cheesecloth into a large container. Add the shrimp and refrigerate. Serve well chilled.

Jeanne Radocaj - Bridesburg, Pa.

JOANNE'S CIOPPINO

Moderate

Serves: 6
Prep Time: 20 to 25 Minutes
Cooking Time: 15 Minutes

¼ cup vegetable or olive oil
2 cloves garlic, minced
2 medium onions, chopped
2 green peppers, seeded and
  chopped
1 (32 ounce) jar Newman's Own
  Marinara Sauce

1 cup dry white wine
1½ pounds cod, sliced and cut
  into pieces
8 ounces frozen lobster tails,
  shelled and cut up
1 pound mussels and/or small
  clams

Heat oil in a deep, heavy skillet or Dutch oven; add garlic, onions and green peppers. Cook until golden. Add marinara sauce, wine, fish and lobster; simmer 6 minutes. Add mussels and/or clams. Cover and cook 5 minutes more, until fish is done and shellfish open. Serve with crusty Italian bread and salad of romaine lettuce.

Joanne Woodward - Westport, Ct.

SEAFOOD TUREEN

Easy

Yield: 8 Cups
Prep Time: 20 Minutes
Cooking Time: 20 to 30 Minutes

¼ cup butter or margarine
1 (16 ounce) package frozen
  flounder fillets, thawed
1½ cups dry white wine
1 (12 ounce) package frozen
  shelled cooked shrimp,
  thawed
1 cup cooked lobster meat,
  canned or frozen

1 (6 ounce) can sliced broiled
  mushrooms
1½ cups evaporated milk,
  undiluted
1 (10¾ ounce) can cream of
  mushroom soup, undiluted
½ cup sherry
Salt and pepper to taste

Melt butter in a large saucepan, add flounder fillets and wine. Cover and simmer 10 minutes. Add remaining ingredients except sherry and seasonings. Simmer another 5 minutes. Add sherry and seasonings to taste. Serve in large tureen with buttered toast. *Lobster and flounder should be in chunks or flakes; shrimp should remain whole.*

Julie M. Camburn - East Falls, Pa.

SEAFOOD

FLOUNDER EL CAPITAN

Moderate

Serves: 3 to 4
Prep Time: 15 Minutes
Oven Temp: 350°
Baking Time: 30 Minutes

1 pound flounder fillets
½ lemon
Paprika
2 tablespoons butter or
  margarine
2 tablespoons flour

Dash of salt and pepper
¾ cup milk
¼ cup dry white wine
1 cup shredded extra sharp
  cheese

Wash and pat dry fillets. Place in greased shallow baking pan making sure not to overlap. Squeeze lemon juice over fillets and sprinkle with paprika. Melt butter in medium saucepan. Add flour, salt and pepper. Stir until mixed. Add milk and white wine. Bring to a boil, stirring constantly. Remove from heat and add shredded cheese. Pour over fillets and bake at 350° about 30 minutes. Place under broiler for 1 minute to lightly brown on top. Serve immediately.

Kit Kelly - Roxborough, Pa.

GRAVLAKS SÅS

Easy
Make Ahead

Yield: About ½ Cup
Prep Time: 10 Minutes

1 tablespoon Swedish or sweet
  German mustard
1 teaspoon dark French mustard
1 tablespoon sugar

2 tablespoons white vinegar
¼ cup olive oil
Small bunch fresh dill, finely
  chopped or about ⅓ cup

In blender or food processor, mix mustard, sugar and vinegar. Gradually add the oil through the feed tube. Add dill to taste. *This sauce is tasty with fish, shrimp, lobster and crab.*

Lisa Lindbom Fetterman - Wyndmoor, Pa.

SHRIMP SCAMPI

Easy
Make Ahead

Serves: 6
Prep Time: 15 to 30 Minutes
Oven Temp: 350°
Baking Time: 20 Minutes

**1 cup butter or margarine,
  melted**
1 teaspoon Dijon mustard
**1 teaspoon Worcestershire
  sauce**
3 cloves garlic, pressed
½ teaspoon chili powder
1 lemon, sliced

Chopped parsley
Salt
Pepper
Paprika
2 tablespoons white wine
**2 pounds large cooked shrimp,
  peeled with tails intact**

Combine first 11 ingredients to make sauce. Place shrimp in 15x10x1 inch jelly-roll pan. Pour sauce over shrimp and let stand at least 24 hours in refrigerator. Bake at 350° for 20 minutes. Broil 1 or 2 minutes; serve hot.

Susan Miller - Philadelphia, Pa.

BAKED SHRIMP PICCATA

Easy

Serves: 6 to 8
Prep Time: 10 Minutes
Oven Temp: 450°
Baking Time: 10 to 15 Minutes

**1 cup melted butter or
  margarine**
¼ cup dry white wine
¼ cup minced parsley
2 tablespoons fresh lemon juice
3 large garlic cloves, minced
2 teaspoons basil

**1 teaspoon Worcestershire
  sauce**
1 teaspoon hot pepper sauce
**2 pounds large shrimp, shelled
  and deveined, tails left intact**
**½ cup dry unseasoned
  breadcrumbs**

Combine first 8 ingredients in shallow 2 quart baking dish and mix well. Remove ¼ cup of this mixture and set aside. Add shrimp to baking dish and mix thoroughly. Combine breadcrumbs with reserved butter sauce and sprinkle over shrimp. Bake at 450° for 10 to 15 minutes; serve immediately.

MaryAnn Veneziale - East Falls, Pa.

SOMERTON

Somerton, known as Smithfield until 1850, has been part of Philadelphia for more than 125 years. Somerton can trace its history to the early 18th century when stagecoaches from Philadelphia changed horses at the Smithfield Inn, which is still "alive" but not so "well" on Bustleton Avenue.

Long gone are the log cabins that the local people called home for many years. Progress promoted sites such as the Somerton Springs Country Club. Stay-at-home vacationers and many city dwellers enjoyed a cool dip on a hot summer's afternoon.

Until the progress of several decades ago, Somerton was rural and remote and was dotted with cornfields and cow pastures. In the 1960's, planned developments of rowhouses, apartment buildings, shopping centers and industrial parks came to Somerton.

Somerton is still a residential section that offers a feeling of rustic living with the convenience of the city.

Cakes

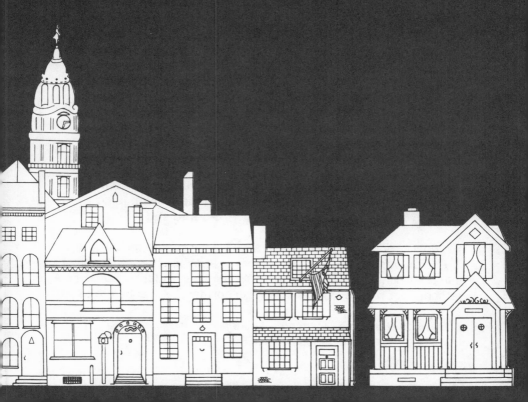

CAKES

FAVORITE APPLE CAKE

Easy
Make Ahead

Serves: 12
Prep Time: 40 Minutes
Oven Temp: 350°
Baking Time: 1 Hour, 15 Minutes

1½ cups oil
2 cups sugar
3 eggs
3 cups flour
1 teaspoon salt
1 teaspoon baking soda

1 teaspoon cinnamon
1 teaspoon vanilla extract
3 cups peeled, thick Delicious
  apple slices
1 cup chopped walnuts
1 cup raisins (optional)

Beat the oil and sugar together in large mixer bowl while assembling the remaining ingredients. Add the eggs and beat until the mixture is creamy. Sift together the flour, salt, baking soda and cinnamon. Stir into the batter. Add all remaining ingredients and stir to blend. Turn the mixture into a buttered and floured 10 inch tube pan. Bake at 350° for 1¼ hours or until done. Cool in pan before removing. Serve at room temperature with ice cream if desired.

Ginny Thornburgh - Governor's Mansion - Harrisburg, Pa.
Joyce Foster - Lafayette Hills, Pa.

DR. BIRD CAKE

Easy

Prep Time: 25 Minutes
Oven Temp: 350°
Baking Time: 1 Hour, 20 Minutes

3 cups sifted all-purpose flour
1 teaspoon baking soda
1 teaspoon salt
1 teaspoon cinnamon
2 cups sugar
3 eggs

1 cup vegetable oil
1½ teaspoons vanilla extract
2 cups diced bananas
1 (8 ounce) can crushed
  pineapple with juice
Powdered sugar

Sift dry ingredients in bowl; make a well in the center and break eggs into it. Add oil, vanilla, and fruit. Stir, do not beat. When blended together, pour into a 10 inch tube pan. Bake at 350° for 1 hour and 20 minutes; cool and refrigerate. Sprinkle top and sides with powdered sugar before serving.

J. Dawson Ransome - Ransome Airlines
Mary Lou Alexander - Chestnut Hill, Pa.

JEWISH APPLE CAKE

Easy
Make Ahead

Serves: 12 to 16
Prep Time: 20 to 30 Minutes
Oven Temp: 350°
Baking Time: 1 Hour, 15 Minutes

**5 apples, peeled, cored and
  sliced
5 tablespoons plus 2 cups sugar,
  divided
2 teaspoons cinnamon
1 cup oil**

**4 eggs
¼ cup orange juice
2½ teaspoons vanilla extract
3 cups all-purpose flour
1 tablespoon baking powder
1 teaspoon nutmeg**

Prepare apples; let stand in mixture of 5 tablespoons sugar and cinnamon for 10 minutes. Combine oil, remaining sugar and eggs; add orange juice and vanilla. Slowly add dry ingredients and beat slowly (do not overbeat). Pour half of batter into a greased 12 cup tube pan. Spread with half of apple mixture. Add remaining batter then remaining apple mixture. Bake at 350° for 1¼ hours.

Howard Eskin - KYW-Channel 3 Sports - Philadelphia, Pa.

1-2-3-4 CAKE

Moderate
Make Ahead

Prep Time: 30 Minutes
Oven Temp: 350°
Baking Time: 1 Hour

**1 cup butter or margarine
2 cups sugar, divided
4 eggs, separated
1 tablespoon lemon or orange
  juice**

**1 teaspoon vanilla extract
3 cups sifted all-purpose flour
1 tablespoon baking powder
¼ teaspoon salt
1 cup milk**

In a large bowl cream butter until light. Gradually beat in 1 cup sugar. In a separate bowl, beat egg yolks until thick and light. Then beat the other cup sugar into them. Beat the juice into the egg yolks and add to the butter mixture, beating in a big tablespoon at a time. Mix in vanilla then add sifted dry ingredients alternately with milk. Beat egg whites until stiff and fold into batter. Pour batter into a tube pan that has been buttered and floured filling no more than ¾ full. Bake at 350° for 1 hour. Let cake cool on a rack before removing from pan. *A cake made from scratch and worth it!*

Barbara M. O'Neill - Norristown, Pa.

CAKES

CHOCOLATE MOUSSE CAKE

Moderate
Make Ahead

Serves: 8 to 10
Prep Time: 40 Minutes

2 (4 ounce) packages
  ladyfingers
½ cup orange juice
1 pound cream cheese, softened
¾ cup sugar
½ teaspoon salt

2 teaspoons vanilla extract
3 eggs, separated
3 (4 ounce) packages German
  chocolate, melted
2 cups heavy cream, whipped

Arrange ladyfingers, round side down, on a baking sheet. Sprinkle with orange juice then arrange along the sides and bottom of a 9 inch springform pan. Combine cream cheese, sugar, salt and vanilla. Beat until well blended and smooth. Add egg yolks and beat. Blend in cooled chocolate. In another bowl beat egg whites until stiff and fold in whipped cream. Fold cream cheese and egg white mixtures together. Pour into pan and chill until firm.

Loretta Burton - Plymouth Meeting, Pa.

SPECIAL CHOCOLATE CAKE

Easy
Make Ahead
Freeze

Prep Time: 20 Minutes
Oven Temp: 350°
Baking Time: 40 Minutes

Cake:
2 cups all-purpose flour
2 cups sugar
¾ cup cocoa
2 teaspoons baking soda
1 teaspoon salt
1 teaspoon baking powder

2 eggs
½ cup vegetable oil
1 cup milk
1 teaspoon vanilla extract
1 cup cold coffee (may use
  instant)

Frosting:
¼ cup all-purpose flour
1 cup milk
1 cup powdered sugar

1 cup butter or margarine
1 teaspoon vanilla extract

216

Cake: Sift together flour, sugar, cocoa, baking soda, salt and baking powder. In a small bowl blend together eggs, oil, milk and vanilla; combine with dry ingredients. Mix thoroughly and then stir in coffee. Batter will be very thin but it bakes into a rich, dark, moist cake. Bake in 9x13 inch pan at 350° (325° if using glass pan) about 40 minutes.

Frosting: Combine flour and milk, adding milk slowly and beating until smooth. Cook over moderate heat and stir constantly until thickened. Set aside to chill. Combine powdered sugar and butter beating until light and fluffy; stir in chilled flour-milk mixture. Beat at high speed until thick and creamy. Add vanilla and beat until thoroughly mixed. Spread on cooled cake. *This is an easy, very moist cake.*

Maria Jones - Roxborough, Pa.
Terri Lambert - Roxborough, Pa.

HOT FUDGE SUNDAE CAKE

Easy
Make Ahead

Serves: 9
Prep Time: 15 Minutes
Oven Temp: 350°
Baking Time: 40 Minutes

1 cup all-purpose flour
¾ cup sugar
2 teaspoons baking powder
¼ teaspoon salt
2 tablespoons plus ¼ cup
   unsweetened cocoa, divided
½ cup milk

2 tablespoons vegetable oil
1 teaspoon vanilla extract
1 cup chopped nuts
1 cup firmly packed brown sugar
1¾ cups hot water
Ice cream

In ungreased 9 inch square pan stir together flour, sugar, baking powder, salt and 2 tablespoons cocoa. Mix in milk, oil and vanilla with fork until smooth. Stir in nuts. Spread evenly in pan. Sprinkle with brown sugar and remaining ¼ cup cocoa. Pour hot water over batter. Bake at 350° for 40 minutes. Let stand 15 minutes. Spoon into dessert dishes or cut into squares. Invert each square; top with ice cream and spoon sauce over each serving. Also good cold.

Jo Anderson - Mt. Airy, Pa.

CAKES

CHOCOLATE CHIP CAKE

Easy

Serves: 8
Prep Time: 20 Minutes
Oven Temp: 350°
Baking Time: 50 to 55 Minutes

1 cup butter or margarine
2 cups sugar
4 eggs, separated
2 teaspoons vanilla extract
2⅔ cups all-purpose flour

2 teaspoons baking powder
1 cup milk
½ cup whole chocolate morsels
¼ cup powdered sugar

Cream butter, sugar and egg yolks; add vanilla. Alternate flour, baking powder and milk, adding to butter mixture. Beat egg whites; fold in chocolate morsels and beaten egg whites into mixture. Bake in a greased tube pan at 350° for 50 to 55 minutes. Grate extra chocolate and sprinkle on top with powdered sugar. *This is a nice cake for company.*

Elaine DePaul - Berwyn, Pa.

BLUE RIBBON FUDGE CAKE

Moderate
Make Ahead

Serves: 8 to 10
Prep Time: 20 Minutes
Oven Temp: 350°
Baking Time: 25 to 30 Minutes

2 cups sugar
3 large eggs
1¼ cups oil
4 teaspoons vanilla extract
1⅓ cups boiling water

1 cup unsweetened cocoa
1⅓ teaspoons baking soda
1⅓ teaspoons baking powder
½ teaspoon salt
1⅓ cups unsifted all-purpose flour

Peanut Butter Frosting:
1 pound sifted powdered sugar
½ cup creamy peanut butter

¼ to ⅓ cup milk

In large mixing bowl beat sugar and eggs until creamy. Blend in oil and vanilla and beat 2 minutes. Combine boiling water and cocoa; add to egg mixture and blend thoroughly. Stir in soda, baking powder and salt. Add flour and beat until mixture is thoroughly blended and smooth. Pour into 2 generously greased 9 inch round cake pans. Bake at 350° for 25 to 30 minutes. Remove from oven and let stand 5 minutes in pans, then turn *directly* onto racks. Let cakes cool completely before frosting.

Frosting: Combine sugar, peanut butter and ¼ cup milk in mixing bowl. Beat until smooth and creamy adding more milk if necessary. *A moist, rich cake from Pa. Dutch country.*

Lynda Usuka - Norristown, Pa.

ORANGE-WALNUT CAKE

Easy
Make Ahead

Serves: 8
Prep Time: 20 Minutes
Oven Temp: 325°
Baking Time: 1 Hour, 15 Minutes

1 cup self-rising flour
½ teaspoon salt
¾ cup butter or margarine
¾ cup sugar
3 large eggs
Rind of 1 orange

2 tablespoons chopped mixed
** fruit peel**
¼ cup chopped walnuts
1 tablespoon concentrated
** orange juice**

Frosting:
1 cup powdered sugar
2 to 3 tablespoons concentrated
** orange juice**

Sift flour and salt together. Cream the butter, sugar and beaten eggs. Add half the flour and other ingredients and blend. Add remaining flour. Spoon mixture into a greased cake pan and bake at 325° for 1¼ hours.

Frosting: In a saucepan heat powdered sugar and orange juice until blended. Frost the cake while frosting is still warm.

Margaret Thatcher, Prime Minister - Great Britain

CAKES

CHOCOLATE BABKA

Moderate
Make Ahead

Yield: 2 Babkas
Prep Time: 40 Minutes
Oven Temp: 350°
Baking Time: 1 Hour

4 eggs, separated
1½ cups sugar
½ cup sweet butter or margarine
2 cups all-purpose flour

1 cup milk
1 teaspoon vanilla extract
2 teaspoons baking powder
3 tablespoons bittersweet cocoa

In a mixing bowl, place egg yolks and beat. Add sugar and beat until foamy. Gradually add butter and continue beating. Add flour and milk gradually and continue beating. Mix in vanilla and baking powder until smooth and no lumps appear. Separate dough into 2 equal parts. Put 1 part in a bowl; add cocoa to other part and mix until well blended. Beat egg whites until stiff peaks form. Separate and gently fold half into white dough and half into the dark dough. Spoon a little of the white dough into bottom of two 9x5x2 inch loaf pans that have been buttered and dusted with flour. Spoon a little of the dark dough on top and alternate until you run out of dough. Bake at 350° for 1 hour. Test for doneness; let rest for 5 to 10 minutes before removing from pans. Turn over on rack and let cool completely.

Marta Jarymovych - Cheltenham, Pa.

DAD'S CHOCOLATE SOUR CREAM CAKE

Easy
Make Ahead

Serves: 10
Prep Time: 20 to 30 Minutes
Oven Temp: 350°
Baking Time: 40 Minutes

2 cups all-purpose flour
2 cups sugar
1 cup water
¾ cup sour cream
¼ cup shortening
1¼ teaspoons baking soda

1 teaspoon salt
1 teaspoon vanilla extract
½ teaspoon baking powder
2 eggs
4 ounces melted unsweetened
  chocolate, cooled

Mix above ingredients in a large bowl. Pour into greased and floured tube pan or 8 inch layer pans. Bake at 350° for 40 minutes.

Pam Richardson - Lafayette Hill, Pa.

BANANA SPLIT CAKE

Moderate
Make Ahead

Prep Time: 45 Minutes

1½ cups butter or margarine, divided
2 cups graham cracker crumbs
2 eggs
2 cups powdered sugar
2 (20 ounce) cans crushed pineapple, well-drained

4 medium bananas
1 (12 ounce) container frozen non-dairy whipped topping
Crushed walnuts
Maraschino cherries, cut in half
1 frozen milk chocolate candy bar, grated

Melt ½ cup butter in pan and mix with crumbs. Press into bottom of a 9x13x2 inch glass dish. Combine eggs, remaining butter and powdered sugar; beat 12 to 15 minutes. Spread over crumbs. Spread squeezed pineapple over mixture about ⅛ inch thick. Cover with sliced bananas then whipped topping. Sprinkle walnuts, halved cherries and grated chocolate over top. Refrigerate 2 hours before serving.

Joan Vitello - Somerton, Pa.
Doris Brown - Wadsworth, Pa.
Msgr. Thomas M. Jordan

POUND CAKE

Easy
Make Ahead

Serves: 12
Prep Time: 15 Minutes
Oven Temp: 350°, 325°
Baking Time: 1 Hour, 15 Minutes

3 cups sifted cake flour
2¾ cups sugar
1½ cups solid shortening
2 teaspoons baking powder

6 eggs
2 teaspoons vanilla extract
1 cup milk

Put all ingredients into large mixer bowl. Beat for 5½ minutes. Pour into greased and floured 10 inch tube pan and bake at 350° for 1 hour. Reduce heat to 325° and bake 15 minutes longer. Cool in pan for 10 minutes then turn out to cool completely. *Good served plain, frosted or sprinkled with powdered sugar.*

Marie Panebianco - North Hills, Pa.

CAKES

CHEESE CAKE

Easy
Make Ahead

Serves: 16 to 20
Prep Time: 20 Minutes
Oven Temp: 350°
Baking Time: 1 Hour

5 (8 ounce) packages cream
  cheese, softened
6 eggs
1½ cups sugar

6 tablespoons flour
2 cups sour cream
2 tablespoons vanilla extract

In large bowl mix all ingredients until smooth about 5 to 10 minutes. Pour into greased springform pan; refrigerate 2 hours. Bake at 350° for 1 hour. Turn off heat and leave in oven with door open for about 2 hours to prevent cracking. Refrigerate overnight. Top with favorite topping or enjoy as is.

Edith Koschineg - Lafayette Hill, Pa.
Bea Schiavo - Lafayette Hill, Pa.

PINEAPPLE CHEESE CAKE TOPPING

Easy
Make Ahead

Prep Time: 10 Minutes
Oven Temp: 350°
Baking Time: 15 Minutes

2 cups sour cream
6 tablespoons sugar
2 tablespoons vanilla extract

1 (15½ ounce) can crushed
  pineapple, drained
Cinnamon

Mix all ingredients together, spread on cooled cheese cake, sprinkle with cinnamon. Bake at 350° for 15 minutes. Chill thoroughly before serving.

Theresa Imms - Jenkintown, Pa.

BRANDY CHEESE CAKE

Easy
Make Ahead

Serves: 20 to 24
Prep Time: 15 Minutes
Oven Temp: 225°
Baking Time: 9 to 12 Hours

3 pounds cream cheese
7 eggs
1¾ cups sugar
¼ cup vanilla extract
¼ cup brandy

1 tablespoon butter or
  margarine
¼ to ½ cup graham cracker
  crumbs

Mix together first 5 ingredients until smooth. Pour into 10 cup or larger soufflé dish which has been buttered and dusted with graham cracker crumbs. Set in pan of water. Bake at 225° overnight or 9 to 12 hours. *The beauty of this recipe is the convenience of baking while sleeping.*

Andrew Schloss, Director of Culinary Arts, The Restaurant School and freelance writer

HOLIDAY CRANBERRY CAKE

Easy

Prep Time: 25 Minutes
Oven Temp: 350°
Baking Time: 45 Minutes

1 (16 ounce) package fresh
  cranberries
3 cups sugar, divided
1 cup chopped walnuts
2 cups all-purpose flour

4 eggs
4 teaspoons almond extract
1½ cups melted butter
Vanilla ice cream or whipped
  cream (optional)

Mix together the cranberries, 1 cup sugar and chopped walnuts. Layer on the bottom of a well-greased 9x13 inch pan. Combine flour, remaining sugar, eggs, almond extract and melted butter. Pour over the cranberry-nut mixture. Bake at 350° for 45 minutes. Top with vanilla ice cream or whipped cream.

Rosaria Hosmer - Roxborough, Pa.

CAKES

RHUBARB CAKE

Easy
Make Ahead

Serves: 12 to 14
Prep Time: 25 Minutes
Oven Temp: 350°
Baking Time: 40 Minutes

½ cup butter or margarine
1½ cups firmly packed brown
  sugar
2 eggs
2 teaspoons vanilla extract
1 teaspoon baking soda

1 cup sour cream
2 cups sifted all-purpose flour
1½ cups fresh thinly diced
  rhubarb
½ cup chopped nuts

Topping:
½ cup sugar
1 teaspoon cinnamon
½ teaspoon nutmeg

2 tablespoons butter or
  margarine

Cream butter and brown sugar. Blend in eggs and vanilla. Dissolve soda in sour cream; stir in alternately with flour, nuts and rhubarb. Pour into a greased and floured 9x13 inch pan; sprinkle with topping. Bake at 350° for 40 minutes.

Topping: Combine sugar, spices and butter; mix into crumbs. Sprinkle over batter.

Margaret Himes - Huntingdon Valley, Pa.

BLUEBERRY COFFEE CAKE

Moderate
Make Ahead: Topping

Serves: 16
Prep Time: 35 Minutes
Oven Temp: 325°
Baking Time: 45 Minutes

Coffee Cake:
1 cup butter or margarine
1 cup sugar
1¾ cups all-purpose flour
2 teaspoons baking powder

¼ teaspoon salt
2 teaspoons grated lemon peel
4 eggs
2 cups blueberries

Topping: (Prepare two hours in advance.)
½ cup butter or margarine
1 cup all-purpose flour

½ cup chopped pecans
¼ cup sugar

Coffee Cake: In large bowl beat butter and sugar at medium speed until light and fluffy. Reduce to low speed, add flour, baking powder, salt, lemon peel and eggs; beat until just blended. Increase to medium speed and beat until smooth. Spread batter evenly in greased and floured 9x13 inch glass dish; top with blueberries. Pinch topping into small pieces, sprinkle on cake. Bake at 325° for 45 minutes until golden. Serve warm or cool.

Topping: Melt butter in small saucepan. Stir in flour, nuts and sugar. Let topping stand for 2 hours before making cake.

Lois Wilson - Chestnut Hill, Pa.

CRANBERRY SWIRL NUT CAKE

Moderate
Make Ahead

Serves: 12
Prep Time: 20 Minutes
Oven Temp: 350°
Baking Time: 55 Minutes

½ cup butter or margarine
1 cup sugar
2 eggs
2 cups sour cream
2 cups all-purpose flour
1 teaspoon baking soda

1 teaspoon baking powder
½ teaspoon salt
8 ounces whole-berry cranberry
  sauce
½ cup crushed walnuts or
  almonds

Glaze:
1 teaspoon almond extract
Water

Powdered sugar

Cream butter and sugar; add unbeaten eggs. Add sour cream and dry ingredients alternately ending with dry ingredients. In 10 inch tube or bundt pan put a layer of batter, cranberries and nuts and swirl through. Repeat procedure. Bake at 350° for 55 minutes; let cool 5 minutes before removing pan. Run glaze over top.

Glaze: Combine ingredients to make thin sauce to drizzle over cake.

Donna J. Bartynski - Maple Glen, Pa.

CAKES

PENNSYLVANIA DUTCH FUNNEL CAKES

Easy

Yield: 2 Dozen Cakes
Prep Time: 30 Minutes

⅔ cup milk
1 egg, beaten
1¼ cups all-purpose flour
2 tablespoons sugar

1 teaspoon baking powder
¼ teaspoon salt
Fat for frying

Beat milk with egg. Blend dry ingredients and gradually add the milk mixture, beating constantly until batter is smooth. Holding finger over the bottom of a ⅜ or ½ inch funnel, fill with batter. Holding funnel as near surface of fat as possible, remove finger and drop batter into deep fat heated to 375° using a circular movement from center outward to form a spiral cake about 3 inches in diameter. Immediately replace finger on bottom of funnel and form other cakes. Fry cakes until they are puffy and golden brown, turning them once. Remove from fat with a slotted spoon to absorbent paper to drain. Sift powdered sugar lightly over cakes or drizzle with molasses and serve at once.

Jill Nichols - Wadsworth, Pa.

RUM CAKE

Easy
Make Ahead

Serves: 12
Prep Time: 20 Minutes
Oven Temp: 325°
Baking Time: 1 Hour

Cake:
1 cup chopped pecans
1 (18½ ounce) package yellow
    cake mix
4 eggs
½ cup cold water

½ cup vegetable oil
½ cup dark rum
1 (3¾ ounce) package vanilla
    flavor instant pudding mix

Glaze:
½ cup butter or margarine
¼ cup water

1 cup sugar
½ cup dark rum

Cake: Sprinkle pecans over bottom of greased and floured 10 inch tube pan. Mix all cake ingredients together. Pour batter over pecans. Bake at 325° for 1 hour. Top with glaze while cake is hot and still in pan. Let cool in pan for 1 hour.

Glaze: Melt butter in saucepan. Stir in water, sugar and rum. Boil 3 to 4 minutes. *If desired decorate with whole maraschino cherries and whipped cream or serve with seedless grapes dusted with powdered sugar.*

Jeanne Dolaway - Blue Bell, Pa.

STRAWBERRY SHORTCAKE
(Chiffon Cake)

Moderate

Prep Time: 45 Minutes
Oven Temp: 350°
Baking Time: 1 Hour

Chiffon Cake:
2 cups all-purpose flour
1½ cups sugar
2 teaspoons baking powder
1 teaspoon salt
¾ cup vegetable oil

7 eggs, separated
¾ cup water
2 teaspoons vanilla extract
2 teaspoons lemon juice
½ teaspoon cream of tartar

Strawberry Short Cake:
4 cups heavy cream, whipped   **1 quart strawberries**

Chiffon Cake: Sift together flour, sugar, baking powder and salt into large bowl. Make a well in center and place oil, egg yolks, water, vanilla and lemon juice in it. Mix all together with wooden spoon. Beat egg whites with cream of tartar until stiff in separate bowl. Fold batter into egg whites. Pour into ungreased tube pan. Bake at 350° for 1 hour.

Strawberry Short Cake: Cut cake into 3 layers. Spread with whipped cream and sliced strawberries; garnish with whole berries on top, half berries around sides of cake.

Bonnie Piecyk - Blue Bell, Pa.

CAKES

AUNT LIDDY BELLE'S PARTY CAKE

Easy
Make Ahead
Freeze

Serves: 12
Prep Time: 30 Minutes
Oven Temp: 300°
Baking Time: 90 Minutes

1 cup butter or margarine,
   softened
2 cups sugar
6 eggs
12 ounces vanilla wafers,
   crumbled

⅓ cup milk
1 cup chopped walnuts
1 (7 ounce) package flaked
   coconut

Beat butter and sugar; slowly add eggs 2 at a time. Stir in other ingredients.
Bake in well-greased and floured 10 inch tube pan at 300° for 90 minutes.
Best to let this cake set for a day before serving.

Charlotte Rodgers, Country Craft Shoppe - Flourtown, Pa.

THE BEST EVER CARROT CAKE

Moderate
Make Ahead
Freeze

Serves: 12 to 15
Prep Time: 15 to 20 Minutes
Oven Temp: 350°
Baking Time: 70 to 80 Minutes

Cake:
2 cups all-purpose flour
¾ cup whole-wheat flour
1 tablespoon baking soda
1 teaspoon salt
1 tablespoon cinnamon
1 teaspoon nutmeg

4 large or 5 medium eggs
1¼ cups vegetable oil
2 teaspoons vanilla extract
2¼ cups sugar
4 cups grated carrots
¾ cup chopped nuts

Frosting:
1 cup butter or margarine,
   softened
1 (8 ounce) package cream
   cheese

½ to 1 pound powdered sugar,
   depending on taste
1 teaspoon vanilla extract

Cake: Mix dry ingredients together. In separate bowl, mix eggs, oil, vanilla and sugar. Combine the 2 mixtures; fold in grated carrots and nuts. Pour into greased and floured springform tube pan or any springform pan. Bake at 350° for 70 to 80 minutes until firm to touch. Cool before frosting.

Frosting: Combine all ingredients and spread on cooled cake.

Joan Forde - Chestnut Hill, Pa.

SPONGE ROLL CAKE

Moderate
Make Ahead

Serves: 8 to 10
Prep Time: 25 Minutes
Oven Temp: 375°
Baking Time: 12 Minutes

¾ **cup cake flour**
¼ **teaspoon salt**
1 teaspoon baking powder
4 eggs, separated

¾ **cup sugar, divided**
½ **teaspoon vanilla extract**
Powdered sugar
1 cup raspberry preserves

Sift flour with salt and baking powder; set aside. Beat egg yolks until light; add ¼ cup sugar and vanilla. In separate bowl beat egg whites until stiff. Gradually add remaining ½ cup sugar. Add beaten yolk mixture to egg whites; fold in dry ingredients. Spread batter in lightly greased, waxed paper-lined 15x10x1 inch jelly roll pan. Bake at 375° for 12 minutes. Meanwhile sift powdered sugar on a clean tea towel. Invert cake on sugar; gently peel off waxed paper. Starting with narrow end, roll up cake (towel and all); allow to cool 20 minutes. Gently unroll cake; remove towel. Spread with raspberry preserves, roll up again. Sift powdered sugar on top; slice on diagonal. *Variation: Spread cake with 2 cups whipped cream topped with 1 (10 ounce) package frozen strawberries, thawed. Roll up and sift powdered sugar over top; refrigerate before serving. A delicious, pretty, and quick summer treat.*

Annette Rafalowski - Mt. Airy, Pa.

STRAWBERRY MANSION

A modest streetcar community, Strawberry Mansion takes its name from the large federal house located in Fairmount Park, the nation's oldest municipal playground. This country mansion is the only single house in the area of otherwise red brick houses. Originally a summer home away from the hot city, the Mansion is furnished with many antiques that reflect the tastes of its various owners.

Mobility and homogeneity have always been the characteristics of this neighborhood from its incorporation into the city in the 1850's until the present. As different ethnic groups arrived and departed from its boundaries, a sense of continuity still remained. This continuity was emphasized by the character of the rising working class.

In the 19th century, Strawberry Mansion was a desirable address for the working middle class, and there were no factories or industries nearby to mar its desirability. The trolley car became emblematic with this neighborhood since it was the only mode of transportation, and the entire area depended on it to move them out into other parts of the city.

The first immigrants to Strawberry Mansion were the Germans who were stonecutters and masons for the headstones, crypts and obelisks of those entombed in the fashionable Laurel Hill Cemetery, the area's first and chief attraction.

In the 1930's, Strawberry Mansion had a strong Jewish population which provided a stability that was seldom found during the Depression. Just as the Jewish population had replaced the Germans, so too, the Black population has, since the 1950's, replaced the Jews. The Blacks continued to demonstrate a sense of civic responsibility and neighborhood pride which characterized Strawberry Mansion from the beginning.

Cookies, Cupcakes & Brownies

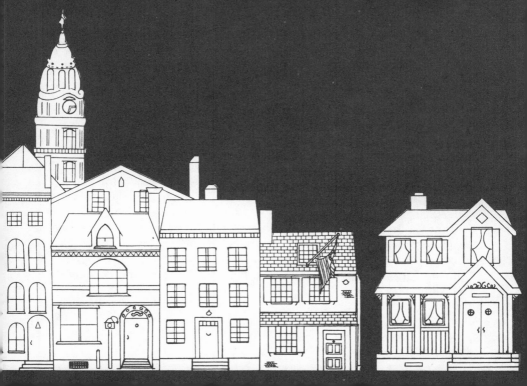

COOKIES, CUPCAKES & BROWNIES

AUSTRIAN CUT-OUT BUTTER COOKIES

Moderate

Yield: About 4 Dozen
Prep Time: 30 Minutes
Oven Temp: 350°
Baking Time: About 10 Minutes

2 eggs
1 cup sugar
1 cup butter or margarine,
  softened
1 teaspoon baking powder

1 teaspoon vanilla extract
¼ teaspoon salt
5 tablespoons milk
4 or 5 cups flour, enough to
  make a flexible ball

Mix all ingredients, roll out to ⅛ to ¼ inch thickness. Use cookie cutters then bake at 350° about 10 minutes or until slightly golden. Remove to cooling rack immediately.

Maria Aduso - Roxborough, Pa.

CREAM WAFERS

Easy

Yield: 5 Dozen
Prep Time: 30 Minutes
Oven Temp: 375°
Baking Time: 7 to 9 Minutes

1 cup butter or margarine,
  softened
2 cups all-purpose flour

⅓ cup heavy cream
Sugar

Filling:
¼ cup butter or margarine,
  softened

¾ cup powdered sugar
1 teaspoon vanilla extract

Mix butter, flour and cream thoroughly. Cover and chill. Roll about ⅓ of dough at a time on floured board to ⅛ inch thickness. Cut into 1½ inch circles. Coat each side with sugar. Place on ungreased baking sheet. Prick rounds with fork about 4 times. Bake at 375° for 7 to 9 minutes just until set but not brown. Remove carefully to wire racks. Cool then fill.

Filling: Cream butter, sugar and vanilla until smooth and creamy. Tint if desired.

Marie Caldwell - Roxborough, Pa.

COCONUT COOKIES

Yield: 4½ Dozen
Prep Time: 30 Minutes
Oven Temp: 350°
Baking Time: 10 Minutes

1 cup butter or margarine
⅔ cup firmly packed brown
  sugar
1 egg

2 teaspoons vanilla extract
¼ teaspoon salt
1¾ cups all-purpose flour
1⅓ cups coconut

Cream butter and sugar together; mix in egg, vanilla and salt. Add flour in 4 parts; add coconut and blend. Drop by teaspoonfuls onto greased cookie sheet. Flatten with bottom of a floured glass. Sprinkle with additional coconut. Bake at 350° for 10 minutes or until edges are browned.

Bernie Handler - Huntingdon Valley, Pa.

RICOTTA COOKIES

Easy

Yield: 6 to 7 Dozen
Prep Time: 30 Minutes
Oven Temp: 350°
Baking Time: 15 Minutes

Cookies:
3 eggs
2 cups sugar
1 cup butter or margarine
2 teaspoons vanilla extract

1 pound ricotta cheese
4 cups all-purpose flour
1 teaspoon baking soda
1 teaspoon salt

Frosting:
1 (16 ounce) package powdered
  sugar
¼ cup butter or margarine

2 teaspoons vanilla extract
Milk

Cookies: Cream eggs, sugar and butter together. Add vanilla and ricotta cheese. Beat well while adding flour, soda and salt. Drop by teaspoon onto ungreased cookie sheet. Bake for 15 minutes at 350° (these will be very light colored, not browned, when done). Cool and frost.

Frosting: Beat sugar, butter and vanilla together. Add milk and beat until smooth. Sprinkle with jimmies or non-pareils. *Soft cookie that kids love!*

Mary Lou Longo - Chestnut Hill, Pa.

COOKIES, CUPCAKES & BROWNIES

ANNIE GLENN'S CHOCOLATE CHIP COOKIES

Easy

Prep Time: 15 Minutes
Oven Temp: 350°
Baking Time: 10 to 12 Minutes

2¼ cups all-purpose flour
1 teaspoon baking soda
1 teaspoon salt
½ cup shortening
½ cup butter or margarine,
　softened
¾ cup sugar

¾ cup lightly packed brown
　sugar
1 teaspoon vanilla extract
2 eggs
1 (12 ounce) package semisweet
　chocolate morsels

Mix together flour, soda and salt and set aside. Cream together shortening, butter, sugars and vanilla. Add eggs, 1 at a time, blending after each addition. Mix in the flour mixture. Fold in chocolate morsels. Spoon onto greased cookie sheet. Bake at 350° for 10 to 12 minutes or until golden brown.

John Glenn - U.S. Senate, Ohio

CHOCOLATE CHIP/OATMEAL COOKIES

Easy
Freeze

Yield: 3 Dozen
Prep Time: 30 Minutes
Oven Temp: 350°
Baking Time: 12 Minutes

1 cup firmly packed brown sugar
1 cup sugar
1 cup butter or margarine
2 eggs
2 tablespoons milk
2 teaspoons vanilla extract
2 cups all-purpose flour

½ teaspoon salt
1 teaspoon baking soda
1 teaspoon baking powder
2½ cups rolled oats
18 ounces chocolate morsels
1½ cups chopped walnuts

Beat sugars and butter until smooth. Add eggs, milk and vanilla. Combine flour, salt, soda and baking powder; add to mixture and blend. By hand add oats, chocolate morsels and nuts. Drop (golf ball size) onto ungreased baking sheets. Bake at 350° for 12 minutes.

Trish Lynch - Norristown, Pa.

COOKIES, CUPCAKES & BROWNIES

FORTUNE COOKIES

Moderate

Yield: 2 to 3 Dozen
Prep Time: 20 Minutes
Oven Temp: 375°
Baking Time: 15 Minutes

¾ cup butter or margarine
2 cups sugar
1 teaspoon vanilla extract

3 eggs
1 cup sifted flour

Mix together butter and sugar; add vanilla. Beat in eggs. Add flour. Drop by teaspoonfuls onto greased and floured cookie sheets. Allow 2 inches between drops. Bake 15 minutes at 375°. Drop folded message on each cookie; fold cookie in half. *The ways of using fortune cookies to teach a lesson are endless. In place of a fortune, I put whatever message or questions I want in the cookie. All subject areas may be used and if you are really clever you can come up with many more ideas. Have fun!*

Mary Ann Powell - Roxborough, Pa.

GRANDMA'S MOLASSES COOKIES

Moderate

Yield: Approximately 4 Dozen
Prep Time: 15 Minutes
Oven Temp: 375°
Baking Time: 12 to 15 Minutes

1 cup sausage drippings
1 cup sugar
2 eggs
1 cup natural, dark molasses
4 cups all-purpose flour

1 teaspoon baking soda
1 tablespoon cinnamon
1 tablespoon nutmeg
1 teaspoon ground ginger
1 scant cup warm coffee

Beat together sausage drippings, sugar and eggs. Add molasses and beat again. Add flour and all other ingredients; mix well. The dough will be soft, but do not add any more flour. Drop from tablespoon onto well-greased cookie sheets. Bake at 375° for 12 to 15 minutes. *Lard may be substituted for sausage drippings, but for the original flavor of this Civil War recipe, refrigerate sausage drippings in a jar until you are ready to use.*

C.A. Schenck - Fox Chase, Pa.

COOKIES, CUPCAKES & BROWNIES

HEAVENLY CARAMEL BROWNIES

Easy

Yield: Approximately 25
Prep Time: 40 Minutes
Oven Temp: 350°
Baking Time: 25 Minutes

**1 (18½ ounce) package German
chocolate cake mix**
**¾ cup butter or margarine,
melted**

⅓ cup evaporated milk
1 cup chopped nuts
1 cup chocolate morsels

Topping:
12 to 14 ounces caramels

⅓ cup evaporated milk

In a large bowl mix by hand the cake mix, butter, milk and nuts. Press half of mixture into greased 13x9 inch baking pan. Bake at 350° for 6 minutes. Remove and sprinkle with chocolate morsels. Spread topping over, then crumble remaining cake mixture on top. Bake 18 minutes longer and cool. Refrigerate 30 minutes before cutting into squares.

Topping: Melt caramels and milk in saucepan; stir until smooth.

Mary Leaness - Norristown, Pa.

FAT MARY'S OATMEAL LACE COOKIES

Easy

Yield: 3 Dozen
Prep Time: 30 Minutes
Oven Temp: 375°
Baking Time: 7 to 10 Minutes

1 egg
1 cup rolled oats
1 cup brown sugar
1 tablespoon flour

1 teaspoon baking powder
½ cup butter or margarine
1 teaspoon vanilla extract
Dash of salt

Mix all ingredients together. Roll into small balls and place on well-greased cookie sheet about 1½ inches apart. Bake at 375° for 7 to 10 minutes.

Josephine Santa Maria - Chestnut Hill, Pa.

WHITE BROWNIES

Moderate

Yield: About 20
Prep Time: 30 Minutes
Oven Temp: 350°
Baking Time: About 30 Minutes

¾ cup butter or margarine
1½ cups firmly packed light
brown sugar
1½ teaspoons vanilla extract
2 extra large eggs

¼ teaspoon salt
1½ cups sifted flour
1½ teaspoons baking powder
½ pound broken walnuts
4 ounces chocolate morsels

Put butter in large oven-proof bowl and place in oven to melt while preheating oven. Let stand until cool. Add all remaining ingredients; mix together. Bake in greased 8 or 9 inch square pan on middle rack of oven at 350° for about 30 minutes. *Recipe may be doubled.*

Lisa Evans - Roxborough, Pa.
Bonnie Piecyk - Blue Bell, Pa.

SOUR CREAM-CHOCOLATE BIT SQUARES

Easy

Yield: 20 (2 inch) Squares
Prep Time: 5 Minutes
Oven Temp: 350°
Baking Time: 35 Minutes

6 tablespoons butter or
margarine, softened
1 cup plus 1 tablespoon sugar,
divided
2 eggs
1⅓ cups all-purpose flour

1½ teaspoons baking powder
1 teaspoon baking soda
1 teaspoon cinnamon
1 cup sour cream
1 (6 ounce) package semisweet
chocolate morsels

Mix butter with 1 cup sugar until blended; beat in eggs 1 at a time. Stir flour with baking powder, soda and cinnamon and blend with creamed mixture. Mix in sour cream. Pour batter into greased and floured 9x13 inch pan. Scatter chocolate morsels evenly over batter; sprinkle with remaining 1 tablespoon sugar. Bake at 350° for 35 minutes. Cut into squares.

Lillian W. Owings - Germantown, Pa.

COOKIES, CUPCAKES & BROWNIES

MICHIGAN ROCKS

Easy

Yield: 6 Dozen
Oven Temp: 375°
Baking Time: 8 to 10 Minutes

1 cup butter or margarine
2 cups firmly packed light brown
   sugar
4 eggs
3½ cups all-purpose flour
1 teaspoon cream of tartar
1 teaspoon cinnamon
1 teaspoon allspice

1 teaspoon vanilla extract
½ teaspoon salt
2 teaspoons baking powder
1 teaspoon baking soda
   dissolved in a little water
1 pound raisins, cooked until
   soft and strained
Chopped black walnuts to taste

Cream butter and sugar; add eggs, flour and next 7 ingredients. Stir in raisins and walnuts. Drop by teaspoon onto greased and floured cookie sheet. Bake at 375° for 8 to 10 minutes.

Lois Brady - Chestnut Hill, Pa.

BLACK BOTTOM CUPCAKES

Easy

Yield: 6 Dozen Miniatures
Prep Time: 15 Minutes
Oven Temp: 350°
Baking Time: 15 to 18 Minutes

Cupcakes:
1½ cups all-purpose flour
1 cup sugar
¼ cup cocoa
1 teaspoon baking soda
½ teaspoon salt

1 cup water
⅓ cup oil
1 teaspoon vinegar
1 teaspoon vanilla extract

Topping:
1 (8 ounce) package cream
   cheese
1 egg
⅓ cup sugar

⅛ teaspoon salt
1 (6 ounce) package chocolate
   morsels

COOKIES, CUPCAKES & BROWNIES

Cupcakes: Sift together flour, sugar, cocoa, soda and salt. Add water, oil, vinegar and vanilla. Fill muffin cups half full. Drop ½ teaspoon of topping to each tin of batter. Bake at 350° for 15 to 18 minutes.

Topping: Cream until smooth the cream cheese, egg, and sugar. Add salt and chocolate morsels.

Julie M. Camburn - East Falls, Pa.

PEANUT BUTTER CUPCAKES

Microwave

Yield: 13 or More Cupcakes
Prep Time: 25 Minutes
Oven Temp: 350°
Baking Time: 12 to 14 Minutes

1 cup all-purpose flour
¾ cup firmly packed brown
    sugar
1 teaspoon baking powder
½ teaspoon salt
½ teaspoon vanilla extract

¼ cup shortening
¼ cup peanut butter
2 eggs
½ cup milk
Pinch of cinnamon

Place all ingredients in a small mixing bowl. Blend at low speed with mixer then at medium speed 2 minutes. Place 2 paper cupcake liners in each 5 or 6 ounce custard cup or microwave muffin dish. Fill each paper liner about ⅓ full. An old-fashioned ice cream scoop makes a good measure. Use less batter if you use muffin pans. Cut through batter with wooden pick to prevent large air spaces which can form because cupcakes bake so quickly. Arrange dishes in a ring in the oven. Microwave on High. If oven holds 3 to 6 cupcakes, rotate or rearrange after half the time. Microwave until almost dry on top. Small moist spots will dry on standing. Overmicrowaving will make dry and tough cupcakes. Remove cupcakes from cups as soon as they are microwaved. Let stand on wire cooling rack. May bake in regular oven at 350° for 12 to 14 minutes.

Alice Brogan - Ambler, Pa.

COOKIES, CUPCAKES & BROWNIES

MRS. BALDERSON'S ORIENTAL CRUNCH

Easy
Make Ahead
Freeze

Yield: 10x15 Inch Pan
Prep Time: 20 Minutes
Oven Temp: 350°
Baking Time: 25 to 30 Minutes

1 cup butter or margarine
1½ tablespoons instant coffee
   powder
½ teaspoon salt
1 teaspoon vanilla extract
½ teaspoon almond extract

1 cup sugar
2 cups sifted all-purpose flour
1 (6 ounce) package semisweet
   chocolate morsels
½ cup nuts, coarsely chopped

Blend butter, coffee, salt, vanilla and almond flavoring. Gradually beat in sugar, then flour; add chocolate. Spread in ungreased 10x15x1 inch pan. Sprinkle nuts over the top; press them in. Bake at 350° for 25 to 30 minutes. Cut into squares then cool. *My daughter once called home long distance from college for this recipe. That's a pretty strong recommendation!*

Louise Daft - Lafayette Hill, Pa.

PEANUT BUTTER SQUARES

Easy
Make Ahead

Serves: Lots!
Prep Time: 30 Minutes
Oven Temp: 350°
Baking Time: 20 to 25 Minutes

1 cup milk
2 tablespoons butter or
   margarine
4 eggs
1 teaspoon vanilla extract
Pinch of salt

2 cups sugar
2 cups all-purpose flour
2 teaspoons baking powder
Peanut butter
1 (8 ounce) milk chocolate
   candy bar

Scald milk and butter and set aside. Mix the remaining ingredients except peanut butter and candy bar together. Then add the milk mixture. Bake in greased jelly-roll pan at 350° for 20 to 25 minutes. Spread peanut butter on hot cake; let cool in refrigerator. Melt candy bar in top of double boiler. Spread over top of cake; refrigerate for ½ hour before serving.

Sally Beil - Oreland, Pa.

LEMON BARS

Moderate

Yield: 15x10x1 Inch Pan
Prep Time: 20 Minutes
Oven Temp: 350°
Baking Time: 40 Minutes Total

1 cup butter or margarine
2 cups powdered sugar
2¼ cups all-purpose flour,
 divided
4 teaspoons lemon juice
Rind of 2 lemons

4 eggs, well-beaten
2 cups sugar
1 teaspoon baking powder
1 cup shredded coconut
 (optional)

Combine butter, powdered sugar and 2 cups flour. Mix and spread out (batter is stiff) in a jelly roll pan (15x10x1 inch). Bake at 350° for 15 minutes until pale tan or paler; cool. Mix lemon juice, lemon rind, eggs, sugar, baking powder, remaining flour and coconut. Pour over crust and bake at 350° for 25 minutes.

George and Barbara Bush, Vice-President of the United States
Rosalynn Sumners, 1984 Olympic Silver Medalist - Edmonds, Washington

MOCHA FROSTING

Easy

Yield: 1 Cup
Prep Time: 25 Minutes

1 cup powdered sugar
1 teaspoon cocoa
1 teaspoon butter or margarine

2 tablespoons hot coffee
¼ teaspoon vanilla extract

Mix together the sugar and cocoa. Add butter and hot coffee blending until smooth with back of spoon. Add vanilla and stir. Spread on cooled cake.

Paul Towhey - Norristown, Pa.

TACONY

Until the American Revolution, bands of Lenni Lenape Indians frequently returned to the hunting villages of "Taconiac". And so Tacony, along with several other Philadelphia neighborhoods, has the distinction of still bearing an Indian name.

Settled first by the Swedes in the late 1600's, Tacony's close proximity to the Delaware River made it attractive to farm the rich soil. Summer mansions were built along the river's white beaches.

Industrial progress crept up on Tacony, and by the 1880's, the metal works industry was the dominant employer. It was the Tacony Iron and Metal Works that had the distinction of casting the statue of William Penn that stands atop City Hall.

The Tacony-Palmyra Bridge is one of the four bridges connecting Philadelphians with New Jersey. In 1929, a nickel could buy a trip across the Delaware River—quite a bargain. Today, it costs a quarter, which is still comparably low, but motorists must be prepared to wait and take in the scenery on the Delaware if there is a merchant ship approaching—it's a drawbridge.

Pies, Pastries & Desserts

JULY 4TH BLUEBERRY PIE

Moderate
Make Ahead

Serves: 10 to 12
Prep Time: 30 to 45 Minutes
Oven Temp: 425°, 350°
Baking Time: 45 Minutes

4 to 5 cups fresh blueberries
1 cup sugar
½ cup sifted all-purpose flour
¼ teaspoon salt
¼ teaspoon ground cloves

½ teaspoon ground cinnamon
3 tablespoons butter or
margarine
1 (10 inch) double pie pastry

Stem and wash berries thoroughly; drain well. Place in large bowl and sprinkle with next 5 ingredients; toss to mix. Roll out bottom pastry and transfer to 10 inch deep dish pie pan. Spoon blueberry mixture into pan and dot with butter. Roll out top crust and place over blueberries. Trim overlapping pastry, leaving enough to make a decorative edge. Brush top with about 1 tablespoon of milk and sprinkle with about ½ teaspoon sugar. Make a few slits in top to vent. Refrigerate about 10 minutes while preheating oven. Place pie pan on cookie sheet in case of spillage. Bake at 425° for 15 minutes; reduce heat to 350° and bake 30 minutes longer. Cool at least 1 hour before serving. May serve with a scoop of vanilla ice cream.

Joe and Nancy Rocks, State Senate, Pa.

HERSHEY BAR PIE

Moderate
Make Ahead

Yield: 1 Pie
Prep Time: 30 Minutes
Oven Temp: 375°
Baking Time: 8 to 10 Minutes

Crust:
1½ cups butter or margarine
1 cup sugar
1 egg
1 teaspoon vanilla extract
1¼ cups unsifted all-purpose
flour

½ cup cocoa
¾ teaspoon baking soda
¼ teaspoon salt

Filling:
½ pound milk chocolate bar
⅓ cup milk
1½ cups miniature or 15 regular
marshmallows

1 cup heavy cream

PIES, PASTRIES & DESSERTS

Crust: Cream butter, sugar, egg and vanilla. Combine flour, cocoa, baking soda and salt; add to creamed mixture. Shape soft dough into two 1½ inch rolls. Wrap in waxed paper and plastic wrap; chill until firm. Cut 1 roll into ⅛ inch slices; arrange, edges touching, on bottom and up side of greased 9 inch pie pan. (Small spaces in crust will not affect pie.) Bake at 375° for 8 to 10 minutes; cool. Yield: 2 crusts. *Leftover dough may be frozen.*

Filling: Break chocolate bar into pieces; melt with milk in top of double boiler over hot water. Add marshmallows, stirring until melted; cool completely. Whip cream until stiff; fold into chocolate mixture. Spoon into crust. Cover; chill several hours until firm. Garnish with whipped topping or chilled cherry pie filling.

Hershey Foods - Hershey, Pa.

PRETZEL PIE

Easy
Make Ahead

Serves: 8 to 10
Prep Time: 15 Minutes
Oven Temp: 375°
Baking Time: 8 Minutes

Crust:
1¼ cups high quality pretzels
¼ cup sugar

¼ cup softened butter or margarine

Filling:
1 to 1½ quarts of your favorite ice cream, softened
⅓ cup coarsely chopped pretzels

Chocolate sauce

Crust: In blender, crush pretzels. In a bowl, mix pretzel crumbs, sugar and butter until well blended. Form a crust in a 9 inch pie pan and bake at 375° for about 8 minutes; cool or freeze.

Filling: Fill the prepared crust with softened ice cream and freeze. When serving, garnish with extra thin pretzel stick design or coarsely chopped pretzels. Top with chocolate sauce. *This is a pretzel and ice cream lovers' delight.*

Evelyn P. Olivieri - Mt. Airy, Pa.

PEACHES AND CREAM PIE

Easy
Make Ahead

Serves: 10
Prep Time: 20 Minutes
Oven Temp: 350°
Baking Time: 30 to 40 Minutes

¾ cup all-purpose flour
1 teaspoon baking powder
½ teaspoon salt
1 egg
½ cup milk
3 tablespoons oil or butter
1 (3⅜ ounce) package vanilla
  pudding and pie filling (not
  instant)

1 (16 ounce) can sliced peaches,
  drained (reserve 3
  tablespoons)
1 (8 ounce) package cream
  cheese, softened
½ cup sugar
Cinnamon

In a bowl, combine first 7 ingredients. Beat for 2 minutes and pour thin batter into greased 9 or 10 inch deep dish pie pan. Drain peaches, reserving 3 tablespoons of juice. Decoratively arrange peach slices on batter. Using same bowl, mix cream cheese, sugar and peach juice. Spoon mixture on peaches. Sprinkle additional sugar and cinnamon on top. Bake at 350° for 30 to 40 minutes.

Nelia Rosqueta - Conshohocken, Pa.

SOUR CREAM APPLE PIE

Easy
Make Ahead

Serves: 14 to 16
Prep Time: 30 Minutes
Oven Temp: 350°
Baking Time: 40, 15 Minutes

Filling:
1 (8 ounce) carton sour cream
1 (8 ounce) package cream
  cheese
1 egg
1½ cups sugar
¼ cup flour

2 teaspoons vanilla extract
½ teaspoon salt
6 to 9 large cooking apples,
  sliced
2 (9 inch) pastry shells

Topping:
½ cup butter or margarine
½ cup flour
½ cup sugar
½ cup firmly packed brown
  sugar

1 tablespoon cinnamon
¼ teaspoon salt
2 cups chopped walnuts

Filling: Combine sour cream, cream cheese, egg, sugar, flour, vanilla and salt in large bowl. Beat until mixture is well blended. Add sliced apples to mixture (paring and slicing apples into cream mixture helps to retard browning), stirring to coat. Pour filling mixture into pastry shell(s) and bake at 350° for 40 minutes until cream mixture is firm.

Topping: Blend together butter, flour, sugars, cinnamon, salt and walnuts. After pie is baked, remove from oven and stir top of filling gently. Place topping mixture evenly over top of pie. Return to oven for 15 minutes more. Makes 2 (9 inch) pies.

Evelyn Coleman - Laverock, Pa.

DESIGNER CHEESE PIE

Easy
Make Ahead

Serves: 8 to 10
Prep Time: 10 Minutes
Oven Temp: 350°
Baking Time: 30 Minutes

3 (8 ounce) packages cream cheese, softened
1 cup sugar
3 eggs

1 teaspoon vanilla extract
3 ounces semisweet chocolate
3 tablespoons strong coffee

Blend first 4 ingredients in electric mixer for a few minutes or until smooth. Pour into greased 9 inch pie pan. In a double boiler, melt chocolate and mix in coffee until well blended. Spoon 2 tablespoons of chocolate into center of cheese mixture and pour remaining chocolate in a thin ring about 2 to 3 inches from edge. Use a knife and slowly make lines of chocolate from center or make an "S" shape and twirl design. Be creative! Bake at 350° for 30 minutes.

Mary Kinneman - Lansdale, Pa.

FRENCH SILK CHOCOLATE PIE

Easy

Serves: 6
Prep Time: 15 Minutes

½ cup butter or margarine
¾ cup sugar
2 ounces unsweetened
   chocolate, melted
1 teaspoon vanilla extract

2 eggs
1 (8 inch) baked pastry shell
Heavy cream, whipped
Chopped walnuts or chocolate
   shavings

Cream butter; gradually add sugar with mixer. Blend in melted chocolate when it is fairly cool. Stir in vanilla. Add eggs 1 at a time, beating 5 minutes at medium speed after each addition. Pour into cool pastry shell. Chill at least 2 hours. Top with whipped cream and chopped walnuts or chocolate shavings if desired. *Recipe may be doubled for a larger pie. Do not freeze.*

Marie Schilling - Conshohocken, Pa.

GRAHAM CRACKER PIE

Moderate

Serves: 12 to 14
Prep Time: 20 Minutes
Oven Temp: 350°
Baking Time: 8, 10 Minutes

Crust:
3 packages graham crackers,
   crushed
¾ cup butter or margarine,
   melted

½ cup sugar

Filling:
10 tablespoons sugar
5 tablespoons cornstarch
¼ teaspoon salt

5 cups milk
6 egg yolks, slightly beaten

Meringue:
6 egg whites
½ teaspoon baking powder

1 teaspoon sugar

Crust: Combine crumbs, melted butter and sugar and press into 1 large or 2 small pie pans. Bake at 350° for 8 minutes.

Filling: Mix together sugar, cornstarch and salt. Slowly add milk and slightly beaten egg yolks. Heat until it begins to thicken then pour into crumb crust.

Meringue: Beat egg whites until stiff but not dry; add baking powder and beat. Gradually add sugar. Spread over filling. Place in oven at 350° for about 10 minutes.

Jacquelyn DeBlasi - Hatboro, Pa.

JO'S LEMON TARTS

Moderate

Yield: 15 to 18 Tarts
Prep Time: 30 Minutes
Oven Temp: 325°
Baking Time: 25 Minutes

Tart Shells:
½ cup butter or margarine
1 cup flour

2 tablespoons sugar
2 tablespoons milk

Lemon Filling:
½ cup plus 2 tablespoons sugar
1 tablespoon butter or
** margarine, melted**
1 egg

1 medium potato, cooked and
** finely grated**
Rind and juice of 1 medium
** lemon**

Tart Shells: Cut butter into flour and sugar until mixture has texture of fine crumbs. Add milk and mix with fork until soft dough forms. Divide dough into 15 to 18 walnut-size balls and press into cupcake tin, pressing dough ½ inch up sides of cups. (If desired, dough can be refrigerated until ready to fill.)

Lemon Filling: Blend together all filling ingredients and spoon into tart shells. Bake at 325° for 25 minutes. Cool for a few minutes before removing tarts from pan. Dust with powdered sugar before serving. *This is an old family treasure that is a favorite with family and friends.*

Peggy Miller - Chestnut Hill, Pa.

PIES, PASTRIES & DESSERTS

YOGURT PIE

Easy
Make Ahead
Freeze

Serves: 6
Prep Time: 10 Minutes

2 (8 ounce) containers fruit-
flavored yogurt
1 (8 ounce) container frozen
non-dairy whipped topping,
thawed

½ cup mashed fruit to
complement yogurt (optional)
1 (9 inch) graham cracker crust

Fold yogurt into whipped topping, blending well. Add fruit and spoon into crust. Freeze until firm, about 4 hours. Remove from freezer 30 minutes (or longer for softer texture) before cutting and keep chilled in refrigerator. Store any leftover pie in freezer. *This is a nice summer dessert-very light. Especially liked by children.*

Eileen Madden - Elkins Park, Pa.

ABBY'S PECAN PIE

Easy

Serves: 8
Prep Time: 20 Minutes
Oven Temp: 350°
Baking Time: 45 Minutes

1 cup light corn syrup
1 cup firmly packed dark brown
sugar
⅓ teaspoon salt
⅓ cup melted butter or
margarine

1 teaspoon vanilla extract
3 eggs, slightly beaten
1 (9 inch) unbaked pastry shell
1 heaping cup shelled pecans

Mix syrup, sugar, salt, butter and vanilla. Blend in eggs; pour into pastry shell. Sprinkle pecans over filling. Bake at 350° approximately 45 minutes.

Abigail Van Buren, Columnist

LEMON FLUFF

Easy
Make Ahead

Serves: 10 to 15
Prep Time: 30 Minutes
Oven Temp: 375°
Baking Time: 15 Minutes

Crust:
**1½ cups chopped walnuts
(reserve ½ cup for topping)
3 tablespoons sugar**

**½ cup flour
¾ cup butter or margarine
1 teaspoon vanilla extract**

Filling:
**2 (8 ounce) packages cream
cheese, softened
1½ cups powdered sugar
1 (12 ounce) container frozen
non-dairy whipped topping,
divided**

**3 (3¾ ounce) packages lemon
flavor instant pudding mix
4 cups milk**

Crust: Mix all 5 ingredients. Spread in bottom of 13x9x2 inch pan. Bake at 375° for 15 minutes; cool completely.

Filling: Beat cream cheese and powdered sugar together. Add half the whipped topping, mix and spread on crust. Beat instant pudding with milk on low speed of mixer. Spread over cream cheese mixture. Top with remaining whipped topping and sprinkle with remaining nuts; refrigerate overnight.

Ann Messina - Norristown, Pa.

ED'S FAVORITE DESSERT

**Carob ice cream
Vanilla ice cream
Banana liqueur**

**Cookie stick
Whipped cream**

Scoop carob and vanilla ice cream into dish; pour banana liqueur over and serve with cookie stick and whipped cream. Enjoy!

Ed McMahon - Tonight Show

PIES, PASTRIES & DESSERTS

GOLDEN PUFFS

Moderate

Serves: 12 to 15
Prep Time: 10 Minutes
Cooking Time: 15 Minutes

Oil for deep fat frying
2 cups flour
1 tablespoon baking powder
¼ cup sugar
1 teaspoon salt

1 teaspoon nutmeg
¼ cup vegetable oil
¾ cup milk
1 egg
Cinnamon or powdered sugar

Heat oil 3 to 4 inches in pan. Mix remaining ingredients except cinnamon until smooth. Drop batter by teaspoon into hot oil and fry until golden brown. Roll in cinnamon or powdered sugar.

Sharon Avato - Roxborough, Pa.

DANISH PUFF

Moderate

Yields: 28 Squares
Prep Time: 20 Minutes
Oven Temp: 350°
Baking Time: 1 Hour

First Layer:
1 cup flour
½ cup butter or margarine,
  softened

⅛ teaspoon salt
2 tablespoons water

Second Layer:
1 cup water
½ cup butter
1 teaspoon almond extract

1 cup flour
3 eggs, at room temperature

Frosting:
2 cups powdered sugar
¼ cup butter or margarine
1 teaspoon vanilla extract

3 tablespoons milk
Nuts

First Layer: Combine first 3 ingredients in food processor until mixture is crumbly. Add water until mixture forms ball. Divide in half and press dough into 2 strips, 2x14 inches on an ungreased cookie sheet.

PIES, PASTRIES & DESSERTS

Second Layer: Add water, butter and almond extract to a saucepan and bring to a rapid boil. Remove from heat; add flour all at once and mix thoroughly. Add eggs, 1 at a time, beating well after each addition. Spoon this mixture over first layer. Bake at 350° for 1 hour. When cooled, spread with frosting and sprinkle with nuts. Slice into 1 to 2 inch pieces to serve.

Frosting: Beat all except nuts with mixer and spread on cooled puff. Sprinkle with nuts.

Flossie Narducci - Blue Bell, Pa.

LES CRÊPES SOUFFLÉES, FLAMBÉES À L'ORANGE

Moderate

Serves: 1
Prep Time: 45 Minutes
Oven Temp: 450°
Baking Time: 3 Minutes

2 crêpes
1 orange
3 large sugar cubes
2 eggs, separated (2 whites, 1 yolk; for each additional person add 1 white, 1 yolk)

3½ tablespoons sugar
1½ tablespoons butter or margarine
2 tablespoons orange liqueur

Make the crêpes using your favorite recipe. Rub the orange peel with the sugar cubes and juice the orange. Boil sugar cubes and orange juice together to make a sugar syrup (stop just when the syrup is about to turn a light caramel color). When the syrup has cooled slightly but is still workable, mix in the egg yolk. Beat the egg whites until stiff, add the sugar and beat until glossy, a few seconds. (Don't overbeat; the whites must have some force left to rise nicely in the oven.) Fold the syrup-yolk mixture into the egg whites. Place the crêpes on a well-buttered oven-proof platter and spoon the soufflé mixture into each crêpe. Bake at 450° about 3 minutes until puffed. Pour orange liqueur over crêpes, flame and serve. Serves 1. *Mr. Clement feels that these crêpes are rich enough to be served without a crème anglaise or any sauce other than the flamed orange liqueur.*

Christian Clément, Chef - Bordeaux, France

TROPICAL CHARLOTTE

Easy
Make Ahead

Serves: 10 to 12
Prep Time: 45 Minutes

2 (4 ounce) packages
   ladyfingers
4 (1.4 ounce) envelopes whipped
   topping mix
2 cups milk
1 (6 ounce) package any fruit-
   flavored gelatin

2 cups boiling water
12 ounces cream cheese
1 (8 ounce) container frozen
   non-dairy whipped topping
Kiwi, peeled and sliced, or
   berries, oranges, bananas or
   combinations

Line the bottom and sides of a springform pan with ladyfingers. Make whipped topping mix with milk; refrigerate. Make gelatin with boiling water; set aside to cool slightly. Beat cream cheese; add gelatin mixture then mix with prepared whipped topping. Spoon into pan and chill. Top with non-dairy whipped topping and fruit before serving.

Annmarie Vozzo - Wyndmoor, Pa.

IRISH COFFEE MOUSSE

Easy
Make Ahead
Freeze

Serves: 8 to 10
Prep Time: 20 to 30 Minutes

3 cups heavy cream, chilled
4 tablespoons instant coffee
⅓ cup Irish whiskey
⅓ cup kahlua

¾ cup powdered sugar
Whipped cream
Grated or shaved chocolate for
   garnish

Whip heavy cream until it starts to thicken. Stir in instant coffee and liqueurs. Continue beating, adding sugar gradually, until stiff peaks form. Pour into attractive container or individual Irish coffee or parfait glasses. Top with thin layers of whipped cream or rosettes. Sprinkle with grated or shaved chocolate; chill well or freeze.

Irene Rothschild - Wyncote, Pa.

RICOTTA MOUSSE

Easy

Serves: 6 to 8
Prep Time: 20 Minutes

1 (15 ounce) container ricotta
  cheese
5 tablespoons sugar, divided
2 tablespoons plus ¾ cup heavy
  cream, divided

2 tablespoons rum
2 tablespoons amaretto
1 teaspoon vanilla extract

Combine ricotta, 3 tablespoons sugar and 2 tablespoons heavy cream; whip these together until smooth (5 minutes). Add rum and amaretto. In a separate bowl whip together ¾ cup heavy cream, remaining sugar and vanilla. Fold this into ricotta mixture. Serve in an ice cream or sherbet cup with a cookie, chopped nuts or shaved chocolate.

Monica Sinker - Erdenheim, Pa.

CHOCOLATE CHARLOTTE RUSSE

Moderate

Serves: 6
Prep Time: 25 Minutes

1 (3⅛ ounce) package vanilla
  pudding mix
1 teaspoon unflavored gelatin
2 cups milk
1 (4 ounce) bar sweet baking
  chocolate

1½ cups heavy cream
2 (4 ounce) packages
  ladyfingers, split

In saucepan combine pudding mix and gelatin; stir in milk. Cook and stir over medium heat until boiling; remove from heat. Break chocolate into squares and add to hot pudding. Stir until chocolate is melted. Cool completely, then beat smooth. Whip cream; reserve 1 cup for garnish; fold remainder into pudding. Line a 9x5x3 inch loaf pan with waxed paper extending paper beyond rim. Line bottom and sides with ladyfinger halves. Pour in half the chocolate mixture. Add a layer of ladyfinger halves and the remaining pudding. Top with remaining ladyfinger halves. Chill 3 to 4 hours or until firm. Using the waxed paper, remove dessert from loaf pan and carefully transfer to serving plate; remove waxed paper. Garnish with the reserved whipped cream.

Betty Jane Whalen - Erdenheim, Pa.

PIES, PASTRIES & DESSERTS

FRENCH CREAM CHEESE MOLD

Easy
Make Ahead

Serves: 8
Prep Time: 20 Minutes

1 cup sour cream
1 cup heavy cream
¾ cup sugar
1 envelope unflavored gelatin

¼ cup warm water
1 (8 ounce) package cream
cheese
½ teaspoon vanilla extract

Combine sour cream and heavy cream in a saucepan and cook over low heat; slowly stir in sugar. In a small bowl dissolve gelatin in warm water, stir into warm cream mixture; remove from heat. In separate bowl beat cream cheese; stir into mixture; add vanilla. Beat entire mixture with electric mixer on high speed until well blended. Pour into an oiled 4 cup mold; refrigerate 4 hours. Serve with frozen strawberries or raspberries.

Bonnie Courtney - Holmesburg, Pa.

APPLE COBBLER WITH HARD SAUCE

Easy

Serves: 8 to 9
Prep Time: 30 Minutes
Oven Temp: 350°
Baking Time: 35 to 40 Minutes

Filling:
5 cups peeled, sliced apples
¾ cup sugar
2 tablespoons flour
1 tablespoon lemon juice
1 teaspoon vanilla extract

½ teaspoon cinnamon
¼ teaspoon salt
¼ cup water
2 tablespoons butter or
margarine

Batter:
½ cup unsifted flour
½ cup sugar
½ teapoon baking powder
¼ teaspoon salt

2 tablespoons butter or
margarine, softened
1 egg, slightly beaten

Hard Sauce:
4 cups milk
1 (3⅛ ounce) package vanilla
pudding mix

Filling: In medium bowl combine all ingredients except butter. Turn into greased 8x8x2 inch baking dish. Dot with butter.

Batter: In medium bowl combine all batter ingredients. Beat with wooden spoon until smooth. Drop in portions over filling, spacing evenly. Bake at 350° for 35 to 40 minutes until apples are tender and crust is golden. Serve warm with Hard Sauce.

Hard Sauce: Heat milk and whisk in vanilla pudding until thickened.

Chris Thistle - Glenside, Pa.

CHOCOLATE SOUFFLÉ

Moderate

Serves: 10
Prep Time: 40 Minutes
Oven Temp: 425°
Baking Time: 5 to 7 Minutes

15 ounces bittersweet chocolate
10 ounces unsalted butter
Pinch of salt
Sugar and butter for soufflé
   dishes

1 cup water
10 egg yolks
3 cups egg whites
1 cup sugar

Cut the butter and chocolate into small pieces and put them together in a bowl with a pinch of salt. Melt them over a pot of hot water. While the chocolate is melting, brush the inside of the soufflé bowls with a thin coating of softened whole butter. Coat the bowls with sugar simply by filling the first one with sugar, turning it to coat the sides entirely, and then pouring the sugar into the next bowl. Add the water, which should be lukewarm, to the yolks and beat them for 10 minutes at high speed of electric mixer. Put the whites and sugar into the large bowl of a mixer. Warm them over low heat until they are at room temperature. Start beating the whites at high speed. While they are beating, fold the beaten yolks into the chocolate mixture. Beat the whites until they are quite glossy and moderately stiff. Fold them into the chocolate-yolk mixture, ⅓ at a time. Ladle the finished mixture into the sugared bowls. Bake the soufflés at 425° for 5 to 7 minutes depending on their size. Immediately upon removing them from oven, drop a scoop of coffee ice cream into the centers and cover the holes with a dollop of whipped cream.

Quilted Giraffe Restaurant - New York, N.Y.

CHOCOLATE MINT FREEZE

Moderate
Make Ahead

Serves: 8
Prep Time: 20 Minutes

¾ cup butter or margarine, divided
2 ounces unsweetened chocolate
3 eggs, separated
1½ cups sifted powdered sugar

1½ cups chopped pecans
1 teaspoon vanilla extract
1¼ cups fine vanilla wafer crumbs
1 quart peppermint ice cream

Melt ½ cup butter and chocolate over low heat. Gradually stir into well beaten egg yolks with sugar, nuts and vanilla. Cool thoroughly. Beat egg whites until stiff peaks form. Beat chocolate mixture until smooth and fold into egg whites. Toss together crumbs and remaining butter (melted). Reserve ¼ cup for topping. Press remainder into 9x9x2 inch pan. Spread ice cream over crumbs followed by chocolate mixture. Top with reserved crumbs; freeze.

Jo Ann Seeger - Oreland, Pa.

POTS DE CRÈME AU CHOCOLAT

Easy

Serves: 6
Prep Time: 15 Minutes

1 package frozen patty shells
1 (6 ounce) package semisweet chocolate morsels

2 tablespoons sugar
1 cup heavy cream, divided
3 egg yolks

Prepare patty shells according to package directions. In the top of a double boiler, melt chocolate morsels over simmering water. Stir in sugar and ½ cup heavy cream; cook, stirring constantly, until smooth. Slowly pour in chocolate mixture while constantly beating yolks; set aside. When cooled to room temperature, fold in remaining ½ cup heavy cream which has been whipped. Spoon evenly into patty shells and refrigerate until serving time. If desired, garnish with a rosette of whipped cream.

Patricia Boris - Roxborough, Pa.

CREAMY RICE PUDDING

Easy

Serves: 6 to 8
Prep Time: 5 Minutes
Cooking Time: 30 Minutes

1 cup rice
2 quarts milk, divided
1 cup sugar
3 eggs
2 teaspoons vanilla extract

1 (13 ounce) can evaporated milk
Raisins (optional)
Cinnamon
Nutmeg

Cook rice in 1½ quarts milk. Bring to a boil and simmer. Cook until well done, allowing milk to evaporate. While rice is cooking, combine ½ quart milk, sugar, eggs, vanilla and evaporated milk in a large bowl. Beat with a whisk. When rice is cooked, raise heat to medium and pour egg mixture over rice and mix well. Stir constantly until mixture comes to a boil. Boil for less than 1 minute; add raisins if desired. Pour into serving dish(es) and top with spices.

Bea Schiavo - Lafayette Hills, Pa.

"NO BAKE" RICE PUDDING

Easy

Serves: 4 to 6
Prep Time: 20 Minutes
Cooking Time: 1 Hour

1 quart milk
½ cup long grain rice
2 tablespoons butter or
 margarine
¼ cup sugar

Speck of salt
2 eggs
1 teaspoon vanilla extract
½ cup raisins (optional)
Cinnamon

Stir together milk, rice, butter, sugar and salt in top of double boiler. Set over boiling water and cook 1 hour, stirring occasionally. Beat eggs and blend in a small amount of the hot pudding. Add this back to double boiler and stir. Add vanilla and raisins; blend well. Sprinkle with cinnamon to taste.

Vince Madden '61 - Elkins Park, Pa.

PIES, PASTRIES & DESSERTS

PARIS-BREST
(Cream Puff Pastry Ring with Whipped Cream Filling)

Moderate
Make Ahead

Serves: 8
Prep Time: 10 Minutes
Oven Temp: 450° for 10 Minutes
           350° for 10 Minutes
           325° for 20 Minutes

Pâte à Choux:
1 cup water
6 tablespoons butter, cut into
   small pieces
1 cup flour
1 tablespoon sugar

5 large eggs, divided
½ teaspoon water
3 tablespoons blanched,
   slivered almonds

Filling:
2 cups heavy cream
1 tablespoon powdered sugar

2 teaspoons vanilla extract

Pâte à Choux: In a heavy 2 or 3 quart saucepan, bring 1 cup water and butter to a boil over moderate heat. Stir and as soon as butter has completely melted, remove pan from heat and pour in the flour and sugar all at once. Beat the mixture vigorously with a wooden spoon until well blended. Return to moderate heat and cook, beating vigorously for 1 or 2 minutes or until the mixture forms a mass that leaves the sides of the pan and moves freely with the spoon. Immediately remove the pan from the heat and use the spoon to make a well in the center of the paste. Break an egg into the well and beat it into the paste. When the first egg has been absorbed, add 3 more eggs 1 at a time, beating well after each addition. The finished paste should be thick, smooth and shiny. Butter a baking sheet, scatter a little flour on it. Lay an 8 inch plate on baking sheet pressing down hard to make a circular impression in the flour; remove the plate. Using a pastry tube with a large plain tip, make a circle or crown of *pâte à choux* 2 inches wide and 1 inch high around the pattern in the flour. If you don't have a pastry tube, drop the paste by the spoonfuls, placing the mounds side by side around the ring. With a spatula, smooth the mounds into a continuous strand 2 inches wide and 1 inch high. Beat 1 egg and ½ teaspoon water together and paint the top of the crown with the mixture. Sprinkle it with slivered almonds. Bake at 450° for 10 minutes, reduce heat to 350° and bake 10 minutes more. Reduce heat to 325° and bake 20 minutes or until the crown has more than doubled in size and is golden brown, firm and crusty. Turn oven off and make 3 or 4 tiny cuts near bottom of crown with sharp knife. Let crown rest in oven for 5 minutes to dry out. Slice it in half horizontally and spoon out any soft dough inside.

Filling: Whip cream; add sugar and vanilla. Using a pastry bag with a decorative tip, fill bottom of crown with whipped cream. Gently replace the top of the crown so that it floats on the cream. Sprinkle the top with powdered sugar and refrigerate until serving time.

Robbyn O'Neill - Oreland, Pa.

BAVARIAN APPLE TORTE

Easy
Make Ahead

Serves: 8 to 10
Prep Time: 20 Minutes
Oven Temp: 450° for 10 Minutes
         400° for 25 Minutes

Crust:
½ cup butter
⅓ cup sugar

¼ teaspoon vanilla extract
1 cup flour

Filling:
1 (8 ounce) package cream
   cheese
¼ cup sugar

1 egg
½ teaspoon vanilla extract

Topping:
⅓ cup sugar
½ teaspoon cinnamon

4 cups peeled thin apple slices
¼ cup sliced almonds

Crust: Cream butter, sugar and vanilla. Blend in flour; spread dough on bottom and sides of 9 inch springform pan.

Filling: Combine cream cheese and sugar. Add egg and vanilla; mix well and pour into crust.

Topping: Combine sugar and cinnamon; toss with apple slices. Spoon apple mixture over cream cheese filling; sprinkle with nuts. Bake at 450° for 10 minutes; reduce heat to 400° and bake 25 minutes; cool before removing from pan.

Marilyn Anderson - Roxborough, Pa.

BANANAS LONGSTRETH

Easy

Serves: 4
Prep Time: 10 Minutes

2 tablespoons butter
4 small bananas, peeled
2 tablespoons brown sugar

¼ cup light rum
Vanilla ice cream

Melt butter and add bananas which have been halved lengthwise. Sauté until golden. Sprinkle with brown sugar and rum. Heat through and pour over vanilla ice cream.

W. Thacher Longstreth, City Council - Philadelphia, Pa.

MOCHA SAUCE

Easy
Make Ahead

Yield: 2 Cups
Prep Time: 5 Minutes

1 (6 ounce) package semisweet
  chocolate morsels
1 ounce unsweetened chocolate

3 tablespoons coffee-flavored
  liqueur
½ cup heavy cream

Melt chocolates in top of a double boiler; add liqueur, blending as chocolate melts. When melted, slowly add cream; stir. (Add more or less cream for thicker or thinner sauce.) Serve hot over coffee ice cream-sauce will harden on ice cream.

Claudia Patterson - Mt. Airy, Pa.

ZABAGLIONE

Easy

Serves: 4
Prep Time: 20 Minutes

4 egg yolks
¼ cup sugar

½ cup marsala
Ladyfingers

Put the egg yolks and sugar in top of a double boiler, over boiling water, and beat until pale and fluffy, making sure the water does not touch the bottom of the double boiler. Beat in the marsala. Remove from boiler and place pan in bowl of ice to stop cooking. Continue beating until the mixture begins to thicken and doubles in volume. Spoon into wine glasses and serve immediately with ladyfingers.

Kas Breslin - Roxborough, Pa.

HELLO DOLLY BARS

Easy
Make Ahead

Yield: 13x9x2 inch pan
Prep Time: 5 Minutes
Oven Temp: 350°
Baking Time: 25 to 35 Minutes

10 tablespoons butter
1½ cups graham cracker
crumbs
1 cup shredded coconut
6 ounces semi-sweet chocolate
pieces

6 ounces butterscotch pieces
1 cup chopped nuts
1 (14-ounce) can sweetened
condensed milk

Melt butter in 9x13x2 inch pan. Pour crumbs over butter; mix; form crust. Sprinkle next 4 ingredients over crust. Dribble milk over all. Bake at 350° for 25 to 35 minutes. Cut while still warm.

Susan Cinalli-Wyndmoor, Pa.

UNIVERSITY CITY-POWELTON VILLAGE

This section of the city gets its name from the many educational facilities within its boundaries. Philadelphia's probable only Puritan, William Warner, purchased its 1500 acres from the Indians in 1677, but over the years much of the original "grand" residential atmosphere has been altered by the growth of the city's educational complexes.

The University of Pennsylvania, Drexel University and the Philadelphia College of Pharmacy and Science create a scholarly environment. A coordination of Philadelphia's twenty-eight colleges and universities, the University City Science Center and Institute, is the newest addition.

The architecture in the area is among the best in Philadelphia. University buildings mingle with blocks of unusual single, twin and rowhouses throughout this section in the western part of the city.

Powelton Village, one of the University City's communities, is now seeing a rebirth of growth. This 19th century residential neighborhood is home to a diversity of people with a spectrum of lifestyles, but all have one concern in common, their "community". The residents of Powelton live here by design, not chance, and are committed to its survival.

A happy contradiction to most Philadelphia communities, University City is often referred to as Philadelphia's "other city".

Children's

CHILDREN'S

SWEETHEART PUNCH

Easy

Serves: 12 to 14
Prep Time: 10 Minutes

2 quarts cranberry juice
3 cups pineapple juice

2 teaspoons fresh lemon juice
1 quart ginger ale or club soda

Combine juices and chill for 2 hours. Add ginger ale or club soda at serving time. *A good children's or Valentine's Day punch.*

Donna Wiser - Fort Washington, Pa.

SMOOTHIES

Easy

Serves: 2
Prep Time: 10 Minutes

1 cup orange juice
1 cup strawberry yogurt

1 egg (optional)
1 sliced banana

Put all ingredients into a blender and mix until smooth. *You may substitute any favorite juices, yogurts and fruits. The possibilities are endless!*

Ann M. Gray - East Falls, Pa.

WITCHES' BREW

Easy

Serves: 8
Prep Time: 10 Minutes

1 quart apple juice
1½ cups pineapple juice
2 tablespoons honey

2 tablespoons fresh lemon juice
3 cinnamon sticks

Mix all ingredients in 1½ to 2-quart saucepan over low heat until ready to serve. *Good for Halloween!*

Jeffrey Brogan - Ambler, Pa.

BANANA MILK SHAKE

Easy

Serves: 1
Prep Time: 5 Minutes

1 cup milk
½ banana or any fruit

1 scoop ice cream

Pour milk into blender container. Add banana and ice cream and blend on high until smooth. Pour into a 10-ounce glass and enjoy!

Dina Roman - Flourtown, Pa.

PEANUT BUTTER CELERY

Easy

Prep Time: 15 Minutes

Celery
Peanut butter

Raisins (optional)

Clean the celery, spread with peanut butter and cut into small pieces. May top with raisins if desired. *This filling may also be used in core of an apple.*

Billy Nichols - Wadsworth, Pa.

PHILADELPHIA HOMEMADE PRETZELS

Easy

Yield: 12 to 15
Prep Time: 20 Minutes
Oven Temp: 425°
Baking Time: 12 to 15 Minutes

1 cake yeast
1½ cups warm water
1 teaspoon salt
1 tablespoon sugar

4 cups flour
1 egg
Coarse salt

Dissolve yeast in warm water. Add salt and sugar. Blend in flour; knead dough until smooth. Cut into small pieces. Roll in ropes and twist into shape. Place on lightly greased cookie sheets. Brush pretzels with beaten egg. Sprinkle with coarse salt. Bake at 425° 12 to 15 minutes.

Mary Ann Powell - Roxborough, Pa.

CHILDREN'S

POPSICLES

Easy

Yield: 2 to 4
Prep Time: 10 Minutes

Chocolate:
8 ounces plain yogurt
2 tablespoons brown sugar or honey

2 tablespoons cocoa or carob powder

Fruit-Flavor:
1 (6-ounce) can frozen fruit juice concentrate

Dash of vanilla extract and/or honey

Place ingredients in blender and liquify; pour into molds and freeze.

Jeffrey and Jamey Brogan - Ambler, Pa.

BEST EVER BAKED CHICKEN

Easy
Make Ahead

Serves: 4
Prep Time: About 20 Minutes
Oven Temp: 350°
Baking Time: 1 Hour

⅓ cup grated Parmesan cheese
1 to 2 tablespoons chopped parsley
1 teaspoon salt
⅛ teaspoon pepper
½ teaspoon paprika

⅔ cup breadcrumbs
1 egg
2 tablespoons water
1 chicken, cut into pieces (have a parent do the cutting)

Mix the dry ingredients in a paper bag. In a bowl beat the egg and water together. Dip chicken pieces in egg mixture; put into bag of crumbs and shake to coat chicken. Place chicken in a greased baking pan; bake at 350° for 1 hour, basting chicken twice with juices from pan. *This recipe is always a favorite with kids in the children's cooking classes at our store.*

Mary Walsh Thorell - Thorell's Quality Cookware - Chestnut Hill, Pa.

HEATHER'S CHICKEN

Easy

Serves: 4
Prep Time: 25 Minutes
Oven Temp: 350°
Baking Time: 30 Minutes

1 pound boned chicken meat
½ teaspoon salt
¼ teaspoon pepper
1 tablespoon flour
1 tablespoon butter or
   margarine
½ cup chicken broth
1 bay leaf

1 clove garlic, minced
Pinch of thyme
Pinch of parsley
1 (10¾ ounce) can cream of
   celery, chicken or mushroom
   soup
½ teaspoon juice
2 cups cooked rice

In a large saucepan combine first 11 ingredients and bring to a boil. Add lemon and cook for 1 minute longer. Pour over cooked rice which has been placed in a casserole dish and bake at 350° about 30 minutes until hot.

Heather Sudul - Olney, Pa.

QUICK PIZZA DOUGH

Moderate

Yield: 2 (13 Inch) Pies
Prep Time: 15 Minutes
Oven Temp: 425°
Baking Time: 20 to 25 Minutes

2 cups flour
2 teaspoons baking powder
½ to 1 teaspoon salt

⅔ cup milk
¼ cup vegetable oil plus 2
   tablespoons, divided

Combine flour, baking powder, salt, milk and ¼ cup oil in a mixing bowl. Stir vigorously until the mixture leaves the side of the bowl. Gather dough together and press into a ball. Knead dough in bowl 10 times to make smooth. Divide dough in half. On a lightly floured cloth-covered board, roll each half into a 13 inch circle. Place on pizza pan or baking sheet. Turn up edge ½ inch and pinch or pleat. Brush circles with remaining 2 tablespoons oil. Fill with tomato sauce and preferred toppings. Bake at 425° for 20 to 25 minutes.

Alice Brogan - Ambler, Pa.

CHILDREN'S

TOFU BURGERS

Easy

Yield: 5 Burgers
Prep Time: 15 Minutes

1 cup chopped onions
3 tablespoons oil
20 ounces firm tofu
⅔ cup breadcrumbs
2 tablespoons Worcestershire
  sauce

1 tablespoon soy sauce
Garlic salt to taste
3 eggs, beaten
Butter for frying

Cook chopped onions in oil until tender, but not brown; cool. Drain tofu and crumble with fingertips. Add onion and remaining ingredients to crumbled tofu and mix well. Make into patties. Fry in butter until crisp and evenly browned on both sides.

Fred Rogers - Mister Rogers' Neighborhood

TIP

On special occasions-or whenever you feel like it-include a note ("I Love You," "You're Great," "Happy Birthday," "Happy Valentine's Day," etc.), a funny drawing, a small toy or a game in your child's lunch box/bag.

Alice Brogan - Ambler, Pa.

FINGER GELATIN

Easy

Yield: 30 Cubes
Prep Time: 20 Minutes

3 envelopes unflavored gelatin
1 (12-ounce) can frozen juice
  concentrate, (any flavor),
  thawed

1½ cups water

Soften gelatin in juice. Boil the water and add the juice mixture and stir until gelatin dissolves. Remove from heat, pour into a lightly greased 9x13 inch pan and chill. Cut into squares when firm. Refrigerate in a covered container. Unrefrigerated will keep about 4 hours. *Variation: add a little honey and 1 cup of sliced fruit.*

Martha Jankiewicz - Hatboro, Pa.

SUGARLESS CARROT FRUIT COOKIES

Moderate

Yield: 36 Cookies
Prep Time: 35 Minutes
Oven Temp: 375°
Baking Time: 12 Minutes

¼ cup shortening
1 egg
4 tablespoons frozen orange
  juice concentrate
4 tablespoons water
½ teaspoon orange extract
1 teaspoon vanilla extract
1 cup self-rising flour

¼ teaspoon baking powder
¼ cup instant nonfat dry milk
1 teaspoon cinnamon
1 small banana, chopped very
  fine
12 dates, chopped fine
1 cup shredded carrots
18 small walnuts, chopped fine

Cream shortening, add egg, orange juice, water and flavorings. Mix flour, baking powder, milk and cinnamon. Add banana, dates, carrots and nuts to creamed mixture. Add dry ingredients and mix well. Drop onto greased cookie sheet and bake at 375° for 12 minutes.

Alice Brogan - Ambler, Pa.

NATURAL APPLE CRISP

Easy

Serves: 6
Prep Time: 15 Minutes
Oven Temp: 350°
Baking Time: 30 Minutes

6 large apples, peeled and sliced
¼ cup apple juice
1 cup rolled oats, uncooked
⅓ cup whole wheat flour

½ cup corn oil
⅛ cup water
1 teaspoon cinnamon

Prepare apples and layer in loaf pan, then pour apple juice over apples. Mix remaining ingredients together and spread over apples. Bake at 350° for 30 minutes. May be served warm or cold.

William W. Scranton, III - Lieutenant Governor of Pennsylvania

CHILDREN'S

HARDY RICE PUDDING

Easy

Serves: 5
Prep Time: 10 Minutes
Oven Temp: 350°
Baking Time: 25 to 30 Minutes

1 cup milk
1 teaspoon vanilla extract
2 eggs
⅓ cup honey
2 cups cooked brown rice

1 cup raisins or chopped dates
½ teaspoon cinnamon
½ teaspoon lemon rind
Dash of nutmeg
1 cup plain yogurt

Combine milk and vanilla. Mix eggs and honey together and blend with milk. Add rice, raisins, cinnamon, lemon rind and nutmeg. Pour mixture into buttered 1 quart casserole. Bake at 350° for 25 to 30 minutes. Stir every 10 minutes adding yogurt after first 10 minutes. Remove from oven and let cool and thicken. *Excellent for children as there is little sugar and it is very nutritious. 325 calories per serving; 225 sodium.*

The Phillie Phanatic - The Phillies

PORCUPINES

Easy

Yield: 24
Prep Time: 10 Minutes

1 cup creamy peanut butter
½ cup sweetened condensed milk

¼ cup powdered sugar
½ cup finely chopped peanuts

In a bowl blend peanut butter, milk and sugar together thoroughly with a wooden spoon, then knead by hand. Divide the candy mixture into small pieces. Roll each piece into a ball about 1 inch in diameter then roll balls in chopped peanuts.

D.J. Murphy - Chestnut Hill, Pa.

CHOCOLATE CHIP CAKE

Easy

Prep Time: 15 Minutes
Oven Temp: 350°
Baking Time: 40 to 45 Minutes

2 cups all-purpose flour
½ cup firmly packed brown
  sugar
½ cup sugar
1 tablespoon baking powder
½ teaspoon baking soda

½ cup shortening
1¼ cups milk
3 eggs
½ cup semisweet chocolate
  mini-morsels

In a large mixer bowl combine all ingredients on low speed for 30 seconds scraping bowl constantly. Beat on high speed, scraping bowl occasionally, for 3 minutes. Pour into greased and floured oblong pan (13x9x2 inch) or 2 round layer pans. Bake at 350° for 40 to 45 minutes. Cool before frosting.

Mary Kate Kelly - Mt. Airy, Pa.

SUNNY HONEY PEANUT BUTTER BALLS

Easy

Yield: 25 to 30
Prep Time: 20 Minutes

2 cups freshly shelled peanuts
3 tablespoons oil (peanut
  preferably)
½ cup honey
1 cup instant nonfat dry milk
½ cup chopped nuts, sunflower
  seeds, soy nuts or
  combination

1 cup raisins
½ cup wheat germ
Chopped seeds or coconut
  (optional)

For fun have a peanut hunt first then shell the peanuts. In small batches chop peanuts in blender with oil. Add honey, milk and chopped seeds. Stir in raisins. Shape into ½ inch balls. Roll balls in wheat germ, chopped seeds or coconut. Store in covered airtight container and refrigerate. *Tried, tested and approved by girls' science classes. So much fun, they'll never guess it's nutritious!*

Maura Bock - Hatboro, Pa.

CHILDREN'S

CHOCOLATE AND BUTTERSCOTCH CRUNCHIES

Easy
Make Ahead

Yield: 20 to 25 Squares
Prep Time: 30 Minutes

½ cup sugar
1 cup light corn syrup
1 cup peanut butter
6 cups crispy rice cereal

1 cup semisweet chocolate
  morsels
1 cup butterscotch morsels

In a saucepan combine sugar, corn syrup and peanut butter; bring to a boil. Pour over crispy rice cereal that has been placed in a baking pan; allow to cool. Melt chocolate and butterscotch morsels together; spread over mixture in pan. Cool and cut into squares to serve. *Kids like to prepare this recipe.*

Gerry Aspen - Willow Grove, Pa.

PEANUT BUTTER CRUMB CRUST

Easy

Prep Time: 10 Minutes
Oven Temp: 350°
Baking Time: 10 Minutes

¼ cup butter or margarine
1½ cups graham cracker
  crumbs

¼ cup creamy peanut butter
3 tablespoons sugar

Melt butter in saucepan over low heat. Remove from heat and stir in graham cracker crumbs, peanut butter and sugar with a fork. Spoon mixture into pie pan and press firmly and evenly against bottom and side of pan with back of spoon. Bake at 350° for 10 minutes; cool. *Fill with ice cream, whipped cream or pudding.*

Jocie Pritz - Roxborough, Pa.

BIRDS' NESTS

Easy

Prep Time: 15 Minutes

**1 (12 ounce) package chocolate
  chips
9 to 12 ounces chunky peanut
  butter**

**10 shredded wheat biscuits
Jelly beans**

In top of double boiler melt the entire package of chocolate chips. Stir in peanut butter. Smash shredded wheat into fine pieces before adding to pot. Stir until coated with mixture. Remove from heat. Spoon out and shape into nest form with indented center for placing jelly beans to resemble bird eggs. Cool before eating. *Pre-schoolers can make these.*

Maura Bock - Hatboro, Pa.

DELICIOUS HEALTH CANDY

Easy

Yield: 60 to 80
Prep Time: 20 Minutes

**1 cup honey
1½ cups instant nonfat dry milk
1 cup peanut butter**

**1½ cups wheat germ or oats
1 teaspoon nutmeg or cinnamon
  (optional)**

Place all ingredients into a bowl and mix well. Shape into small balls. *Variation: May roll balls in crushed nuts, cornflakes or coconut.*

Jamey Brogan - Ambler, Pa.

IRISH POTATOES

Easy

Yield: 25 to 30 Potatoes
Prep Time: 15 Minutes

**½ cup softened butter or
  margarine
¼ teaspoon salt
1 teaspoon vanilla extract**

**14 ounces powdered sugar
1 (3½ ounce) can flaked coconut
Ground cinnamon**

In a mixing bowl combine butter, salt, vanilla, sugar and coconut; mix with hands. Shape into balls about ½ inch in diameter. Roll in ground cinnamon. *The family favorite—easy for children.*

Sharyn Vergare - Chestnut Hill, Pa.

SUGGESTED FAMILY ACTIVITIES

January: Mummers' Day Parade (along Broad Street)
Philadelphia, Pa.   (215) 568-6599

February: Maple Sugar Festival, Tyler Arboretum
Media, Pa. (Delaware County)   (215) 566-9133

Washington's Birthday Weekend
Valley Forge, Pa.   (215) 278-3558

Welcome Spring Display, Longwood Gardens
U.S. Route 1, Kennett Square, Pa.   (215) 388-6741

March: Philadelphia Flower and Garden Show
Civic Center, Phila., Pa.   (215) 625-8250

April: Pennsylvania Crafts Fair Day, Brandywine River Museum
Delaware County, Pa.   (215) 388-7601

May: Folk Fest
Doylestown, Bucks County, Pa.   (215) 345-0210

Devon Horse Show
Devon, Chester County, Pa.   (215) 964-0550

Lehigh County Historic Covered
Bridge Festival   (215) 437-9661

June: Rittenhouse Square Art Annual, 18th & Walnut Streets
Philadelphia, Pa.   (215) 423-7254

Elfreth's Alley Fete Days (18th century crafts)
Front and 2nd Streets, Phila., Pa.   (215) 574-0560

Delco Scottish Games & Country Fair
Devon, Chester County, Pa.   (215) 566-2898

July: Port Indian Regatta
Norristown, Montgomery County, Pa. (215) 666-5478

Independence Day
Philadelphia, Pa.   (215) 568-6599

August: Philadelphia Folk Festival
Schwenksville, Pa.   (215) 247-1300

SUGGESTED FAMILY ACTIVITIES

German Festival
Penn's Landing, Delaware Avenue, Phila., Pa.

September: Polish Festival
Doylestown, Bucks County, Pa.   (215) 345-0600

Re-enactment of Battle of Brandywine
Chadds Ford, Delaware County, Pa.   (215) 459-3342

Italian Festival, St. Thomas Aquinas
17th & Morris Streets, Phila., Pa.   (215) 334-2312

Traditional Irish Music & Dance Festival
Lansdale, Montgomery Co., Pa.   (215) 849-8899

Fairmount Park Fall Festival
Philadelphia, Pa.   (215) 568-6599

In-Water Boat Show
Philadelphia, Pa.   (215) 923-9030

October: Radnor Hunt
Malvern, Chester County, Pa.   (215) 644-9918

Linvilla Orchards Pumpkin Harvest
Media, Delaware County, Pa.   (215) 876-7116

Re-enactment of Battle of Germantown at "Cliveden"
6401 Germantown Ave., Phila., Pa.   (215) 848-1777

Super Sunday
Benjamin Franklin Parkway, Phila., Pa.   (215) 568-6599

November: Pennsylvania Hunt Cup Races
Unionville, Chester County, Pa.   (215) 431-6365

Gimbels Thanksgiving Day Parade
Philadelphia, Pa.   (215) 568-6599

Army-Navy Football Game
Philadelphia, Pa.   (215) 568-6599

SUGGESTED FAMILY ACTIVITIES

December: Festival of Lights American-Swedish Museum
1900 Pattison Avenue, Phila., Pa.   (215) 389-1776

Re-enactment of Washington Crossing the Delaware
Washington Crossing State Park, Pa.   (215) 493-4076

Christmas Evening Display, Longwood Gardens
U.S. Route 1, Kennett Square, Pa.   (215) 388-6741

Bartram's Garden
54th & Lindbergh Blvd., Phila., Pa. (215) 729-5281
Begun in 1728, learn about colonial days and botany on 27 acres.

Lenape Indian Cultural Center
Park Avenue & Route 152, Chalfont, Pa. (215) 822-3265

Moravian Pottery and Tile Works
Swamp Road & Route 313, Doylestown, Pa. (215) 345-6722
"Children's Art Festival" held in September

Mule-Drawn Barge Rides (the last of its kind in nation.)
New Street, New Hope, Bucks County, Pa. (215) 862-2842

Perelman Antique Toy Museum
270 South 2nd Street, Phila., Pa. (215) 922-1070

Smith Playground (6½ acre playground for young children)
33rd & Oxford Streets (2 blocks from East River Drive
& Grant's Statue, Phila., Pa. (215) 765-4325

Strasburg Railroad
Route 741, East of Strasburg Pa. (717) 687-7522
9 mile ride on restored 1900 vintage steam locomotive

Swiss Pines Oriental Garden
Charlestown Road off Route 29, Phoenixville, Pa. (215) 933-6916
A 70 acre garden paradise.

John Wanamaker (Center City)
Daily organ concerts, Christmas musical light show.
13th and Market Streets, Phila., Pa. (215) 422-2000

INDEX OF CELEBRITIES & RESTAURANTS

INDEX OF CELEBRITIES & RESTAURANTS

INDEX

INDEX

282

INDEX

INDEX

Philadelphia Homestyle
Norwood-Fontbonne Academy
8891 Germantown Avenue, Dept. C
Philadelphia, Pennsylvania 19118

Please send me _____copies of **Philadelphia Homestyle** at $12.95 each plus $1.50 per book for postage and handling. Add sales tax where applicable. (6% in Pennsylvania).

My check or money order is enclosed for $_____.

Name:_____

Address:_____

City:_____State:_____Zip:_____
Make checks payable to: *Norwood-Fontbonne Home and School Association.*

Philadelphia Homestyle
Norwood-Fontbonne Academy
8891 Germantown Avenue, Dept. C
Philadelphia, Pennsylvania 19118

Please send me _____copies of **Philadelphia Homestyle** at $12.95 each plus $1.50 per book for postage and handling. Add sales tax where applicable. (6% in Pennsylvania).

My check or money order is enclosed for $_____.

Name:_____

Address:_____

City:_____State:_____Zip:_____
Make checks payable to: *Norwood-Fontbonne Home and School Association.*

Philadelphia Homestyle
Norwood-Fontbonne Academy
8891 Germantown Avenue, Dept. C
Philadelphia, Pennsylvania 19118

Please send me _____copies of **Philadelphia Homestyle** at $12.95 each plus $1.50 per book for postage and handling. Add sales tax where applicable. (6% in Pennsylvania).

My check or money order is enclosed for $_____.

Name:_____

Address:_____

City:_____State:_____Zip:_____
Make checks payable to: *Norwood-Fontbonne Home and School Association.*

Reorder Additional Copies